GM10
CONFABULATIONS.
COLOGNE LIFE AND HUMANISM
IN HERMANN SCHOTTEN'S
CONFABULATIONES TIRONUM LITTERARIORUM
(COLOGNE, 1525)

Copyright © Manchester University Press 2007

While copyright in the volume as a whole is vested in Manchester University Press, copyright in individual chapters belongs to their respective authors, and no chapter may be reproduced in whole or in part without the express permission in writing of both author and publisher.

Published by Manchester University Press
Oxford Road, Manchester M13 9NR, UK
and Room 400, 175 Fifth Avenue, New York, NY 10010, USA
www.manchesteruniversitypress.co.uk

Distributed exclusively in the USA by
Palgrave, 175 Fifth Avenue, New York NY 10010, USA

Distributed exclusively in Canada by
UBC Press, University of British Columbia, 2029 West Mall,
Vancouver, BC, Canada V6T 1Z2

British Library Cataloguing-in-Publication Data
A catalogue record for this book is available from the British Library

Library of Congress Cataloging-in-Publication Data
A catalog record for this book is available from the Library of Congress

ISBN 13: 978 0 7190 8186 6

First published 2007
First digital paperback edition published 2010

Printed by Lightning Source

Confabulations

Cologne Life and Humanism in Hermann Schotten's
Confabulationes tironum litterariorum
(Cologne, 1525)

By

Peter Macardle

Durham Modern Languages Series 2007

Non-Bibliographic Abbreviations

b.: born.
BA: Baccalaureus Artium.
BDecr: Baccalaureus Decretorum (Bachelor of Canon Law).
BFTh: Baccalaureus Formatus Theologiae.
BJur: Baccalaureus Jurium.
BJurCiv: Baccalaureus Jurium Ciuilium.
BMed: Baccalaureus Medicinae.
BM: Bibliothèque Municipale.
BN: Bibliothèque Nationale.
BSB: Bayerische Staatsbibliothek.
BTh: Baccalaureus Theologiae.
d.: died.
DDecr: Doctor Decretorum (Doctor of Canon Law).
DJur: Doctor Jurium.
DTh: Doctor Theologiae.
LB: Landesbibliothek.
LicA: Licentia Artium.
LicJur: Licentia Jurium.
LicLeg: Licentia Legum.
LicTh: Licentia Theologiae.
MA: Magister Artium.
matr.: matriculated, matriculation.
ÖNB: Österreichische Nationalbibliothek.
StBPK: Staatsbibliothek Preußischer Kulturbesitz.
UB: Universitätsbibliothek.
UL: University Library.

Contents

Non-Bibliographic Abbreviations — iv
List of Illustrations — vi
Acknowledgements — vii

Introduction — 1

CHAPTER 1 — 19
Through a Glass Darkly. Hermann Schotten's Career

CHAPTER 2 — 55
Space, Time and Culture. The *Confabulationes* and Early Modern Cologne

CHAPTER 3 — 91
The *Confabulationes* and other Humanist Colloquy Collections

CHAPTER 4 — 129
Schotten's Latinity

CHAPTER 5 — 151
Visible Means of Support? Traces of Schotten's Networks

Conclusions — 205

Select Bibliography — 211

List of Illustrations

Titlepage of the second edition of the *Confabu-* 54
lationes (Cologne: P. Quentel, 1526).

Master and scholars, titlepage of the *Manuale* 128
scholarium (Cologne: H. Quentel, *ca.* 1490).

Hans Weiditz, *St Anthony*, woodcut, *ca.* 1522. 150

Cologne, St Maria im Kapitol, from Anton 203
Woensam, *Große Ansicht von Köln* (1531).

Hermann Schotten's handwriting, at the start of 204
the record of his deanship of the Cologne Arts
Faculty, HAStK, 150, A 481, fol. 187^v (lower
half).

Boats designed for the central Rhine (left) and 210
the lower Rhine (right), from Anton Woensam,
Große Ansicht von Köln (1531).

Acknowledgements

Many years ago, looking for background information on Hermann Schotten, I came across the *Confabulationes* in the British Library. I was immediately charmed by the colloquies, and their vivid depiction of early modern Cologne, and determined there and then that they should be made properly known to modern scholarship. If, after a long time, I have succeeded in doing this, it is only thanks to a very great number of people.

Many colleagues in Durham and elsewhere, by no means all in the early modern field, have offered encouragement, information and expert criticism: especially Jenny and Richard Britnell, Anna Carrdus, David Cowling, Ian Doyle, Gabriele Fischer, John Flood, Margaret Harvey, Tim Jackson, Jonathan Long, Ann Moss, Nigel Palmer, Nicholas Saul and Michael Straeter.

A great deal of help has come from the various libraries and archives where my research has been done; above all the magnificent Historisches Archiv der Stadt Köln. I am grateful to the Director, Dr Joachim Deeters, to Dr Manfred Huiskes, and to Dr Manfred Groten, now Professor of History at the University of Bonn, for a great deal of specialist information and advice. Thanks too to all the helpful staff who brought me (quite literally) trolley-loads of fascinating material, much of which has been directly used in this study, and answered queries of the most diverse kinds. Other Cologne collections, too, have been extremely helpful, notably the Universitäts- und Stadtbibliothek Köln, especially the Historic Collection, the Erzbischöfliche Diözesan- und Dombibliothek, and the Historisches Archiv des Erzbistums Köln.

It has always seemed a good omen that Wilhelm Levison, once Professor of History at the University of Bonn, spent his last years (1939–1947) in exile from the Nazi regime at Durham, and that many obscure, but to me extremely relevant works were in the collection he bequeathed to Durham University Library. To that library, especially the helpful and accommodating staff of Archives and Special Collections, Palace Green, go sincere thanks; as also to the Chapter Library and the Meissen Library of Durham Cathedral, and the library of Ushaw College. Beyond Durham, I must thank particularly the British Library, the library of the Warburg Institute, the Herzog August Bibliothek, Wolfenbüttel, and the Stadtbibliothek Trier.

It is a pleasure to acknowledge the support of the British Academy, whose award of a Small Research Grant made possible an intensive two months of archival research in Cologne, which allowed me to make out at least the outlines of the career of a strangely elusive humanist. I am also profoundly grateful for generous financial support, towards both research visits and publication costs, from the Durham University School of Modern Languages and Cultures.

Everyone connected with the Durham University Modern Languages Series has my sincere gratitude: Mike Thompson, the General Editor; Leah Tether, who has helped to design such an attractive book cover. Very special thanks must go to the Assistant Editor Janet Starkey, who has been efficiency and good humour incarnate as she has coped with every aspect of taking this study through the press with remarkable dispatch.

Best thanks of all must go to my wife Fiona, for companionship, support and encouragement at every stage of a long and sometimes arduous project.

This book is dedicated to my friends Gabriele Fischer and Michael Straeter, scholars and connaisseurs of medieval and modern Cologne.

Introduction

Some time in the earlier part of 1525 there appeared a collection of Latin colloquies, dialogues for teaching schoolboys Latin. The *Confabulationes tironum litterariorum*, which roughly translates as *Dialogues for the Lower Forms of Grammar Schools*, contained one hundred and twenty-three short dialogues covering a wide range of topics and conversational situations. It was composed in a distinctly humanist Classical Latin, modelled mainly on the elegant but racy colloquial language of Terence. Its author, Hermannus Schottennius Hessus (or Hermann Schotten), was a young humanist as yet unknown to the world of letters. He was probably about twenty-two, and was working as a schoolmaster somewhere in the city of Cologne. The fuller understanding of this still relatively unknown humanist, and of his remarkable book of colloquies, is the aim of this monograph, and of the critical edition of the *Confabulationes*, to which it is a companion.[1]

In 1525, a new set of Latin colloquies was not in itself an unusual occurrence. Since the Middle Ages, Latin teachers had made use of manuscript collections of dialogues; and the later fifteenth century had seen the appearance of the first printed collections. Well known is the anonymous *Manuale scholarium* (*ca.* 1490),[2] an adap-

---

[1] Hermannus Schottennius Hessus, *Confabulationes tironum litterariorum (Cologne, 1525)*, ed. by Peter Macardle (Durham: Durham Modern Languages Series, 2007), hereafter Schotten, *Confabulationes*, ed. by Macardle.

[2] *Manuale scholarium qui studentium vniversitates aggredi ac postea proficere in eis intendunt* ([Cologne]: [H. Quentel], after 6 April 1490]). *Manuale scholarium*, ed. by Zarncke; *The*

1

tation of an earlier book of dialogues, the *Latinum ydeoma* by Paulus Niavis.³ Most of the *Manuale* was given over to conversations between two students on topics related to university life, allegedly in Heidelberg, though in fact the *Manuale* author had taken over many of Niavis's Leipzig details, adapting them only minimally to the quite different Heidelberg situation.⁴ It presented a shaky Latinity, retaining many Medieval Latin features, and introducing a fair share of solecisms.⁵

But much better was to come. In Germany, the early sixteenth century brought the beginnings of serious humanist engagement both with Latinity and with pedagogy, and the first two decades of the century had seen the appearance of some of the most influential colloquy collections. In undisputed first place were Erasmus's *Colloquia familiaria*: they had appeared in 1518, and the edition of 1522 had established them as the leading humanist colloquy collection. The *Paedologia* of the Leipzig professor Petrus Mosellanus, containing thirty-seven eloquent dialogues, had appeared in 1518, and had been reprinted in a definitive edition two years later. Christoph Hegendorff's slim volume of *Dialogi pueriles* of 1520 went on to be printed along with the *Paedologia*. The Flemish humanist Hadrianus Barlandus's *Dialogi* were published in Louvain in 1524. The relationship of the *Confabulationes* to other colloquy collections is discussed in Chapter 3.

---

3   *Manuale Scholarium*, trans. by Seybolt.
    Paulus Niavis, *Latinum ydeoma pro novellis studentibus* (Leipzig: K. Kachelofen, [*ca.* 1488]). Bömer, *Die lateinischen Schülergespräche der Humanisten*, p. 27, wrongly states that Niavis copied the *Manuale*; cf. Barth, 'Manuale scolarium', esp. col. 321.
4   Barth, 'Manuale scolarium', cols 326–28; Streckenbach, 'Paulus Niavis, "Latinum ydeoma [...]"', passim.
5   Barth, 'Manuale scolarium', col. 325; Berry, 'A Fifteenth-Century Guide to Latin Conversation for University Students', esp. pp. 528–30.

Nor would the *Confabulationes* be the last of this line. The next decades saw more new colloquy collections, including Sebald Heyden's *Formulae puerilium colloquiorum*, itself based on Schotten, which was probably first printed in 1527; and one of the most prestigious examples of the genre, the elegant *Exercitatio linguae Latinae* of the Spanish humanist Juan Luís Vives, who was then living in Louvain (1538).

But Schotten's *Confabulationes* were distinctively different from what had gone before and what would come after, and they were an instant success. The first surviving edition (Augsburg: S. Ruff, 1525) has up till now been regarded as the princeps; but Schotten had no connection with Augsburg, no obvious need to publish outside Cologne, and a consistent history of having his works printed there by Peter Quentel. There are in fact very strong indications that Ruff had swiftly pirated a now lost Cologne first edition. An expanded Cologne second edition appeared in 1526; it contained an additional thirty *conuiuia*, 'banquets'. It was reprinted most enthusiastically. By the end of the sixteenth century fifty-seven editions are recorded; almost certainly there were more which have not survived.[6] This is a truly impressive number of editions for an early-sixteenth-century colloquy collection.

All the more surprising, then, that this book, once a best-seller, is now almost forgotten; that this milestone of Latin pedagogy and humanist culture, which is also a singularly pleasurable read, has never had a modern edition, and that Schotten's biography, career and other work have gone almost uninvestigated. Schotten may not have been a 'major humanist', yet his first substantial work made a major contribution to humanist pedagogy, and deserves a modern critical appraisal. St Jerome's dictum,

---

[6] See the the list of all known editions of the *Confabulationes*, pp. 9–12; and the detailed discussions of the earliest editions in Schotten, *Confabulationes*, ed. by Macardle, Section I.

used as a motto in Mosellanus's *Paedologia*, applies equally to the *Confabulationes*: 'Non sunt contemnenda quasi parua sine quibus magna constare non possunt'.[7]

The Confabulationes

It is impossible in a short space to give an adequate idea of the range, variety and charm of Schotten's colloquies. They must be read in their entirety; and the reader is referred to the companion edition of the *Confabulationes* for the complete text of many passages referred to in this study. The list of the titles of the colloquies and *conuiuia* at the end of this introduction will give an idea of the scale and scope of the collection.

The one hundred and twenty-three colloquies of Schotten's first edition cover a large sweep of the life and concerns of the early modern schoolboy. The world of school itself is prominent: the learning of Latin, the difficulties and possible approaches (e.g. colloquies 23–26, 42, 73, 74 and many others). This includes references to the various duties of the typical schoolboy, such as singing in the church choir, with its associated tedium and discomfort, especially in winter (colloquy 35). Some of the colloquies move beyond immediate practical concerns to more generalized discussion of the aims of education and the value and ideals of humanist culture (e.g. colloquies 64, 73, 103, 104, 118).

But the horizon extends well beyond the classroom. A good number of the colloquies thematize the major feasts of the Christian year: Christmas, Maundy Thursday, Easter, Pentecost, (colloquies 35, 58, 38, 39); and some of the main saints' days: St Gall, St Lambert, the Purification of the Blessed Virgin (colloquies 31, 32, 95). Many of

---

[7] Jerome, *Epistola CVII, ad Laetam, PL*, XXII, col. 872, on the titlepage of Mosellanus, *Paedologia*, ed. by Michel, p. LV.

them are associated with schoolboy customs and rituals, like electing a 'Boy Bishop' on St Nicholas's Day, 6 December (colloquy 33); or going round the houses asking for gifts on the eve of St Martin, 10 November (colloquy 40) or on St Blasius's Day, 2 February (colloquy 102). In many cases Schotten's dialogues provide very helpful evidence on details of contemporary popular culture in Cologne.

Other details of the boys' leisure time are introduced. There are sports: ball games, marbles, a croquet-like game, jumping and running, all staples of humanist colloquy collections (colloquies 44–50). Schotten is realistic, and unidealistic, enough to include descriptions of less acceptable leisure activities, such as clandestine drinking in one of the city's more remote alehouses (colloquies 26, 97).

Life is no mere round of superficial pleasures, however. The boys are acquainted with some of the harder realities of life, such as the need to beg for at least part of one's food and money (colloquies 40, 45, 120), especially if one is a 'foreigner' to the city, without parents or relatives (e.g. colloquy 55). There are intimations, too, of public as well as private discontents. There are references to the Reformation, still a new phenomenon, but already infiltrating the Catholic bastion of Cologne, where the previously automatic deference to Catholic clergy can no longer be relied upon (e.g. colloquies 88, 107). Occasionally popular causes of resentment are aired. Two colloquies on funerals (89 and 90) talk about how lucrative they are for the city's parish priests – a genuine grievance of the period, and one that played a part in a 1525 citizens' uprising (see the detailed discussion in Chapter 2). And there are also glimpses of plague, war and famine (colloquies 81–83), none of which was ever far enough away for comfort in the early sixteenth century. Lesser evils, too, are alluded to: the danger of the city streets at night (colloquy 10), the expense of everyday living, the inconveniences of bad weather (e.g. colloquies 28, 29).

The sheer number of topics dealt with in so many discussions makes the *Confabulationes* one of the longest of such collections: only Erasmus's *Colloquia familiaria*, which had expanded edition by edition from 1518 on, were more substantial, and Mosellanus's slim *Paedologia*, Hegendorff's even slimmer *Dialogi* and Heyden's *Formulae puerilium colloquiorum*, were not in the same league at all as far as size is concerned. But if the *Confabulationes* were extensive overall, their individual scale was modest. They are nearly all of the same length, about a page of printed text, between thirty and forty lines. Only the final colloquy 123, set at a Shrove Tuesday party, is rather longer: at almost 150 lines it is a foretaste of the thirty longer *conuiuia*, 'banquets', which Schotten added to the 1526 second edition of the work.

Limiting the length of the colloquies was pedagogically realistic, for boys at the start of their Latin studies would obviously find shorter dialogues easier to digest and master. It was also realistic in another, literary and aesthetic, sense. The short colloquies were made up of realistically short conversational turns. Rarely does one of Schotten's boys speak more than two lines. This contrasts with most other colloquy collections, where the authors' pedagogical idealism forces into the mouths of schoolboys speeches of a length and polish which no one could possibly expect them to attain. In length and syntactical and rhetorical complexity Schotten writes Latin not of a kind which one might ideally, or idealistically, wish boys to aspire to, but of a kind which they could realistically be expected to master, and which would in some measure correspond to the kind of language which they actually used when speaking in German.

This compositional realism is of a piece with other aspects of the *Confabulationes*. Again and again they give the impression of having been written on the basis of actual classroom experience. This correlates convincingly with aspects of Schotten's career which are discussed in Chapter 1. Schotten began a conventional university career at Cologne, gaining his MA and going on to further study to become a full member of the Arts Faculty board. But for one reason or another (the various possibilities are also discussed in Chapter 1) he left the Faculty for several years, from 1522 or 1523 till 1528 or so, and worked as a master at a 'trivial' (grammar) school somewhere in Cologne before eventually returning to take up a university lectureship. It was here that he authored the *Confabulationes*, as class texts for his pupils; and as examined in Chapter 3, internal evidence confirms that several were written in late 1524 and early 1525.

The colloquies, then, were not composed in the abstraction of the study for a generic or merely imagined readership, but were forged to respond to the specific classroom needs of real boys whom Schotten was teaching at the time. This too is part of Schotten's pedagogical and cultural realism. For as will be explored, particularly in Chapters 1 and 5, Schotten seems to have held strong views on the proper education of boys in Cologne, which was a sensitive topic in the Arts Faculty at the time. Humanists like Schotten not only deplored the exclusively Aristotelian and scholastic nature of the traditional Arts curriculum; they also felt that that it gave schoolboys very little that was applicable to the lives that most of them would go on to lead in the mercantile and administrative world of Cologne. It is notable that the *Confabulationes*, though couched in humanist Classical Latin, remain thematically close to actual early modern concerns. Never do the boys lose themselves in a reconstructed classical Roman past. The city they live and move in is recognizably an early modern one, and in many respects demonstrably Cologne: the frequent incorporation of the topography, customs and even some of the personalities of Cologne into the dialogues is explored in detail in Chapter 2.

For some, these 'realistic' aspects of Schotten's dialogues have seemed deserving of criticism. For Hermann Michel, the early-twentieth-century editor of Mosellanus's *Paedologia*, Schotten was culpably unidealistic. The undoubted liveliness of the *Confabulationes* had come at the unacceptable cost of overly informal language and a perspective excessively close to that of schoolboys.[8] The French scholar Louis Massebieau was more ambivalent. He conceded that the *Confabulationes* are 'simples, naturels [...] et parfaitement appropriés à leur but'; Schotten's short, punchy dialogues 'indiquent plus de connaissance de l'enfance et de l'art du dialogue que les périodes oratoires de la Pédologie'.[9] Yet his subsequent depiction of the *Confabulationes* is ironically dismissive of Schotten's values and pedagogical effectiveness: whereas Mosellanus 'corrige les mœurs', Schotten, 'le maître vulgaire de Cologne', 'encourage les mauvaises habitudes en les décrivant.'[10]

From a twenty-first-century perspective, however, at a time when, at least in the west, idealistic and ethically normative aspects of education are emphasized less than before (and where ethical norms are in many cases less rigid and more pluralistic), Schotten's approach seems interestingly similar to modern language learning with its emphasis on 'authenticity' of language and situation. And of course, this emphasis means that for a modern reader the *Confabulationes* are not only a work of pedagogy but also an amazingly important cultural document, recording many fascinating details of everyday life in early modern Cologne, only some of which are mentioned in other sources. This aspect of the *Confabulationes* is examined closely in Chapter 2, and also in the detailed notes to the individual colloquies in *Confabulationes*, edited by Macardle.

---

[8] Mosellanus, *Paedologia*, ed. by Michel, p. XL.
[9] Massebieau, *Les colloques scolaires du seizième siècle*, p. 119.
[10] Ibid., pp. 120–30 (p. 122).

Introduction 9

Editions of the Confabulationes

The *Confabulationes* were recognized at the time as an important collection. There seem to be no surviving documents recording the use of the *Confabulationes* in identifiable schools, though there are many such references to the use of Erasmus and Mosellanus; but it is quite evident that such use was made, from the sheer number of contemporary editions. There has never been a detailed bibliographic study of the editions of the *Confabulationes*, and such information as has been published has relied on the limited range of library catalogues in print in the earlier part of the twentieth century. The extensive printed and electronic catalogue resources now available, however, allow the following comprehensive list of editions to be drawn up.

The printed and online sources cited here in abbreviated form are:

CCFr: *Catalogue Collectif de France.*
KVK: *Karlsruher Virtueller Katalog.*
N&K: Nijhoff and Kronenberg, *Nederlandsche Bibliographie van 1500 tot 1540.*
NUC: *The National Union Catalog*
VD 16: *Verzeichnis der im deutschen Sprachbereich erschienenen Drucke des XVI. Jahrhunderts.*

Full details of all these are found in the bibliography.

Where the major printed sources (*VD 16*, N&K) give adequate information on library holdings, this is not included here. Where editions are known from individual library catalogues, or from electronic catalogues (*VD 16 online, KVK, CCFr*) details of library holdings have been added.

First edition: 123 colloquies only:

Augsburg: S. Ruff, July 1525. *VD 16*, S 4005; Munich, UB, 8° Misc. 604a; *KVK*: Stuttgart, Evangelischer Oberkirchenrat, 443.

Editions including the *conuiuia*:

Cologne: P. Quentel, 1526. *VD 16 online*, ZV 14151; Trier, Stadtbibliothek, 2 an: G 59 8°; *KVK*: Besançon, BM, 246809.

Augsburg: A. Weißenhorn, 1529. *VD 16*, S 4006; *NUC*, 529, 615.

Antwerp: M. de Keyser, September 1530. N&K, 3861.

[Antwerp]: M. [Hillen van Hoochstraten], n.d. [1531?]. N&K, 3865.

Vienna: J. Singriener, 1531. *NUC*: Cornell UL, Rare PA 8577 S27C7 1531.

Zwickau: W. Meyerpeck, 1531. *VD 16*, S 4007; Berlin, StBPK, Prf 2996.

Augsburg: A. Weißenhorn, 1532. Vienna, ÖNB, 74.Y.99*

Leipzig: N. Schmidt, March 1532. *VD 16*, S 4008.

Nuremberg: J. Petreius, 1532. *VD 16*, S 4009.

Antwerp: M. de Keyser, 1533. N&K, 3862.

Augsburg: A. Weißenhorn, 1533. *VD 16*, S 4010.

Augsburg: A. Weißenhorn, 1534. *KVK*: Florence, Biblioteca Nazionale Centrale, MAGL.11.9.142/b.

Augsburg: A. Weißenhorn, 1535. *VD 16*, S 4011; *KVK*.

[Leipzig]: [N. Schmidt], 1535. *VD 16*, S 4012.

Leipzig: N. Schmidt, 1535. *VD 16 online*, ZV 14149.

Augsburg: A. Weißenhorn, 1536. *VD 16*, S 4013; *KVK*.

Nuremberg: J. Petreius, 1536. *VD 16*, S 4014; *CCFr*.

Antwerp: M. Hillen van Hoochstraten, 1536. N&K, 3863.

Antwerp: M. [Hillen van Hoochstraten], [*ca* 1537?]. N&K, 3865.

Antwerp: Widow of M. de Keyser for J. Cock, 1537. N&K, 3864.

Augsburg: A. Weißenhorn, 1537. *VD 16*, S 4015.

Leipzig: N. Schmidt, 1537. *VD 16 online*, ZV 22363: Dresden, Sächsische LB, 3.A.10384, angeb. 2.

Leipzig: N. Schmidt, 1538. *VD 16*, S 4016.

Augsburg: A. Weißenhorn, 1540. *VD 16*, S 4017.

[Leipzig]: [N. Wolrab], [*ca* 1540?]. *VD 16*, S 4018.

Leipzig: N. Schmidt, 1540. *VD 16 online*, ZV 14150.

Leipzig: N. Schmidt, [*ca* 1540?]. *VD 16*, S 4019.

Nuremberg: n.pr., *ca* 1540. Oxford, Bodleian Library, Vet. D1 f. 97.

Augsburg: H. Steiner, 1541. *VD 16*, S 4020.

Ingolstadt: A. Weißenhorn, 1542. *NUC*: Chicago, Newberry Library, Case Y 682 .s3832.

Lyon: J. & F. Frellon, 1543. *KVK*: Mannheim, UB, Sch 072/265 an 1; Florence, Biblioteca Nazionale Centrale, MAGL.5.9.232/a.

Introduction 11

Nuremberg: J. Petreius, 1543. *VD 16 online*, ZV 20803: Munich, BSB, L.lat. 1014v; *KVK*: Vienna, ÖNB, 73.Y.60;

Augsburg: V. Otmar, 1544. *VD 16,* S 4021.

Venice: F. Bindoni and M. Pasini, 1544. *KVK*: Jesi, Biblioteca Comunale Planettiana.

Lyon: J. & F. Frellon, 1545. *CCFr*: Paris, BN, RES P-X-411 1.

Lyon: T. Payen, 1545. *CCFr*: Marseille, BM, 81771/2.

Lyon: A. Vincent, 1545. *CCFr*: Grenoble, BM, F 3711 CGA.

Lyon: T. Payen, 1547. *CCFr*: Toulouse, Bibliothèque d'Etude et du Patrimoine, Fa D 8879, Fonds ancien 2.

Leipzig: n.pr., 1548. *KVK*: Dresden, Sächsische LB, 39.8.5780.

Frankfurt an der Oder: J. Eichorn [*ca* 1550]. *KVK*: Berlin, StBPK, 2 an: @Wp 1232.

Ingolstadt: A. and S. Weißenhorn, 1550. *VD 16 online*, ZV 22001: Munich, BSB, L.lat. 1014y.

[Leipzig]: [N. Wolrab?], [*ca* 1550?]. *KVK*: Wolfenbüttel, Herzog August Bibliothek, QuH 160.1 3.

Augsburg: V. Otmar, 1551. *VD 16,* S 4022. (The colophon carries the date 1546).

N.p., n.pr., 1551. *NUC*: Washington: Folger Shakespeare Library, Folger PA 8577 S25 C5 cage; *KVK*: Bamberg, Staatsbibliothek, 22/L.r.r.o.267-a; Basel, UB, DB IX 28:2.

Lyon: J. Frellon, 1552. *KVK*: Universitat de Barcelona, UL, no shelfmark.

Augsburg: H. Zimmermann, 1553. *VD 16,* S 4023.

Lyon: T. Payen, 1556. *CCFr*: Le Mans, Médiathèque Aragon, 2e st BL 8* 270 Fonds anciens; Lyon, BM, B 510183 CGA.

[Strasbourg?]: n.pr., 1556. *KVK*: Augsburg, Staats- und Stadtbibliothek, Th B V 49.

N.p., n.pr., 1556. *VD 16,* S 4024; Oxford, Bodleian Library, Vet. D1 f. 136.

N.p., n.pr., 1559. *KVK*: Stuttgart, Württembergische LB, Phil. oct. 2306; Augsburg, UB, 221/FX 105001 C25.559.

Nuremberg: U. or V. Neuber, 1561. *KVK*: Regensburg, Staatliche Bibliothek, 999/Lat. rec. 638.

Strasbourg: [C. Mylius], [*ca* 1565]. *VD 16,* S 4025.

Lyon: A. Gryphius, 1566. *KVK*: Rome, Biblioteca Universitaria Alessandrina, M.g.39.

Copenhagen: n.pr., 1576. *KVK*: Copenhagen, Royal Library, 52, -14 8^0.

Lyon: A. Vincent, 1621. *KVK*: Milan, Biblioteca Nazionale Braidense, 25.15.K.0005/01.

Undatable editions:

Frankfurt am Main: n.pr., n.d. *KVK*: Greifswald, UB, 542/Ch 722.

Frankfurt an der Oder: n.pr., n.d. *KVK*: Copenhagen, Royal Library, 166, 1031 051 26.

Between the appearance of the first recorded edition in 1525 and the late Lyon edition of 1621, the *Confabulationes* had been printed fifty-eight times, an impressive number indeed for any sixteenth-century book, let alone one that is now rather obscure. Mosellanus's immensely popular *Paedologia* managed about seventy, not so very many more than Schotten; Sebald Heyden's *Nomenclatura rerum domesticarum*, probably the most successful Latin-German vocabulary book of the century, had forty-four.[11] One edition of the *Confabulationes*, or more, appeared in practically every year till the mid-1550s, and another four between then and the mid-1560s, which seem to mark the end of the work's popularity. The text was printed by leading presses in major German and Dutch printing centres, notably Antwerp, Augsburg, Leipzig and Nuremberg, and even in the great French printing city of Lyon. Printers clearly saw it as a book which, despite some very evident traces it bore of its Cologne Catholic origins, would sell well over a wide geographical and confessional area.

---

[11] Barth, 'Mosellanus, *Paedologia*', cols 427–28. Heyden, *Nomenclatura rerum domesticarum*, ed. by Müller and van der Elst, p. 4* and n. 6.

A book and its contexts; an author and his networks

There is as yet no detailed study of the *Confabulationes*, and no adequate biography of Schotten in any biographic reference work, a sorry state of affairs which this study and the companion edition attempt to remedy. The edition focuses on textual and editorial questions, some of which are surprisingly complex. It presents a critical text of the *Confabulationes*, and detailed critical study of the earliest editions of the work. It also provides comprehensive notes on linguistic and stylistic points of interest, and on literary and cultural references and background.

This study is primarily an attempt to understand the work and its author in contextual terms. How are the *Confabulationes* situated in the material, social and cultural realities of Cologne, the city of their genesis (Chapter 2)? How are they situated in the context of other examples of the same genre of schoolboy colloquies (Chapter 3)? And where did they situate themselves on the spectrum of Latin, the crucially important language of learned European discourse, a language which was in the process of being being re-formed by humanists like Schotten, though at a period when the question of what form(s) humanist 'Classical' Latin could or should take was by no means definitively decided (Chapter 4)?

And then there is Schotten himself. What can reliably be known of his life and career (Chapter 1), and just as importantly, of the various social and institutional contexts in which he must have worked (Chapter 5)? For it is now recognized that understanding humanists as individuals is only half the scholarly battle: we must also strive to understand the contacts, the networks of friendship, intellectual alliance, and patronage which sustained them, materially and intellectually. This is especially important in the case of Cologne, a city which until quite recently was regarded as a bastion of militant, unreconstructed Catholic obscurantism which made very little room for humanists or humanism. It is clear that individuals like Schotten did not conform to that ethos; but our understanding of the structures and networks, personal and institutional, which made that non-conformism possible, especially for relatively obscure figures like Schotten, is still very sketchy. Though the exploration here cannot claim to provide all the answers, I believe that it represents a useful beginning.

The titles of the colloquies and conuiuia

1. Difficile esse Latinum discere sermonem, et unde dicatur sermo Latinus
2. De salutatione matutina
3. De salutatione pomeridiana
4. De salutatione uespertina
5. De uerbis dum itur cubitum
6. De cubitu resurgendo
7. De ientaculo sumendo
8. De prandio
9. De uictu pomeridiano
10. De cena
11. De postcenio
12. De potu postremo a cena
13. De inuitatione ad ientaculum
14. Inuitandi alium ad prandium
15. Vocandi alium ad cibum pomeridianum
16. Vocandi alium ad cenam
17. De modo studendi
18. De epistola conficienda
19. De repetenda lectione
20. De Corycaei metu auscultantis eos qui non Romano utuntur sermone
21. De somno plus aequo extenso
22. De morbo socordiae quem scholasticis ascribunt
23. De metu ferulae
24. De excusatione absentiae a ludo literario

Introduction 15

25. Quare schola dicatur ludus
26. De die qua otiatur a lectione
27. De aestate
28. De autumno
29. De hieme
30. De uere
31. De festo Sancti Galli
32. De festo Sancti Lamberti
33. De eligendo episcopo
34. De eligendo rege
35. De festo natali Christi
36. De tempore Bacchanali
37. De Quadragesima
38. De festo Paschatis
39. De festo Pentecostes
40. De festo Sancti Martini
41. De xeniis mittendis
42. De pecunia danda in nouae scholae ingressu
43. Non semper esse studendum
44. Quem ludum debeant iuuenes exercere
45. De eleemosynis colligendis
46. De ludo pilae
47. De ludo globorum missilium, quos 'omnia' uocant Colonienses tirunculi literarii
48. De ludo globorum qui torquentur per annulum
49. De ludo saltus
50. De certamine cursus
52. De praeceptore eligendo
53. An praeceptor literarius sit colendus tamquam parentes
54. De nundinis et munerum nundinariorum emptione
55. De nundinis Francfordiensibus
56. De uitando mendacio
57. De confessione
58. De cena suprema Christi cum discipulis et die Parasceues
59. De sumptionis Eucharistiae praeparatione

60. De more post gymnasia triuialia accedendi scholas praecelsas, quas bursas appellant
61. De deponendis (ut aiunt) cornibus beanitatis
62. Quod difficile et amarum sit a tepefacto surgere lecto
63. De profectione in peregrinae urbis gymnasium literarium
64. Quando quis satis scientiae habeat, uel sciat
65. De more standi ad cyathos
66. Quibus utendum uerbis, dum uinum foris emptum mensae affertur
67. De modo sternendi mensam
68. Miserum esse in prandio uenire peracta fabula
69. De uuis carpendis
70. De cerasis
71. De fabis, et cur sit prouerbium 'Fabis uirentibus furunt mori'
72. De missa indies audienda
73. Quomodo iuuenis in literis profecturus se gerere debeat
74. Cur scholastici tam desides sint ad laborem
75. Quod promissa stultos exhilarant
76. De omasis deportandis post bouem mactatum
77. De conuiuio opiparo et lauto
78. De conuiuio tenui et frugali
79. De auibus, columbis et piscibus capiendis
80. De balneis ingrediendis
81. De pestis saeuitia
82. De bellorum incommodo
83. De annonae caritate
84. Quam delicate in oppidis, et quam misere ac tenuiter victitent in agris
85. Facile emergi eos, qui opulenti sunt
86. De nuptiis
87. De uino dando in illius Sancti die, cuius nos nomen gerimus
88. De primo sacerdotis sacrificio
89. De exequiis defunctorum peragendis
90. De sepultura

Introduction

91. De Anno Iubilaeo
92. De tempore quo librorum lectiones auspicantur
93. De tempore quo lectionibus librorum colophon imponitur
94. De ebrietate uitanda
95. De cereis gerendis in festo Purificationis Mariae
96. De sertis in die celebri ferendis
97. De conuiuio inter cereuisiae baratra celebrando
98. De conuiuio uicissitudinario, quod sacerdotes inter se agunt
99. Cur conuiuium istud instituerunt sacerdotes uel alii
102. De feriis diui Blasii
103. De eloquentia et barbarie
104. An omne perdatur tempus quod studio non impartitur, ut dixit Plinius
105. Cum aetate esse sapiendum
106. De nouis indumentis
107. Tractare dicunt fabrilia fabros Eberhardus et Fabritius
108. Ad mensam laeta et non tristia debere esse colloquia
109. Ante et post cibum hymnum esse dicendum
110. De capite aperiendo
111. De fertili sacerdotio
112. De officio mechanico addiscendo
113. Eos raro probos fieri, quibus in teneris parentes nimium indulgent
114. Qui parentes suos diligant filios
115. Quis noster sit amicus
116. Quis nobis sit inimicus
117. De monasterii et religionis ingressu
118. Non omnes doctos esse, qui capite redimiti sunt rubeo tegmine
119. Quibus sit utendum uerbis dum aliquid a praeceptore flagitatur
120. De ouis colligendis circa Paschatis ferias
121. Nusquam nunc tutam esse fidem
122. Quod obsequium amicos, ueritas odium pariat
123. Conuiuium Bacchanale, siue ultima cena dierum Lupercalium

The *conuiuia*:
1. Conuiuium Telesphorianum siue esuriale
2. Pythagoricum conuiuium
3. Philosophica mensa
4. Diogenicum conuiuium
5. Aristippicum conuiuium siue aulicum
6. Regium conuiuium post ferias Epiphaniae
7. Conuiuium amicorum
8. Funebre conuiuium
9. Conuiuium nuptiale
10. Conuiuium Epicureum
11. Conuiuium caninum uel cereale
12. Conuiuium plebeium vel uulgare
13. Conuiuium diuitum siue opulentorum
14. Conuiuium Paschale
15. Conuiuium nundinarium siue dedicationis templi
16. Conuiuium campestre
17. Conuiuium satyricum siue inuectiuum
18. Conuiuium laudatorium
19. Conuiuium declamatorium
20. Conuiuium reconciliatorium
21. Conuiuium histrionum siue parasiticum
22. Conuiuium nugatorium
23. Conuiuium tabernarium, ubi certo asse et nummis praesentibus conuiuatur et soluitur
24. Conuiuium natale
25. Conuiuium delicatorum palatorum
26. Conuiuium helluonum poculis sese urgentium
27. Conuiuium commilitonum litterariorum asses suos congerentium
28. Conuiuium lucri lusorii
29. Conuiuium ultimi digressus, dum discessus monumentum compotatur
30. Conuiuium disceptatorium et litterarium

CHAPTER 1

Through a Glass Darkly. Hermann Schotten's Career

> Hermannus Schottenius Natione Hessus,
> Coloniae bonas litteras tradidit.
>
> HAStK, 7030 (C+D), 129, p. 113.

Hermannus Schottennius Hessus, or Hermann Schotten, who authored the *Confabulationes*, has been biographically poorly served. The main details of his career were first listed, briefly but accurately, by Nikolaus Didier in his 1915 monograph on the Luxemburg humanist Nicholas Mameranus: Didier had been apprised of these by Professor Eduard Wiepen of Cologne, who was planning an edition of the *Confabulationes* which unfortunately never saw the light of day.[1] Didier's and Wiepen's data are similar to those which Hermann Keussen published a few years later (though often cryptically abbreviated and with occasional mistakes) in his edition of the Cologne University Matricula in 1918.[2] Unfortunately both these works post-dated the appearance of the first systematic German national biography, the *Allgemeine Deutsche Biographie*, and neither it nor

---

[1] Didier, *Nikolaus Mameranus*, pp. 29–30 and n. 16, mentioning Wiepen's projected *Confabulationes* edition. No trace of Wiepen's preparatory work has been found in Cologne archives.
[2] *Matrikel*, 516,100.

any other biographical dictionary contains a remotely satisfactory entry on Schotten.[3] There are skeletal accounts in Meuthen's 1988 history of Cologne University, and Roloff's 1990 edition of the *Ludus martius*, but they are derivative of Keussen; Tewes's major monograph of 1993 on the Cologne *bursae* gives only a little more detail.[4] An article of my own of 1994 was the first detailed consideration of Schotten's biography.[5] What follows is an updated version of that account, expanded and in a few places corrected.

Schotten lived out his life in Cologne, in close connection with the University, and most of the sparse details of that life are found in the University records now in the *Historisches Stadtarchiv* of Cologne: the fourth Matricula, containing the names of all students admitted by the Rector to the University from 1500 till 1565; the fourth Arts Faculty *Dekanatsbuch* (1500–1565), the dean's official record of the Faculty business; the Arts Faculty Receptor's (Treasurer's) Book; and manuscript extracts copied from the now lost original *Dekanatsbuch* of the Theological Faculty.[6]

The official entries are few and brief. The Matricula records the matriculation on 5 December 1517 of 'Hermannus Scotten':

> Herman[n][us] scotten dyoces[is] magu[n]tine[n]s[is] – ad artes – Jura[ui]t – s[olui]t.

---

[3] *ADB*, XXXII, p. 412; cf. the sparse account in *DBE*, IX, p. 123.
[4] Meuthen, *Universität*, pp. 226–27; Schotten, *Ludus martius*, ed. by Roloff, pp. 8–9; Tewes, *Bursen*, pp. 71, 742, n. 394, 746–47, 794, 803–04.
[5] Macardle, 'Cologne Life and Cologne University Humanism', esp. pp. 142–57.
[6] HAStK, 150, A 39 (Matricula); A 481 (*Dekanatsbuch*); A 516 (Receptor's Book); A 230 (Theological *Dekanatsbuch*).

Hermann Schotten's Career 21

(Hermannus Scotten of the diocese of Mainz – Arts – swore – paid.)[7]

Schotten entered the Arts Faculty ('ad artes'). Since he swore the matriculation oath ('jurauit') he will have been at least fourteen, the minimum canonical age for oaths, and will have been born in 1503 or 1504 at the latest.[8] He may of course have been some years older, as many sixteenth-century university entrants were.[9] 'Scotten', which represents 'Sc[h]ottennius' or 'Sc[h]ottenensis', is presumably a toponymic derived from the town of Schotten in the Vogelsberg region of Hessia, which was indeed in the diocese of Mainz ('dyocesis maguntinensis'). Hessian students were not rare at Cologne, for in the later fifteenth century the University's traditional catchment area (the dioceses of Cologne, Liège and Utrecht) had extended considerably, notably into the Palatinate, Hessia and Franconia: from the end of the century till the Reformation Cologne drew its students from far beyond its own region.[10] Hessian students in early modern Cologne were frequently poor, and Schotten seems to have arrived at the University not in any kind of group, but alone, which tends to correlate with lesser wealth and status.[11] But he paid ('soluit') the matriculation fee, which was

7   HAStK, 150, A 39, fol. 91ʳ; cf. *Matrikel*, 516,100.
8   *Matrikel*, I, p. 37*; cf. Decreti II pars, causa XXII, quaest. V c. XV: 'Pueri ante quatuordecim annos non cogantur iurare', *CIC*, ed. by Friedberg, II, col. 887.
9   *Matrikel*, I, p. 38*; Gingerich and Owen, 'Matriculation Ages in Sixteenth-Century Wittenberg', pp. 135–37.
10 Schwinges, 'Sozialgeschichtliche Aspekte', p. 548; id., *Deutsche Universitätsbesucher*, pp. 244–60, esp. pp. 251, 254, 257.
11 Schwinges, *Deutsche Universitätsbesucher*, pp. 448, 458; Fletcher, 'Wealth and Poverty in the Medieval German Universities', p. 424; Schwinges, 'Studentische Kleingruppen', esp. pp. 336–37. Schotten matriculated in a group of four Laurentiana students (*Matrikel*, 516,99–102); but nothing indicates that he had any personal connection with the other three.

waived for *pauperes*, so he seems not to have been seriously impecunious. The Arts *Dekanatsbuch* reveals that Schotten was a student at the Bursa Laurentiana, once the largest of all the Cologne *bursae* or colleges, though then somewhat in decline.[12]

Schotten gained his BA on 27 January 1519 and his MA on 15 March 1520.[13] The time of just over a year for each degree suggests he was a competent student whose previous schooling had prepared him well for university work. On 15 April 1522 he became a full voting member of the teaching body of the Arts Faculty, 'receptus ad consilium facultatis'.[14] This required him to have been MA for two years, to have lectured, presided over undergraduate disputations, and attended a quota of advanced ones.[15] Schotten seems to have been a bright young man on the threshold of a conventional university career: however, it is precisely now that he simply vanishes from the official Faculty record, not to be heard of for a full nine years, till 19 May 1531, when he appears as one of the five examiners for the BA degree.[16] This long hiatus is not explained in the official Faculty record, but fortunately a few other documents allow us to get some idea of the reasons for it.

One crucial source is a manuscript history of the Bursa Laurentiana, written around 1530 by Arnold Luyde de Tongeren (d. 1540), principal of the *bursa* from 1503 to 1516, in which a dated list of the masters engaged as

---

[12] HAStK, 150, A 481, fol. 126^r, listing Schotten amongst the Laurentiana students presented for the BA. See Schwinges, 'Sozialgeschichtliche Aspekte', p. 549.
[13] HAStK, 150, A 481, fols 125^v, 126^r (BA); 131$^{r, v}$ (MA).
[14] HAStK, 150, A 481, fol. 143^v: 'In die 15 aprilis recepti sunt ad c[on]siliu[m] ffacultat[is] [...] Jtem M[a]g[iste]r Herman[n]us Ortma[n] de Hassia.'
[15] Bianco, I,2, p. 69; *Alte Un.*, p. 299; Meuthen, *Universität*, pp. 29, 119.
[16] HAStK, 150, A 481, fol. 180^v.

lectors in the *bursa* records Schotten's appointment in 1530.[17] This is the key to the gap in the *Dekanatsbuch*: since the mid-fifteenth century the *bursae* had effectively monopolized the Cologne Arts Faculty. Almost all teaching went on there; regular stipends and Faculty offices went exclusively to *bursa* lectors (see pp. 153–54). Before his admission to this realm of privilege in 1530, Schotten could have filled no official Faculty positions, and there would have been nothing to record about him.

After 1530, however, Schotten's career developed conventionally. He read for a higher degree: the Theological *Dekanatsbuch* records his promotion 'ad Lecturam Bibliae', that is to the degree of Baccalaureus Theologiae, on 26 February 1532,[18] and this is confirmed by the Arts *Dekanatsbuch*, which consistently refers to him as BTh from 10 May 1532 on.[19] Although the incomplete Theology records contain no more references to Schotten, he clearly continued his studies: on 26 May 1536 he was still BTh; but from 2 November 1536 the Arts *Dekanatsbuch* refers to him as Baccalaureus Formatus Theologiae: for this more advanced degree the further four years' study was the norm.[20] There is no indication that Schotten was ever ordained as a priest, though this cannot be excluded: his study of Theology may simply point to academic ambition. Theology, far more than the other higher faculties of Law and Medicine, was the discipline of the successful Cologne academics, the men prominent in teach-

---

17 HAStK, 150, A 760, fol. 11^r.
18 HAStK, 150, A 230, fol. 9^r, no. 60: 'Venerandus M[a]g[iste]r noster Pastor Columbae [= Arnold de Dammone] praesentavit M[a]g[ist]rum Hermannum Scholenium [sic] ad Lecturam Bibliae'. Schotten's name may have been misspelt by the eighteenth-century copyist Nikolaus Brewer.
19 HAStK, 150, A 481, fol. 184^r.
20 BTh: HAStK, 150, A 481, fol. 203^r. BFTh: ibid., fol. 203^v; HAStK, 150, A 516, fol. 84^r (1537). Gescher, 'Die Statuten der theologischen Fakultät', esp. pp. 83, 86; Meuthen, *Universität*, p. 27.

ing, examining and promoting graduates, in Arts as well as in Theology, and in university governance.[21] Schotten probably aimed to be one of that number.

Schotten held a number of Faculty offices. From 1531 till 1542 his name recurs repeatedly. Twice a year he was an examiner for the BA or the Licence;[22] in 1537 he was one of the 'Tentatores' who conducted the first part of the Cologne chronicler Hermann von Weinsberg's Licence examination.[23] In December 1531 he presided over the *Disputatio quodlibetica*.[24] In 1533 he was elected dean of the Faculty: he was the first man in the Faculty's history to hold office for a whole year: previously, deans had changed every six months.[25] As dean, he spoke in the 1533 *Quodlibetica*, 'super expositione orationis dominice';[26] in 1534 and 1537 he was the Arts Intrans, the Faculty representative at the election of the rector;[27] on 14 June 1537 and again in 1540 he presided over the inception of three MAs from the Laurentiana.[28] On 22 December 1537 he was made receptor (treasurer) of the Faculty, for the usual period of a year.[29]

By the institutional standards of the time, however, this was a mediocre academic career. Whether Schotten even attempted the next theological degree, the Licence,

---

[21] Tewes, *Bursen*, pp. 116–17.
[22] HAStK, 150, A 481, fols 182^r, 183^r, 184^r, 186^v, 188^r, 189^v, 191^r, 196^v, 203^r, 203^v, 204^v, 206^r, 208^r, 209^v, 212^r, 213^v, 215^v, 219^r, 222^r.
[23] HAStK, 150, A 481, fol. 204^v: Licence *Tentamen*, 3.2.1537; cf. *BW*, I pp. 114–115. On Weinsberg, see p. 56.
[24] HAStK, 150, A 481, fol. 183^r. See p. 29.
[25] HAStK, 150, A 481, fol. 187^v. Cf. n. 36.
[26] HAStK, 150, A 481, fol. 190^v.
[27] HAStK, 150, A 39, fols 144^r, 151^r; HAStK, 150, A 481, fol. 207^r; *Matrikel*, II, pp. 927, 944.
[28] HAStK, 150, A 481, fols 206^r, 218^r; HAStK, 150, A 516, fol. 92^r.
[29] HAStK, 150, A 481, fol. 208^r; HAStK, 150, A 516, fol. 84^r. Schotten's entries in the Receptor's Book: HAStK, 150, A 516, fols 84^r–85^v.

is not known, but he certainly did not attain it, and it was this degree that distinguished the leading teachers of the University and put them in line for principalships at the *bursae* and benefices at the Cathedral and the Cologne parish churches. About two-thirds of Laurentiana lectors with the BFTh gained the Licence, most taking between three and seven years to do so.[30] Perhaps Schotten was working slowly, and was overtaken by illness and death (see below). Since about half of all known Laurentiana masters held the LicTh, Schotten, with his BFTh, was not in the academic first division.[31] This is reflected in the number of Bachelors and Masters over whose determination and inception he presided, the crucial sign of academic success: whereas Schotten's most successful contemporaries notched up hundreds, he himself incepted a mere six MAs.[32]

Schotten died in 1546, on an unrecorded date, a fact noted only by the then Arts receptor under the head of expenses for his funeral.[33] There is no obituary, or indeed any mention of Schotten's death or funeral, in the *Dekanatsbuch*, as there is for a good many members of the University, possibly because he was not regarded as an important figure, and possibly also because he had not been active in the Faculty for several years: he is last recorded, as a BA examiner, on 16 February 1542.[34] This may be why some older authors incorrectly date his death

---

[30] Based on the data on Laurentiana lectors in Tewes, *Bursen*, pp. 47–73.
[31] Tewes, *Bursen*, pp. 116–20, esp. pp. 116, 118.
[32] Tewes, *Bursen*, pp. 116–17. Comparative figures for Laurentiana masters, ibid., pp. 47–73: e.g. Johannes Wanger de Nurtingen: 405 promotions; Johannes Jacobi de Campis: 362; Hermann Blanckenfort de Monasterio: 135. Schotten: see n. 28.
[33] HAStK, 150, A 516, fol. 105^r. Keussen's reference to this source in his note to *Matrikel*, 516,100, is unclear.
[34] HAStK, 150, A 481, fol. 222^r. He is last mentioned in the Receptor's Book on 20 May 1540: HAStK, 150, A 516, fol. 91^v.

as 1543.³⁵ Unless Schotten was a very mature student on matriculation, he had lived only into his early to mid-forties, not particularly long even by sixteenth-century standards. This, together with the four years of apparent inactivity before his death, suggests that he might have been in poor health for the last few years of his life.

These are the only official references to Schotten in the University books, the records made in due form by University officers. But fortunately the official books also contain another, unofficial, stratum of entries: corrections, annotations and marginalia made by those temporarily in possession of the books. Rare indeed was the dean who could resist making some such additions, often outspoken, and regularly fascinating and informative to the later reader. Schotten was no exception. As dean in 1533–1534 he made several retrospective additions to the *Dekanatsbuch* in his own distinctive hand (see p. 204). Against early occurrences of his name in the book he noted that he was to become dean in 1533, the first to hold office for a whole year.³⁶ More helpfully, he emended several references to himself as 'Hermannus de Hassia' and 'Hermannus Ortman', substituting 'Hermannus Schottennius Hessus', the name most frequently given him in later entries.³⁷ This establishes the medieval nomenclature habitually used by colleagues, 'Hermannus

---

[35] E.g. Cratepoleus, *De electorum ecclesiasticorum [...]* (*ca.* 1580), p. 167; Hartzheim, *Bibliotheca Coloniensis* (1747), p. 138.

[36] HAStK, 150, A 481, fol. 125ᵛ: '1533 Decanus facultat[is] effectus'; fol. 131ʳ: 'Tandem Anno 1533 Decanus facultat[is] artiu[m]'; fol. 131ᵛ: 'Postea lec[tor] b[ursae] Lau[rentianae] et el[e]ctus 1533. in Decanu[m] facultat[is] a[r]tiu[m] et primus q[ui] p[er] annu[m] pr[aee]ss[et] Decanatui NB'.

[37] HAStK, 150, A 481, fols 152Aʳ, 180ᵛ ('Hermannus de Hassia'); fol. 187ᵛ ('Hermannus Ortman'). Also HAStK, 150, A 39, fol. 144ʳ ('Hermannus de Hassia', unemended); 150, A 481, fol. 143ᵛ ('Hermannus Ortman de Hassia i. Schotten[ius]', unemended).

de Hassia', and Schotten's real surname, Ortman, a name not mentioned in the Matricula (see note 14). Schotten evidently found both names distasteful, and preferred his semi-classical toponymic: another humanist, Johannes Phrissemius, who matriculated as 'Johannes Ott de Fryckenhusen', recast his own name in the same way.[38] Schotten is absolutely consistent in spelling himself 'Schottennius';[39] by contrast, the spelling by other hands in the *Dekanatsbuch* varies widely (Scotenius, Scattennius, Schutthennius, etc.).[40] 'Schottennius' is also the form found in printed editions of Schotten's works supervised by him. This establishes the correct orthography of his name, in the sense of the form he preferred. The spelling 'Schottenius', widely used in modern sources,[41] is technically more 'correct', because names formed with the toponymic suffix '-ius' should not double the final consonant of the place-name (cf. 'Phrissemius'); but it is clear what Schotten's preference was, and it should be respected.[42]

---

[38] Phrissemius: *Matrikel*, 487,68: 'Johan Ott de Fryckenhusen d. Herbipol.', 3 October 1510; Meuthen, *Universität*, pp. 245–46.
[39] E.g. HAStK, 150, A 481, fols 180^v, 187^v.
[40] HAStK, 150, A 481: 'Scotennius': fol. 219^r; 'Scottennius': fols 182^r, 222^r; 'Schottenius': fols 183^r, 204^v, etc.; 'Scotthennius': fol. 208^r; 'Schottennius': fols 183^r, 206^r, etc.; 'Schottenus': fols 212^r, 213^v; 'Schuttennius': fol. 209^r; 'Schutthennius': fol. 196^v; 'Scattennius': fol. 207^r; 'Schattennius': fol. 208^r. Cf. 'Scotenius', HAStK, 150, A 759, fol. 3^v; A 760, fol. 11^r.
[41] E.g. *ADB*; *DBE*; *KVK*; *NUC*; *VD 16*; Tewes, *Bursen*; Leedham-Green, *Books in Cambridge Inventories*, etc.
[42] Forms in modern sources are inconsistent, sometimes misleading: e.g. 'Schottenus' in Kuckhoff, *Geschichte des Gymnasium Tricoronatum*, p. 3, n. 2; 'Schoten' in Kahl, 'Die Musik an der alten Kölner Universität um 1500', p. 494; 'Schooten' in Bayle and others, *Répertoire automatisé des livres du seizième siècle à la bibliothèque municipale de Rouen*, p. 274.

The official traces, then, are those of a conventional academic career between 1517 and 1522, and again from 1530 onwards. But the very conventionality makes the gap of eight years, from Schotten's admission to the Arts Faculty *consilium* in 1522 to his appointment at the Laurentiana in 1530, all the more intriguing. Why did a clearly competent young man have to wait so long for a permanent position, and what was he doing while he waited? Though there are few definite answers to these questions, there are a number of highly suggestive indications. Unfortunately, it is precisely their suggestiveness that is the problem. Humans crave narrative, and the few documented details of Schotten's life can be used as the basis for a rather gratifying story, but it must be remembered that these details are sparse, ambiguous and their survival probably fortuitous. The entire Schotten narrative, which we will never be able to reconstruct, might make a different overall effect.

To take the later evidence first: in 1528 the humanistically-inclined Konrad Kluppel, former town clerk of Fritzlar, spent about a year's 'study leave' in Cologne, living in Phrissemius's household. In a letter of 23 April 1528 he detailed his daily programme. He attended mainly Law lectures, but also listened to 'Hermann Schottenus [sic] Hessus interpreting the Psalter at four in the afternoon near the Cathedral'.[43] Classes on the Psalms delivered 'near the Cathedral' suggest Theology lectures delivered in the 'Aula' of the faculty near the Cathedral's south tower.[44] Yet it seems unlikely that Schotten was giving official theological classes as early as 1528. After

---

[43] 'Ne profanis studiis omnino deditus videar, Hermannum Schottenum [sic] Hessum prope aedem sacram eminentiorem psalterium interpretantem quarta pomeridiana hora veneror', Kluppel, *Konrad Kluppels Chronik*, ed. by Jürges, pp. 154–55.

[44] *Topogr.*, I, p. 139*; II, 301b, c. A new building had been erected in 1523: HAStK, 150, A 481, fol. 148ʳ; *BRStK*, I, pp. 952–53.

the MA the Theology course involved about six years' study for the first degree, BTh, when the student was admitted to the *Lectura Bibliae*, that is, permitted to lecture on the text of the Bible: yet by the clear testimony of the Theological and Arts *Dekanatsbücher* Schotten achieved this status only in 1532.[45] This suggests either that he had begun Theology only in about 1526, or, perhaps more probably, had started after his MA in 1520 and continued after a break of some years (see p. 47). In these lectures on the Psalms, then, Schotten might have been deputizing for a senior faculty member, or possibly even engaging in a more private intellectual enterprise, maybe even in a humanist-philological vein. The late hour of 4 pm, in an academic day which began at 6 am, suggests so. Whatever the case may have been, Schotten was demonstrably present in, or on the margins of, the University in early 1528.

At the other end of Schotten's long absence from the records, an unofficial source gives a more substantial glimpse of the man in mid-December 1523. This is in the record of the *Disputatio quodlibetica*, a set of disputations on subjects freely chosen by the students and masters, used in medieval universities to extend the range of material for discussion beyond that of the stereotyped 'ordinary' disputations.[46] Schotten had been scheduled to speak in the disputation, but was prevented. His exclusion is recorded in the Arts *Dekanatsbuch* – not in the official minutes of the disputation but in a fascinating, outspoken marginal addition:

---

[45] Gescher, 'Die Statuten der theologischen Fakultät', especially pp. 74–86; Meuthen, *Universität*, pp. 27, 142. Twenty-eight out of forty Laurentiana lectors attained the BTh between four and seven years after the MA (based on Tewes, *Bursen*, pp. 47–73). See n. 18.

[46] Bianco, I,2, pp. 296–97; Meuthen, *Universität*, pp. 23–24; cf. Meuthen, 'Artesfakultät', p. 389 on the stereotyped nature of ordinary disputations.

> Scottennius
> Dixiss[et] quoq[ue] m[a]g[iste]r Herman[n]us
> de Hassia de institution[n]e pueroru[m]
> in patria, nisi ad instantiam
> d[omi]ni licentiati Joh[annis] Campis
> censuris ecclesiastic[is] ob debita
> quedam victus p[rae]peditusq[ue] fuisset
> vbi ob vni[us] m[a]g[ist]ri priuatam
> rem res publica facultat[is]
> artiu[m] pati cogebatur / queritur
> quid sit iuris.[47]

The hand seems to be that in which the main record of Johannes Volsius Lunensis's deanship is written, and so is presumably that of Volsius himself.[48] It is definitely not Schotten's own writing.[49] The 'Scottennius' added above the line is not in Volsius's hand, but not in Schotten's either; despite a slight similarity to Schotten's script, the spelling and the fact that the form 'Hermannus de Hassia' is not deleted are entirely uncharacteristic of him.[50]

---

[47] HAStK, 150, A 481, fol. 152A^r; transcribed, with some mistakes, in Krafft, 'Mittheilungen aus der niederrheinischen Reformationsgeschichte', p. 216, n. 1, and Tewes, 'Die Universität Köln im Umbruch', p. 164; and correctly in Liessem, *Hermann van dem Busche*, p. 65, n. 2.

[48] Volsius's hand (HAStK, 150, A 481, fols 152^v–54^v, 165^r–66^r, 184^r–85^r) varies considerably, and the record of the *Quodlibetica* (152A^r) initially seems to be written by someone else, as I asserted in 'Cologne Life and Cologne University Humanism', p. 148. Subsequent closer inspection suggests that the whole record of Volsius's Deanship was indeed written by him, as stated by Tewes, *Bursen*, p. 747 and n. 421, and id., 'Die Universität Köln im Umbruch', p. 162.

[49] As assumed by Krafft, 'Mittheilungen aus der niederrheinischen Reformationsgeschichte', p. 216, n. 1.

[50] Liessem, *Hermann van dem Busche*, p. 65, n. 2, believes the addition is in Schotten's hand. The hand is very similar to one which has made a number of historical and biographical annotations in the *Dekanatsbuch*: HAStK, 150, A 481, e.g. fols 181^v, 187^v. Recent conservation work on the *Dekanats-*

As so often with documents concerning Schotten there is a certain amount of ambiguity. The clause 'nisi [...] censuris ecclesiasticis [...] victus praepeditusque fuisset' might translate as 'had he not been overcome and impeded by ecclesiastical censures'; but the participle 'victus' ('overcome, defeated') seems an unusual one to associate with 'censura'. More usual would be 'vinctus' ('bound, fettered') which would also fit well with 'praepeditus' ('fettered, impeded') to give 'nisi censuris ecclesiasticis vinctus praepeditusque fuisset': 'had he not been bound and impeded by ecclesiastical censures'. This could easily have been the intended reading: the writer could simply have left out a stroke representing 'n' over the 'i' of 'victus'. However, it is also possible that 'victus' is not a participle but the genitive of the noun 'victus', 'food, necessaries of life'; that the intended reading was 'ob debita quedam victus', and that the suffix '-que' on 'praepeditus' was mistakenly added, the writer having become confused between the two meanings of 'victus'.[51]

The passage, then, translates as:

And Master Hermann of Hessia would have spoken too, on the subject of the education of boys in their home region, had he not, at the instigation of Licentiate Johannes de Campis, been impeded by ecclesiastical censures on account of certain sums he owed for his living expenses [OR 'been bound and impeded by ecclesiastical censures on account of certain debts']. In this way the common good of the Faculty was forced to suffer on account of a single master's private financial affairs; one must ask whether this is right.

---

buch has rendered the word 'Scottennius' nearly illegible.

[51] That 'debita victus' might mean 'misdemeanours in his way of life', as Tewes translates (*Bursen*, p. 747), seems improbable; and indeed three years later, in 'Die Universität Köln im Umbruch', p. 164, l. 26, Tewes reads 'vinctus', and translates as 'wegen gewisser Schulden', 'on account of certain debts' (p. 165, ll. 29–31).

This entry is brief, but it suggests several things. First, that in late 1523 Schotten already had an interest in pedagogy, and ideas of his own on the subject. Second, that he had not completely severed his connection with the University, and that possibly he was still in some sense within the pale of the Laurentiana: for the most likely place to run up debts (especially on living expenses, if that is the correct reading) would be in a *bursa*; and Johannes Jacobi de Campis, who demanded the 'ecclesiastical censures', was principal of the Laurentiana at the time.[52] Third, that there were some – apparently including a figure as important as Dean Johannes Volsius – who sympathized strongly with Schotten and felt that de Campis's action had harmed the Arts Faculty.

This incident is particularly intriguing because this exclusion of Schotten from the formal business of the University comes towards the beginning of his absence from the official Faculty record after April 1522. After it there is no extant reference to Schotten in the University context till Kluppel's letter of April 1528, almost four and a half years later; and Schotten is not back within the official Faculty structures till 1530. Might the exclusion from the Quodlibetica have been the beginning of Schotten's exile from the University, as Tewes concludes?[53] Like so many questions this cannot be answered definitively, but some of the attendant circumstances are distinctly suggestive.

For a start, why should Johannes de Campis have taken such a drastic step on account of some debts? There may well be a connection with the important, albeit abortive, reform of the Cologne Arts curriculum in a humanist direction which was then under way.[54]

---

[52] Johannes de Campis: *Matrikel*, 418,65.
[53] Tewes, *Bursen*, pp. 71, 747.
[54] Nauert, 'Humanists, Scholastics, and the Struggle to Reform the University of Cologne, 1523–1525', esp. pp. 54–59; Meuthen, *Universität*, pp. 229–35.

Despite the presence of numerous humanists in Cologne since the fifteenth century, humanism had been unable to penetrate the official Arts curriculum. In the 1520s, however, Cologne was affected by a serious drop in student numbers: the late-fifteenth-century average of 400 or 500 matriculations a year had dropped to about 300 in the first sixteen years of the sixteenth century. The period 1517–1522 saw the beginnings of a drastic decline which continued till an absolute low of fifty-four in 1535, and from which the university did not really recover till the later seventeenth century; a spectacular casualty was the Bursa Corneliana, which closed for lack of students in 1524.[55] This decline, which affected many other universities, was a consequence of the enormous social, political and religious uncertainties of the Reformation; but the reasons were not fully understood at the time, and the various interest groups in the University offered their own tendentious explanations. Amongst them were the humanists, who claimed that Cologne's refusal to reform the scholastic Arts course was alienating students, and who sought a considerable opening of the curriculum in a classical and humanist direction.[56] It was in this atmosphere of crisis that the first negotiations for curricular reform in the Arts Faculty took place.

The drafting of new Arts statutes which included some classical and humanist authors had begun in 1522. The precise details of this process, and of those involved in it, are far from clear from the surviving documentation; but it is evident that resistance to change, on the part of the more conservative members of the Faculty and University, was considerable at every stage. On 3 January 1523 Phrissemius, then dean, and himself strongly in

---

[55] Eulenburg, *Die Frequenz der deutschen Universitäten*, pp. 285–99; Meuthen, *Universität*, pp. 77–79; Nauert, 'Humanists, Scholastics [...]', pp. 50–51.

[56] Nauert, 'Humanists, Scholastics [...]', pp. 50–53.

favour of curricular change, presented draft revised statutes to the rector, to be put before a congregation of the University as a whole; but disagreements within the Arts Faculty protracted matters for another three months. Only on 27 March did a poorly attended University congregation meet: it seems to have ordered a further draft of the statutes to be submitted for the approval of all the faculty deans.[57] Revised statutes were eventually agreed, and were implemented by early 1524; but they were far from a radical break with previous practice.[58] The Aristotelian and scholastic foundations of the Arts course remained unchanged, the only concessions to humanism being in the inclusion of some works of Cicero, Vergil and Baptista Mantuanus (none compulsory for exams), and permission to use Cicero, Vergil, Mantuan and Filelfo as models of Latin prose style.[59] Moreover, a ban on teaching 'lascivious' authors who write 'comical and disreputable tales' would, if strictly interpreted, have prohibited a good deal of secular humanist writing.[60] The mountains of the University had gone into labour, and given birth to a mouse. The humanist-minded in the Faculty must have seen the 1523 curricular 'reform' as profoundly frustrating. Two years later, in 1525, they were able to console themselves a little when a more thoroughgoing reform leavened the Arts curriculum with

---

[57] Bianco, I, p. 467, n. 1; Nauert, 'Humanists, Scholastics [...]', p. 54.
[58] Revised statutes: Bianco I,2, pp. 288–316, 'C. Statuta reformata Facultatis Artium Ubiorum'.
[59] Bianco I,2, pp. 288–316, esp. pp. 297–99, 'de libris legendis et exercendis', pp. 303–08, BA and MA examination regulations; Nauert, 'Humanists, Scholastics [...]', p. 57.
[60] Bianco, I,2, p. 299: 'ut nemo legere vel audire praesumat lascivos autores qui comicas quasdam et inhonestiores fabulas docent'; cf. Bianco I, p. 468; *Alte Un.*, p. 370; Nauert, 'Humanists, Scholastics [...]', p. 57.

a number of humanist translations of Aristotelian texts and some classical and humanist rhetorical works.[61]

It is not entirely clear who drafted the 1523 revised statutes, exactly what the disagreements within the Arts Faculty were, or who articulated them. The description of the revision of the statutes mentions disagreements amongst the 'regent masters' of the Arts Faculty: this might refer either to the regents or principals of the *bursae*, or simply to the masters officially teaching in the Faculty.[62] This is certainly not specific enough to identify the *bursa* principals as the main obstacles to reform; but it is unlikely that any of them was in favour. The principals at the time were personally 'very elderly and very conservative';[63] and they represented a system which, having functioned in the same way for a long time, had an inbuilt opposition to change.

The 1522 and 1523 quodlibets seem to have been used by the humanists as a platform in this curricular debate, and in the wider humanist/scholastic conflict in the University at the time.[64] By contrast with the theological orientation of earlier and later quodlibets, the disputations of these years had a humanist emphasis. Speakers in 1522 included Phrissemius himself; the eminent Jacobus Sobius, heavily involved in the 1525 reforms; the notable Hellenist and Hebraist Arnold von Wesel; Chrysanthus von Münstereifel, a friend of Heinrich Bullinger; and Petrus Segenensis, schoolmaster and

---

[61] Nauert, 'Humanists, Scholastics [...]', esp. pp. 59–76; Meuthen, pp. 280–87; Tewes, *Bursen*, p. 802.
[62] Bianco, I, p. 467, n. 1: 'propter certas discordias Dominorum Regentium in eadem Facultate'. The meaning 'bursa principals' is understood by Nauert, 'Humanists, Scholastics [...]', pp. 54, 55–56, 59; for the sense of 'official Faculty teaching masters' see Tewes, *Bursen*, p. 15.
[63] Nauert, 'Humanists, Scholastics [...]', p. 55.
[64] Tewes, *Bursen*, pp. 743–44; id., 'Die Universität Köln im Umbruch', p. 162.

associate of Hermann von Neuenahr.[65] Phrissemius and Sobius were accused by the monks and scholastics of heterodoxy. Monks, normally well represented amongst the speakers, stayed away from the disputation, but most unusually it was attended by Johann von Reidt, the humanist-minded mayor, a former pupil of Sobius and friend of Erasmus, who had been involved in the curricular reform, and by Councillor Adolf Rinck. This was an unmistakable signal of solidarity with the humanists.[66]

1523 saw several of the same speakers again. This time their themes were recorded, and several were unmistakeably humanist: Petrus Segenensis's 'De tribus linguis'; Johannes Kempensis's 'De arte dicendi'; Petrus Ubelius Wormariensis's 'De necessitate Hebraicae linguae'; Schotten's cancelled 'De institutione puerorum in patria'; and possibly also Chrysanthus von Münstereifel's 'De vera eruditione'.[67] Once again there was a monastic boycott, and the detailed account in the *Dekanatsbuch* suggests an atmosphere of tension.[68]

The presumption must be that Schotten was in favour of the curricular reform, and of the humanist cause in general. De Campis, by contrast, was neither a humanist by personal bent nor, as a *bursa* principal, likely to have favoured reform. Could this have been what moved the

---

[65] HAStK, 150, A 481, fols 146^v–47^r; Krafft, 'Mittheilungen aus der niederrheinischen Reformationsgeschichte', pp. 216–17; Meuthen, *Universität*, p. 254.

[66] HAStK, 150, A 481, fols 146^v–47^r; Krafft, 'Mittheilungen aus der niederrheinischen Reformationsgeschichte', pp. 214–15; Meuthen, *Universität*, p. 229; Tewes, 'Die Universität Köln im Umbruch', pp. 162–63.

[67] HAStK, 150, A 481, fol. 152A^r. Tewes, *Bursen*, p. 746, plausibly assumes that Chrysanthus's was a secular humanist theme.

[68] HAStK, 150, A 481, fol. 152A^r; Krafft, 'Mittheilungen aus der niederrheinischen Reformationsgeschichte', pp. 215–16; Meuthen, *Universität*, p. 236; Tewes, 'Die Universität Köln im Umbruch', pp. 164–65.

senior academic to debar Schotten from speaking at the Quodlibetica? His reaction seems plausible in context. Schotten, a humanist, was planning to speak in a forum which conservative academics probably felt had been hijacked by the humanists as part of the curricular debate. This may explain why senior Laurentiana masters seem to have boycotted the Quodlibet,[69] and it might have motivated de Campis to discourage or even prevent others from going. Schotten was presumably going to expound humanist ideas on education, and indeed, his title hints that he may have been planning a critique of the methods of the Arts Faculty and the *bursae*. 'De institutione puerorum *in patria*' had an unmistakable resonance in Cologne ears, to understand which a little background information is necessary.[70]

Widespread doubts about the quality of schools in Cologne meant that boys from the burgher classes in search of a serious 'grammar' schooling tended to seek it not 'in patria', 'at home' in Cologne, but 'abroad', 'apud exteros',[71] in the excellent humanist *gymnasia* of the Lower Rhine, the Netherlands or elsewhere, notably Emmerich, Deventer, Zwolle and Münster.[72] The *bursae* of the Cologne Arts Faculty competed in the same educational market: they had long been taking in under-age boys, who circumvented the matriculation oath by promising to swear it when they reached the proper age.[73]

---

[69] Tewes, *Bursen*, pp. 746–47.
[70] The translation 'in ihren Heimatorten' by Tewes, 'Die Universität Köln im Umbruch', p. 165, l. 29, is correct but does not convey the specific Cologne resonance which Schotten probably intended.
[71] The description used by the dean, Hermannus Schilderus Embricensis, in 1542: HAStK, 150, 481, fol. 228r.
[72] E.g. Schwinges, *Deutsche Universitätsbesucher*, pp. 336–37 and n. 168, citing relevant literature; Kuckhoff, *Geschichte des Gymnasium Tricoronatum*, pp. 52–53. Weinsberg records his years at Emmerich, 1531–1534, in *BW*, I, pp. 74–103.
[73] *Matrikel*, I, pp. 35*–37*; e.g. *Matrikel*, 332,75: Bernardus

Such boys were taught 'grammar', sometimes as a *bona fide* preparation for the Arts course, but often with no thought of matriculating them or presenting them for degrees. This was an educational and ethical grey area: where exactly was the line between legitimate introductory, even remedial, teaching and usurping the proper task of the grammar school?[74]

Almost nothing concrete is known about the curriculum, organization and personnel of this pre-university instruction, or of precisely how it related to the official structures of Arts teaching.[75] Two *bursae* which had specialized in this activity in the fifteenth century had by the 1520s long disappeared: the Raemsdonck in the 1470s, the Ottonis by 1503. The Ottonis, which had possibly developed the humanist curricular elements introduced earlier at the Raemsdonck, had been particularly appreciated and patronized by the Cologne burgher class. Students had tended to take their BA there, then to migrate to other *bursae* for the MA and higher degrees.[76] It was not clear that the four remaining 'principal' *bursae* were as successful: they were perceived as leaving boys not linguistically up to the demands of the Arts course to sink or swim in a pedagogically irresponsible way.[77]

---

[74] Eylsich de Colonia: 'Non iuravit, quia minorennis, sed pater promisit, quod, cum venerit ad annos discretionis, prestabit iuramentum consuetum'. This was despite a University statute of 1481 forbidding the practice: *Matrikel*, I, pp. 16*–17*; Kuckhoff, *Geschichte des Gymnasium Tricoronatum*, pp. 24–25. Hence educational endowments of the sixteenth century often stipulated a minimum age or school experience of the beneficiaries: Tewes, *Bursen*, p. 273.

[75] Divergent assessments in Tewes, 'Die Studentenburse des Magisters Nikolaus Mommer von Raemsdonck', pp. 49–55; *Alte Un.*, p. 347; Kuckhoff, *Geschichte des Gymnasium Tricoronatum*, pp. 50–51; Schwinges, *Deutsche Universitätsbesucher*, pp. 335–37; Meuthen, *Universität*, p. 227.

[76] Tewes, *Bursen*, pp. 425–27.

[77] Weinsberg criticizes teaching in the Laurentiana in the 1530s,

These doubts about the *bursae* became more serious as the steep decline in student numbers of the early sixteenth century began to threaten the University's very survival. The proponents of reform, the city council and certain 'progressive' elements in the University, felt that what was needed to assure proper pre-university education in Cologne was a revival of institutions like the Ottonis. In the debate over the 1525 University curricular reform, the Medical Faculty suggested that two *bursae* 'instar Ottonis' should be set up, offering grammar, dialectic and 'politiores literae' up to BA level, after which students could proceed to a philosophical training in one of the principal *bursae*. The hope was that the new *bursae* would attract the sons of Cologne burghers, allowing the city's private schools to be closed.[78] In 1529 the city council was planning a (never realized) municipal humanist *bursa*.[79] Thirteen years later, in 1542, the council, still concerned to stop the continuing decline of the University, again suggested setting up a school along the lines of the Ottonis.[80]

If the council constantly repeated the same proposal, the University doggedly kept raising the same objections. In 1525 the Arts Faculty, dismissing suggestions of pedagogical reform, listed the 'real' reasons for the decline in student numbers. War and plague had raised food prices to prohibitive levels. The University's fiscal privileges had been eroded by the council. Lutheranism had drawn many away from university study, in Cologne

---

    especially the lack of instruction in grammar: *BW*, I, pp. 103–04.
[78] HAStK, 150, A 74, fol. 8ᵛ; cf. 150, A 317, fol. 90ᵛ; Tewes, *Bursen*, pp. 435–36.
[79] *BRStK*, III, p. 631, no. 472, 9 July 1529 (original HAStK, 10 (Rpr), 7, fol. 248ᵛ); *Regesten*, 2953; cf. Ennen, *Geschichte*, IV, p. 673; Tewes, *Bursen*, pp. 437–38.
[80] 'Studium particulare instar domus Ottonis': HAStK, 150, A 481, fol. 220ᵛ, 7 February 1542.

as elsewhere. 'Clandestine' private schoolmasters, many infected by Lutheranism, were seducing students away from the traditional university curriculum. Last but not least, students were lazy.[81]

The University clung to this official line for decades. When in 1542 the Council again suggested a school comparable to the Ottonis, the rector, Theodoricus Alardi de Geldria, simply repeated the objections of 1525, staunchly maintaining that the *bursa* teaching methods were so thorough, so carefully differentiated and gradated as to make the proposed school unnecessary. The next year, the dean, Hermannus Schilderus Embricensis of the Montana, restated exactly the same arguments.[82] Some seem weak and self-contradictory. Both Alardi and Schilderus asked the council to fund extra Arts Faculty teachers, freeing the *bursa* masters to teach more of the basics, which sounds like an implicit admission that what they were offering was not in fact sufficient. Schilderus's claim that extra staff would allow the *bursae* to divide the boys into classes suggests that Alardi's description of the differentiated teaching was highly optimistic; and certainly Weinsberg remembered teaching at the Laurentiana in the 1530s as slack.[83]

Schotten's phrase 'de institutione puerorum in patria' thus almost certainly alluded to the vexed question of how pre-university schooling in Cologne could be improved so as to make going 'abroad' unnecessary; and this question in practice always involved a critique of *bursa* methods and of their Aristotelian-scholastic curriculum, which taught no *bonae litterae*, and little or nothing of relevance to the civic and mercantile life which the youth of the Cologne burgher class would go

---

[81] HAStK, 150, A 74, fol. 7^{r-v}.
[82] Alardi, 1542: HAStK, 150, A 481, fols 220^v–21^v. Schilderus, 1543: ibid., fol. 228^r.
[83] HAStK, 150, A 481, fol. 228^r; *BW*, I, pp. 103–04.

on to lead. Schotten's proposed topic, then, was a hot potato, particularly in the charged situation of factional conflict in which the 1523 Quodlibet was held.

Interestingly, one of the *Confabulationes* relates to the topic. In colloquy 60, 'De modo post gymnasia triuialia accedendi scholas praecelsas, quas *bursas* appellant',[84] Crato tries to dissuade Vinandus from his plan of leaving the *schola trivialis* for a *bursa*, implying that the *bursae* build without proper educational foundations, and quipping that their name is derived from 'bursa', a synonym of 'crumena', a moneybag, because it costs 'bags of money' to study there and take their dubious degrees (ll. 38–42). All this evidence makes it distinctly possible that Schotten's debarment from the 1523 Quodlibet was one of the skirmishes in an ongoing university conflict.

The unofficial evidence on the Quodlibet and in Kluppel's letter reduce the eight years' gap in the official records (April 1522 to August 1530) to about four years (December 1523 to April 1528, or even October 1527). This correlates very well with the speed of Schotten's academic progress. He completed the normally six-year-long BTh course in 1532: this was six years later than he would have done had he begun his theological studies straight after his MA (which would have given him his BTh in 1526); and four years later than if he had started after being *receptus* in the Arts Faculty (BTh 1528).

Into this period of Schotten's absence from the official University record fit most of his surviving printed works, from the *Ludus grammaticus, Meta studii literarii* and *Confabulationes* of 1525 to the *Centuria epistolarum prouerbialium* of 1529. Since all are dated from Cologne, it seems unlikely that he left the city. As the *Confabulationes* and the two plays clearly show, he spent some

---

[84] All in-text references to colloquies are taken from Schotten, *Confabulationes*, ed. by Macardle.

or all of this period teaching boys at a 'trivial' level. As to where Schotten's school was there is no direct evidence, though the chronology of two dedicatory letters makes it almost certain that it was an institution quite separate from the Laurentiana, and not some kind of pre-university instruction offered within the *bursa* itself (see pp. 190–91). It is also uncertain exactly when Schotten started and ended his school career. It seems unlikely that he did so before being *receptus ad consilium* in April 1522, for the required exercises would hardly have left time for schoolmastering, and Schotten took the normal two years, whereas men who were simultaneously schoolteaching usually took longer.[85] He could, however, very well have started in the classroom shortly after April 1522, and have been established by the December 1523 Quodlibet incident. To speak in the Quodlibet Schotten did not have to be teaching in the Arts Faculty or studying in another faculty; he was entitled to take part as an MA and as a member of the Faculty *consilium*. Several speakers at the 1522 and 1523 Quodlibets, including Johannes Kempensis, Antonius Cornelii de Linnich and Petrus Segenensis, were schoolmasters.[86] Matters are not helped by the fact that about half of the year 1523 is simply not recorded in the Arts *Dekanatsbuch*.[87] Nonetheless, de Campis's debarring Schotten from the disputation might have been the cause of his leaving the Faculty.

---

[85] E.g. Nicholas Goswini de Venraij (Laurentiana): LicA 1512, *receptus ad consilium* 1518, simultaneously schoolteaching at St Johann Baptist (*Matrikel*, 484,71; Oediger, 'Die niederrheinischen Schulen', p. 393); see below.

[86] Krafft, 'Mittheilungen aus der niederrheinischen Reformationsgeschichte', pp. 216–17.

[87] HAStK, 150, A 481 records almost nothing from 24 March till 5 October 1523 (fols 149^v–52^v). Fols 150^{r-v}, 151^v and 152^r are blank, as are half of fols 149^v and 151^r.

The dating evidence of the *Confabulationes* does not help. All verifiable references to dates are to 1524 or 1525: though some of the text could well have been written as early as 1522 or 1523, nothing positively establishes that it was (see Chapter 2). This, indeed, is as far as direct evidence can take us: we simply do not know when Schotten's career as a schoolmaster began.

Two considerations, however, suggest that Schotten could have left the University sooner rather than later. One is the fact that he proposed to speak on a pedagogical topic, which on balance seems more likely after some practical classroom experience. The second is the fact that leaving the Arts Faculty for the trivial school was by no means always a desperate or discreditable departure.

The early modern period was familiar with movements between school and university unknown today but clearly visible even in the limited corpus of known schools and teachers in Cologne in the late fifteenth and sixteenth centuries. The sixteenth-century graduate who went into schoolteaching usually saw it as a stop-gap; recorded examples of long-term commitment to the classroom are exceptional.[88] Quite a few of the men who left schoolmastering went, or returned, to the University.

---

[88] E.g. Weinsberg's teacher Antonius Wippervordis (LicA 1502, Ottonis), at the parish school of St Georg and St Jakob, from *ca.* 1504 till his death, at around eighty, in 1564 (*Matrikel*, 437,34: matriculated 1498, thus born by 1484; *BW*, I, pp. 37–38, 136; II, p. 128, recording his death in 1564; Oediger, 'Die niederrheinischen Schulen', p. 392. Johannes (Christiani) Rivius de Attendorn (MA 1519, Montana) taught at the Stiftsschule St Mariengraden in 1522–1523 before a long career as a teacher at, then inspector of, schools in Saxony: *Matrikel*, 511,34; Oediger, 'Die niederrheinischen Schulen', p. 394; Tewes, *Bursen*, p. 742. Goddert von Wulfrath, (MA 1499, Laurentiana) spent many years at the school of St Eligius: *Matrikel*, 430,120; Oediger, 'Die niederrheinischen Schulen', p. 392; *BW*, I, pp. 52–53. Cf. Oediger, 'Die niederrheinischen Schulen', pp. 370–71.

They fall, roughly speaking, into two classes. Some did not have a degree, and decided for whatever reason to take one; others had put in several years of schoolteaching between the MA and a higher degree. Striking about the first group is the brevity of their university careers: matriculation is the last fact recorded about quite a few of them.[89] The admittedly limited Cologne evidence suggests that the non-graduate schoolmaster, perhaps unsurprisingly, had difficulty in progressing in the university environment.

In a very different class, however, are graduates whose schoolteaching was an interlude of several years between the MA and a higher degree. This, which seems to have been Schotten's case, was a path well enough trodden to suggest that it was an effective career strategy. A number of men who interrupted their studies with a period of schoolteaching made a return to the University which was successful at least in that they attained a higher degree. In some cases the length of time they took suggests that they were combining study with schoolteaching.[90] Several men in this category were obviously

---

[89] E.g. Judocus Kunyngzberger de Wynshem, Cathedral school (matr. 1498, Laurentiana; BA 1501): *Matrikel,* 439,28; Oediger, 'Die niederrheinischen Schulen', p. 392. Matthias Herstraijt, St Kolumba (matr. 1515, probably Corneliana) HAStK, 1 (HUA), U 15 726, cit. Kuphal, 'Das Urkundenarchiv der Stadt Köln', VIII, p. 47; *Matrikel,* 507,51; Oediger, 'Die niederrheinischen Schulen', p. 390. Albert de Borkenn, St Kunibert (matr. 1532): *Matrikel,* 575,30; Oediger, 'Die niederrheinischen Schulen', p. 393. Matthias Jacobi Venlensis, St Johann Baptist (matr. 1555): *Matrikel,* 663,167; Oediger, 'Die niederrheinischen Schulen', p. 393.

[90] E.g. Johannes de Bocholdia (matr. in Law, 1485): probably J. Hoiginck de Bocholdia, sub-master, Stiftsschule of St Kunibert, 1488–1490; unusually long seven years to BJur 1492: *Matrikel,* 388,8; Oediger, 'Die niederrheinischen Schulen', p. 393. Hermann Kannengießer von Herford (matr. 1503, BDecr 1508), appointed at Klein-St.-Martin parish school in 1505 for four years: Schaefer, 'Inventare', III, p. 122,

aiming to make the transition back to a university career. Something of a parallel to Schotten's own case is offered by Nicholas Goswini de Venraij who entered the Laurentiana in 1509. The period between his LicA in 1512 and being *receptus ad consilium* of the Arts Faculty in 1518 included an unspecified spell at the parish school of St Johann Baptist. Four years seems likely: from MA to Faculty membership normally took two years, whereas Goswini took six.[91] Goswini's subsequent career, however, was not as successful as Schotten's. He was Arts Intrans in 1529, but is not recorded in any other Faculty office.[92]

Other men's trajectories were more impressive. Heinrich Immendorp (MA 1524, Laurentiana), began a period of schoolteaching during which he taught Hermann von Weinsberg at both St Eligius and St Alban, then returned to the University, lecturing in the Arts Faculty, becoming rector in 1554, then rector of St Johann Baptist and canon of St Georg.[93] Antonius Cornelii de Linnich was appointed to the parish school of St Laurenz after determining BA in 1517 at the Montana.[94] How long he worked there, or whether he combined teaching with further study, is unknown; at any rate, he incepted MA in 1519, spoke in the 1522 Quodlibet, and was BDecr in 1526.[95] He

---

document of 6 March 1505; *Matrikel*, 459,89; BDecr: HAStK, 150, 126, fol. 92ʳ; Oediger, 'Die niederrheinischen Schulen', p. 395.

[91] *Matrikel*, 484,71; Oediger, 'Die niederrheinischen Schulen', p. 393, citing the (surely mistaken) dates 1512–1529. Goswini is not recorded in the list of Laurentiana masters in Tewes, *Bursen*, pp. 47–73.

[92] Intrans, 1529: HAStK, 150, A 11, fol. 94ᵛ.

[93] *Matrikel*, 532,15; *BW*, I, pp. 52–53 (St Eligius), pp. 65–67 (St Alban); p. 67 records him as canon and rector of St Georg; Oediger, 'Die niederrheinischen Schulen', p. 389.

[94] *Matrikel*, 512,22; determined BA as pauper: Receptor's Book, HAStK, 150, A 516, fol. 12ʳ; Oediger, 'Die niederrheinischen Schulen', p. 393.

[95] *Matrikel*, 512,22. MA: HAStK, 150, A 481, fols 126ᵛ, 127ʳ;

developed into a powerful critic of the ignorance and moral turpitude of the Cologne clergy.[96] A friend of Sobius, he assisted him with his edition of Josephus.[97] Theobaldus Aquensis (MA 1531, Montana), spent some time as tutor of the children of the mayor Arnold van Brauweiler and as a schoolmaster at St Laurenz before going on to academic and ecclesiastical distinction: a DTh in 1562, the deanship of the Theological Faculty (1565–1568) and the University rectorship in 1567–1568 are highlights on his path towards consecration as suffragan bishop of Cologne in 1574.[98]

The relatively rich evidence of competent graduates who made schoolmastering an interlude between undergraduate studies and a return to an often successful university career suggests that Schotten's temporary departure from, and his return to, the University could have been a proactive career strategy, not a merely reactive response to institutional harassment. Against this hypothesis, perhaps, would count the fact that de Campis managed to debar him on account of debts which would most likely have been run up in the *bursa*. But these could of course have been debts outstanding from a preceding academic year.

If the 1523 data are scanty but suggestive, so are those relating to Schotten's appointment at the Laurentiana in 1530. It certainly looks as though Schotten was changing, or attempting to change, his main orientation from school

---

Quodlibet: ibid., fol. 147ʳ; BDecr: HAStK, 150, A 126, fol. 129ᵛ.

[96] E.g. *Oratio habita Coloniae coram frequenti clero [...]* (Cologne, 1527); and involvement in diocesan synods, 1527 and 1528: Ennen, *Geschichte*, IV, p. 111.

[97] Krafft, 'Mittheilungen aus der Matrikel der alten Cölner Universität [...]', pp. 493–94; id., 'Mittheilungen aus der niederrheinischen Reformationsgeschichte', p. 216; Ennen, *Geschichte*, IV, pp. 111, 360 and n. 2. *Flavii Iosephi [...] opera* (Cologne: E. Cervicornus for G. Hittorp, 1524) (*VD 16*, J 957).

[98] *Matrikel*, 561,3; Oediger, 'Die niederrheinischen Schulen', p. 393.

back to university in the later 1520s. From 1522 or 1523 to 1527 he was schoolmastering. This is shown by the evidence of the *Confabulationes*, and by the two plays he produced with his boys. The dedication of the second, the *Ludus imperatorius*, is dated 22 October 1527;[99] by April 1528 Kluppel attests Schotten's university lectures on the Psalms. Schotten's regular stream of publications, mainly connected with 'trivial' pedagogy, dries up in 1529 with the *Centuria epistolarum prouerbialium* for six full years, till the *Colloquia philosophica* and *Colloquia moralia* of 1535. It looks as though he had made a transition about 1527–28 from schoolmastering, which provided opportunities for writing and publishing, to a more exclusively university activity which initially left less time for literary pursuits. This could have been due to his studies for the BTh, the precondition for promotion in the University hierarchy, which he must have begun, or more likely taken up again, during this period, in order to gain the degree (usually six years' work) in 1532.

Perhaps the most plausible timetable which would explain these data would be that Schotten put in about two years' theological study after his MA in 1520, left the Arts Faculty, probably shortly after full Faculty membership in April 1522 but perhaps in late 1523, spent four or five years schoolmastering, then completed a further four years or so of Theology from about 1528 to 1532. The lectures on the Psalms that Kluppel attended may well have been in some way connected with this transition from 'trivial' teaching to university theological study. Yet the events surrounding Schotten's return to university teaching raise as many questions as those surrounding his departure. Why, if Schotten was eligible for a lectorship from his inception as MA in 1520, did he gain one only in 1530? If he had abandoned the Arts Faculty to be able to

---

[99] 'Undecimo kalendas Nouembris Anno domini M. D. XXVII': Schotten, *Ludus imperatorius*, sig. A3r.

teach in a more humanist ambience, what induced him to return? If his departure had been forced by the dearth of jobs in the shrinking university, what changed in 1530? If his advancement was being blocked (perhaps by Regent de Campis), what happened to unblock it?

Schotten might have been induced to return to a university career by the 1525 curriculum reforms, which did make a considerable difference to the Arts Faculty courses.[100] His appointment in the Laurentiana in 1530 proves that he was not then irreconcilably opposed to the University and its methods. Yet this very appointment raises another area of uncertainty. Here again the evidence is at various points inconclusive, but highly suggestive and open to narrative construction which may be seriously mistaken.

Johannes Jacobi de Campis's regentship (1516–1530) coincided with the disastrous drop in student numbers at Cologne between 1515 and 1535. Arnold von Tongeren's history of the Laurentiana records the period as a nadir; the Corneliana closed in 1524 for lack of students.[101] Yet numbers of lectors at the Laurentiana do not seem to have declined correspondingly. There are no detailed records of who was teaching in the *bursa* at any one time, but collating Arnold's records of the deaths of lectors, and of those appointed under the various regents, with Keussen's and Tewes's lists of teachers in the Arts Faculty gives a rough picture of the staffing of the Laurentiana in the earlier sixteenth century.[102] On these figures, from 1520 to

---

[100] Nauert, 'Humanists, Scholastics [...]', pp. 60–75; Meuthen, *Universität*, p. 234. Cf. *BW*, I, p. 104: Georgius Trapezuntinus, Rudolf Agricola and Cicero were in use in the Laurentiana in 1534.
[101] HAStK, 150, A 760, fol. 11ʳ; *Festschr. Köln*, ills 91 (historical graph of number of teachers in the Arts Faculty) and 92 (historical graph of numbers of students and teachers). On the Corneliana, see Meuthen, *Universität*, pp. 227–28, 237–45.
[102] HAStK, 150, A 760, fols 10ʳ–11ʳ; *Matrikel*, I, pp. 93*–139*, esp.

1529, when student numbers were approaching an all-time low, there were seven or eight lectors in the Laurentiana in any given year, only slightly below the mean figure of nine or ten for the two preceding decades when student numbers were still buoyant; for many of those appointed between 1510 and 1520, and even some engaged before 1510, remained in the *bursa* till the early 1530s. There would, then, have been hardly any need to add to the numbers of *commensales*; and indeed only four new lectors were engaged in de Campis's time, in 1516, 1519, 1521, and 1528, all, it seems, replacements for dead or retired men; during his regentship at least six lectors left.[103]

The evidence, therefore, does not show Schotten being repeatedly passed over for positions for which he was suitable. He would have been eligible only for the last two lectorships, and it is not certain that he actually was a candidate for both. The 1521 appointee, Jacobus Brandenborch de Campis, was of exactly the same status as Schotten. Both had matriculated and gained their BA and MA together; neither was yet *receptus ad consilium*, and indeed Jacobus took a year longer than Schotten to reach this stage.[104] But he had been Regent de Campis's *servitor*, and was, if not his kinsman, certainly his compatriot from the Kampen–Zwolle–Amersfoort 'power base' of the Laurentiana. The regional prejudices which Schwinges has revealed as operating so powerfully in Cologne University would explain Jacobus's preferment over a Hessian of similar seniority; there need have been no special animosity against Schotten.[105]

---

pp. 104*–15* (Bursa Laurentiana); repr. in *Alte Un.*, pp. 504–78, esp. pp. 523–44 (Laurentiana); Tewes, *Bursen*, pp. 47–73.

[103] HAStK, 150, A 760, fols 10^r–11^r.

[104] HAStK, 150, A 760, fol. 11^r; *Matrikel*, 516,62; Tewes, *Bursen*, p. 71.

[105] Schwinges, 'Sozialgeschichtliche Aspekte', p. 553; on servitors see Fletcher, 'Wealth and Poverty', p. 425.

More problematical is the appointment in 1528 of Hermann Blankenfort de Monasterio (1506–1554), who had incepted MA only in 1527, and would not be *receptus ad consilium* till 1530.[106] Schotten, by comparison, *receptus* in 1522, was, on the evidence adduced above, making a return to the University about 1528: he was indeed probably one of the few unattached masters senior to Blankenfort in the depleted Arts Faculty at the time.[107] At first sight Blankenfort's appointment might suggest continuing personal or anti-humanist animosity on de Campis's part. Yet this may be over-interpretation: whereas Schotten's career, in the University's own terms, was mediocre, Blankenfort was the highest of high-flyers. He worked his way speedily to the LicTh, and became the most successful Laurentiana don of the 1530s and 1540s, laden with most of the prizes the University had to offer: a doctorate in Theology, the rectorship of the prestigious parish of St Kolumba (1542–1554) and a Cathedral canonry.[108] He was also admired for a punctiliousness in teaching entirely uncharacteristic of a senior professor, and for not having deserted the city during the plague epidemic of 1553.[109] At his death this 'pastor vigilan-

---

[106] HAStK, 150, A 760, fol. 11ʳ; *Matrikel*, 543,44; Tewes, *Bursen*, pp. 71–72.

[107] See graphs of staff and student numbers, in *Festschrift Köln*, ills 91 and 92.

[108] *Matrikel*, 543,44: various positions in the Arts Faculty, 1531–1540; BTh and BJur 1531, BFTh 1533, LicTh 1535, DTh and Dean of Theological Faculty 1550; canon of St Andrew 1543, Cathedral canon 1553. Epitaph in St Kolumba (destroyed World War II): Hegel, *St. Kolumba in Köln*, pp. 300–01. See also von Mering and Reischert, *Die Bischöfe und Erzbischöfe von Köln*, I, p. 435; Schaefer, 'Inventare und Regesten', II, pp. 193, nos 233–35; p. 194, no. 240; p. 197, no. 245; Tewes, *Bursen*, pp. 71–72.

[109] Hegel, *St. Kolumba in Köln*, p. 91; *Alte Un.*, p. 50. The canonry rewarded Blankenfort for having stayed during the plague: *BW*, II, p. 32, n. 7.

tissimus' was buried 'cum totius Vniversitatis gemitu et dolore', and the Arts Faculty memorialized a 'magister noster eximius [...] cuius mors multum attulit doloris toti vniversitati et detrimenti.'[110] Even shortly after graduation this academic paragon may have been the obvious candidate for the vacant lectorship.

One intriguing detail of the chronology of Schotten's eventual appointment is, however, suggestive of conflict with de Campis. In early 1530 de Campis, embroiled in litigation over a canonry at St Maria im Kapitol,[111] handed back the principalship to Arnold Luyde von Tongeren, who had initially contracted it to de Campis. Arnold installed his own compatriot Heinrich Buschers von Tongeren as regent with effect from 6 April: de Campis meanwhile kept up his teaching in the *bursa*, but not for long, for on 29 August he died in the plague of that year.[112] Arnold notes that Schotten was appointed lector in 1530, 'ante obitum licentiati de Campis'.[113] Here again is the irritating mixture of detail and imprecision which characterizes most of the data of Schotten's career. If Arnold is speaking of de Campis's death in August in careful contradistinction to his resignation as principal in April, the note would mean that Schotten was appointed in the few months between de Campis's resignation and his death, at a time when – to judge from the staff and student numbers – there was no pressing need for an extra lector.[114] A scenario suggests itself in which as soon

---

[110] HAStK, 150, A 11, fol. 179^r; HAStK, 150, A 481, fol. 256^v (12 October 1554).
[111] Tewes, *Bursen*, p. 65. A letter on this complex case in *Regesten*, 3006.
[112] HAStK, 150, A 760, fols 11^{r-v}; Tewes, *Bursen*, p. 67. *Regesten*, 3004: J. de Campis's will (bequests to poor Laurentiana students); ibid., 3005: inventory of de Campis's books and other possessions.
[113] HAStK, 150, A 760, fol. 11^r. Tewes, *Bursen*, p. 747, wrongly states that Schotten was appointed after de Campis's death.
[114] It is unclear whether the statement that Jacobus Branden-

as the obstructive obscurantist de Campis is removed from authority, Schotten is ushered into the *bursa* with a pointed haste by a more sympathetic Heinrich von Tongeren.¹¹⁵ But this interpretation is by no means certain. Arnold's phrase may simply be an approximate way of saying 'before the end of de Campis's period of office', which would make Schotten the last of de Campis's appointees. Arnold does not divide the list of lectors clearly into the various regentships. He ends his manuscript with the start of Heinrich von Tongeren's regentship; he records Schotten's appointment at the bottom of the previous page; and he lists no lectors appointed by Heinrich: Schotten's precise status must remain doubtful. Nor is Heinrich von Tongeren positively known as a humanist. Tewes notes moderate humanist tendencies in writing and expression in the record of his deanship, but also sees him as a representative of the morally strict theological tradition of the Albertist *bursae* which included the Laurentiana (see pp. 155–58): he was in fact recommended to Arnold by de Campis.¹¹⁶ Here again we must beware of over-imaginative construction on too little evidence; the precise details of Schotten's appointment to the Laurentiana remain uncertain.

For all their ambiguities, however, the University documents and related materials allow a relatively detailed reconstruction of the skeleton of Schotten's career. Interesting is the centrality of the University in this humanist's life. Nearly all the direct evidence of his life relates in some way to the University. At most a block

---

borch de Campis died in 1530 (*Matrikel*, 516,62; Tewes, *Bursen*, p. 71) confuses him with Johannes Jacobi de Campis who died in the plague of 1530. If Jacobus did die then, this may have created a vacancy which Schotten filled.
¹¹⁵ This is Tewes's interpretation of the events, *Bursen*, p. 747.
¹¹⁶ 'De eius [= Johannis Jacobi de Campis] consilio [...] institui [...] M. Henricum de Tungri': HAStK, 150, A 760, fol. 11ᵛ; Tewes, *Bursen*, p. 70; cf. pp. 742–43.

of six years is unaccounted for in University documentation; and even during this period Schotten seems to have retained some University connections. Most significant, perhaps, is the fact that even having pursued an apparently successful career in schoolteaching Schotten still wished to return to the Laurentiana. Clearly the two worlds were not for him completely antithetical; indeed he seems to have fitted into the University structures with relative ease. Though never one of the club of senior Cologne professors, Schotten does not give the impression of a marginalized maverick. His record of his own deanship, for example, is complete and punctilious, and beyond a moderate classicism in Latinity reveals nothing subversive, disaffected, or even particularly reforming in his attitude; by contrast, a more militantly humanist dean like Phrissemius was consciously 'oppositional' in his humanist script, his demonstratively classical language and his sometimes unorthodox and critical content.[117] Schotten's conformity to the expected pattern of theological study, and his peripheral theological activity (the Psalm-lectures of 1528 and his Quodlibet address on the Lord's Prayer in 1533) suggest a religious orthodoxy in line with the earnest piety particular to the Albertist *bursae*. It is evidenced also by his writings, where nothing is found beyond a mild humanist persiflage of clerical manners and popular religiosity; indeed the *Confabulationes* look like a consciously orthodox Catholic version of Erasmus's *Colloquia* (see Chapter 3).

Schotten's modest academic career seems to confirm the much more positive evaluation of the place of humanism and humanists in early-sixteenth-century Cologne which has emerged in recent scholarship. Not only were there humanist 'niches' outside the University, as will be

---

[117] Schotten: HAStK, 150, A 481, fols 187ᵛ–93ʳ. Phrissemius: ibid., fols 145ʳ–49ʳ.

explored further in Chapter 5; there were also real opportunities for the humanists in the *bursae*, at the very heart of the University structures, as the curriculum was gradually, undramatically, but inexorably 'humanized'.

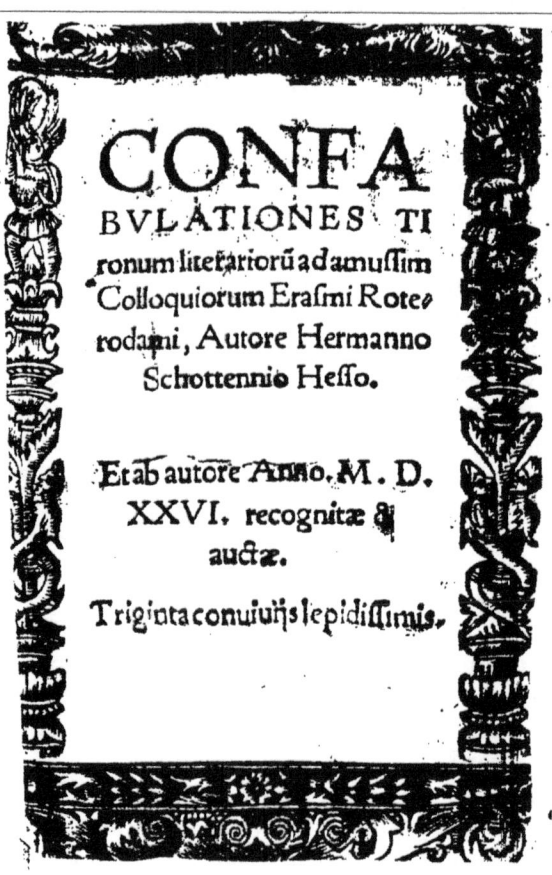

Titlepage of the second edition of the *Confabulationes* (Cologne: P. Quentel, 1526).

CHAPTER 2

Space, Time and Culture. The *Confabulationes* and Early Modern Cologne

The Schotten biography which emerges from the university documents is skeletal, giving no sense of Schotten as a rounded human being, and very little sense of any friendships or networks he may have cultivated. The only other clues to this humanist's life are to be found in his works: the *Confabulationes* themselves, which are the subject of this chapter; and the dedications of them and his other writings, which point to some of the networks of interest and patronage in which he seems to have operated. These will be examined in Chapter 5.

Schotten, as far as can be seen, lived out his entire adult life in Cologne, and the *Confabulationes* are in a profound sense a Cologne book. Local referentiality in humanist colloquies has still not received a great deal of scholarly attention. Yet most colloquy collections were conceived not in a geographical and cultural vacuum, but against the background of a particular place, usually a city. The *Manuale scholarium* relates ostensibly to Heidelberg, though in fact to Leipzig, like Mosellanus's *Paedologia* and Hegendorff's *Dialogi*; Vives's *Exercitatio* refers to Louvain.[1] The *Confabulationes* reflect, to a

---

[1] *Manuale scholarium*: Barth, 'Manuale scolarium', cols 326–28; Streckenbach, 'Paulus Niavis, "Latinum ydeoma [...]"', passim. Mosellanus: Barth, 'Petrus Mosellanus, *Paedologia*', col. 417. Hegendorff: ibid., col. 425. Vives: *CoE*, III, pp. 410, 412;

remarkable extent, specifics of life in the Cologne of the 1520s. This 'Cologne stratum' has both an intrinsic and an antiquarian interest, but more importantly it casts light on Schotten, on his place in the still imperfectly understood humanist world in and around the University, and on his literary approach with its emphasis on describing the authentic, even if it fell short of the pedagogically ideal.

The city in which the boys of the *Confabulationes* live out their juvenile burgher existence is recognizably Cologne. Again and again there are precise and specific references to late-medieval Cologne reality, which has been recorded in greater detail than that of any other German city. One important source of information on the sixteenth-century city is the diary-cum-chronicle of the Cologne burgher Hermann von Weinsberg (1518–1597), a large selection of which was published between 1886 and 1926 as *Das Buch Weinsberg*.[2] Weinsberg is a prolix, opinionated, sometimes pedestrian but always fascinating chronicler of Cologne reality; and he often parallels or illuminates Schotten. References to him will be frequent here.

The Cologne background is seen even in the most basic details. Many of the boys' names are redolent of the Lower Rhine: Arnoldus, Emmericus, Gisbertus, Goswinus or Iaspar. Some are specific to Cologne; the names of local saints and bishops, and the patrons of city parishes: Albanus; Albertus; Balthasar; Bruno; Euergislus; Herebertus; Hilgerus; Melchior; Pantaleon; Quirinus; Seuerinus. The currency is that in circulation in Cologne in Schotten's time (apart from the generic 'nummus' for any coin, 'teruncius' to denote an insignificant sum, and 'corona

---

Noreña, *Juan Luis Vives*, pp. 118–19.

[2] *Das Buch Weinsberg*, ed. by Höhlbaum and others (*BW*). There is now an online transcription of the whole manuscript on the Weinsberg research project website: http://www.weinsberg.uni-bonn.de.

aurea' in a reference to French grain prices).³ The denominations are the Heller, the Schilling (six Hellers), the Albus (two Schillings) and the Gulden or Goldgulden (twenty-four Albus).⁴ These equivalences are notional: both the gold Gulden and the silver Albus were gradually losing weight and value, so that when the *Confabulationes* appeared, there were more Albus to the Gulden than the notional twenty-four. In 1524 there were thirty; between 1527 and 1532, twenty-seven.⁵

The Gulden is 'aureus nummus', sometimes abbreviated to 'aureus'. Also frequent is 'albus', which translates 'Wyspennynge', so called because its high silver content made it almost white. Thus 'albus', in this sense a medieval Latin usage, is criticized as unlearned ('indoctus'). The Schilling is 'solidus'. The Heller is translated as 'obolus'. This word can signify any trifling amount, but is regularly used for 'Heller' by humanists, including Schotten himself when Arts Faculty receptor. These are the only denominations mentioned in the *Confabulationes*. Schotten reflects the actual usage of contemporary Cologne. Particularly indicative is the fact that he never mentions two denominations: the Pfennig (two to the Heller) and the Mark (a quarter Gulden) which in Cologne were units of account only: no coins of those values were actually minted in the city.⁶

---

3 See Schotten, *Confabulationes*, ed. by Macardle, colloquies 42, l. 18, 83, ll. 23–24, and note to colloquy 26, l. 34–35.
4 Ebeling and Irsigler, *Getreideumsatz*, I, table LV.
5 Gulden: 1513: 2.32 g; 1525: 2.005 g; 1526: 1.94 g: Ebeling and Irsigler, *Getreideumsatz*, I, p. LV. Albus: 1515: 1.006 g; 1525: 0.9 g; 1526: 0.885 g: ibid.; Schwerhoff, 'Köln rüstet sich zur Gottestracht', pp. 133–34.
6 Ebeling and Irsigler, *Getreideumsatz*, I, table LV. Gulden: see Schotten, *Confabulationes*, ed. by Macardle, notes to colloquies 55, l. 32 and 83, l. 20. Albus: see ibid., note to colloquy 32, l. 33. Schilling: see ibid., note to colloquy 5, l. 28. Heller: see ibid., note to colloquy 32, l. 34.

In numerous other ways the city in which Schotten's boys live and move is recognizably Cologne. Nearly a sixth of all the *Confabulationes* refer to details specific to the city. Some allude to local topography. In colloquies 26 and 97, boys plan drinking bouts at an inn in the 'Platea Ouium', which is a standard Latin form of the Schaafenstraße (Schaepenstraisse, Platea Ouina, etc.), a street leading to the Schaafenpforte (Porta Ouina) in the western wall of the medieval city, in the parish of St Aposteln; it was named after the flocks of sheep driven along it to graze outside the city.[7] Not only the topographical allusion, but also the subject-matter has the ring of authenticity. Schotten cannot have had any positive pedagogical reason for including a discussion of schoolboy drinking. The alehouse was an undesirable place for schoolboys: in Barlandus's colloquies one who spends an evening drinking is threatened with expulsion for a repeat offence.[8] And in early modern Cologne generally, beer caused considerable public order problems, and since 1456 might be publicly sold and consumed only in alehouses attached to the city's sixty-odd breweries.[9] One is recorded on the northern side of the Schaafenstraße, near the tollhouse;[10] these colloquies strongly suggest it was still there in the 1520s. This was an extremely discreet place to drink. An urban backwater even today, the Schaafenstraße was in Schotten's time remote and semi-rural, and an inn near the tollhouse, close to the end of the street, almost at the city wall, was about as far from the attentions of parents and teachers as one could

---

[7] *Topogr.*, I, pl. IX and pp. 437b–40b; Ennen, *Quellen*, VI, pp. 185–86; *KiM*, p. 17; Glasner, II, pp. 149–50; Kellenbenz, 'Wirtschaftsgeschichte Kölns', p. 341.
[8] Barlandus, *Dialogi*, sig. Biij^{r-v}.
[9] *Topogr.*, I, pp. 122*–24*; Stein, II, pp. 374–75, no. 231; von Loesch, *Die Kölner Zunfturkunden*, II, no. 273; *KiM*, pp. 123–24.
[10] In 1363 and 1425: *Topogr.*, I, pp. 438 b 1, 439 a 1.

imagine, a 'tranquillus et solitarius locus', even a hiding-place, 'latebrae' (colloquy 97, ll. 33–34). Given how discreditable most of these details are, Schotten must have included them simply because they were true of his pupils' actual life and behaviour.

Colloquy 69, 'De uuis carpendis', where Petrus and Cornelius talk about the pleasures of the grape-harvest, is less precisely topographical, but equally characteristic of Cologne, where in the 1520s wine was still the dominant alcoholic drink, and where small vineyards covered much of the outlying suburbs. For the burgher class they were also places of recreation: many of Weinsberg's frequent visits to his vineyard were simply for pleasure.[11]

Another slice of Cologne reality is served up in colloquy 55, 'De nundinis Francfordiensibus'. The Frankfurt fairs every March and August were crucial to the Cologne economy: the important Frankfurt–Cologne–Antwerp trade axis had developed out of the trade routes between the fairs. Twice a year Cologne saw feverish activity in preparation for Frankfurt, where Cologne merchants were the largest and most powerful group of traders: so many were city councillors that no important decisions could be made in Cologne for the duration of the fairs.[12] The boys watch the sailors loading their boats for the voyage (ll. 3–5), another authentic detail. The river route from Cologne to Frankfurt was safer and easier for heavy goods than the roads via Siegen or Wetzlar, and the fairs produced the heaviest Rhine traffic of the year. Anton Woensam's woodcut of Cologne (1531) shows the boats specially designed for the Central Rhine southwards

---

[11] *BW*, e.g. V, pp. 75–76, 215, 240, 391. See Schotten, *Confabulationes*, ed. by Macardle, notes to colloquy 69.

[12] Irsigler, 'Köln, die Frankfurter Messen [...]', esp. p. 343; id., 'Kölner Wirtschaft im Spätmittelalter', pp. 271–79; Kellenbenz, 'Wirtschaftsgeschichte Kölns', pp. 397–401; von Ranke, 'Die wirtschaftlichen Beziehungen', pp. 54–55.

from Cologne, distinctively different from the larger craft for the Lower Rhine journey northwards.[13]

A piece of genuine Cologne schoolboy culture is found in the discussion of the game of marbles in colloquy 47, 'De ludo globorum missilium, quos "omnia" uocant Colonienses tirunculi litterarii'. Cologne schoolboys did indeed call marbles 'omnia', a Latinized form of the Ripuarian dialect noun 'Ommer' or 'Ömmer', which in Cologne was (and still is) the common word for a marble rather than 'Murmel' or 'Klicker'.[14] 'Omnia' is much used in early modern times, even in the vernacular; Weinsberg used it when listing the games he played as a boy.[15] Unsurprisingly, the word is criticized as uncouth (l. 11). The variant of the game described in the colloquy was a common one where the marbles were pitched into a small hole in the ground; in Cologne it was known as 'Külche', meaning a small depression.[16]

Colloquy 81, 'De pestis saeuitia', deals with one of the more apocalyptic aspects of life in Cologne. There, as all over Western Europe, a series of plagues beginning with the Black Death in 1348 went on till 1666.[17] Between

---

13   Woensam's woodcut (Geisberg, G. 1562–70) shows boats of both types on one sheet (Geisberg, G. 1566) : see illustration on p. 210. Cf. Irsigler, 'Kölner Wirtschaft im Spätmittelalter', pp. 271–72; Kellenbenz, 'Wirtschaftsgeschichte Kölns', pp. 397–401.
14   Also 'Ommel': *Rheinisches Wörterbuch*, VI, p. 400, 4–20; also 'Ummer', 'Ümmer', 'Ümmes', etc.: ibid., IX, p. 45, 35–37; cf. Beemelmans, 'Bilder aus dem Kölner Volksleben', p. 139. The form 'Ommer', pl. 'Ömmer' is characteristic of Cologne and region: Wrede, *Neuer Kölnischer Sprachschatz*, II, pp. 253–54.
15   'A. 1528, als ich uff der Santkuilen scholen gink, do war uns spill [...] nemlich mit dem topp, koiten [bone dice], omnian', *BW*, I, p. 57. Cf. 'Zwei kleine jungen mit omrian [sic] gespielt', HAStK, Turmbuch 29, quoted in Klersch, II, p. 139. Schotten also uses 'omnia' in *Instructio prima puerorum*, sig. f1ʳ.
16   See Schotten, *Confabulationes*, ed. by Macardle, note to colloquy 47, l. 15.
17   Helmstaedter, 'Pestprävention', p. 87; Isenmann, pp. 38–41.

1500 and the time this colloquy appeared, Cologne had known plague in 1502, 1506–1507, and 1518, when the Bursa Laurentiana, where Schotten was already a student, had probably moved out of Cologne. More were to follow in Schotten's lifetime (1527, 1530, 1540, 1541), and others before the end of the century: Weinsberg recorded several.[18] Other epidemics, such as the English sweating sickness of September 1529, caused a general desertion of the city.[19]

The colloquy does not appear to describe an actual outbreak of plague in Cologne; it may have been inspired by a detailed discussion of the plague in Leipzig in Hegendorff's *Dialogi*.[20] Nonetheless, certain details do reflect Cologne reality. Plague victims are looked after by the lay monks of the order of St Alexius (l. 27). This refers to the still extant Alexian order, founded as a lay brotherhood in the fifteenth century in Mechelen, which had notable German houses in Cologne, Neuss, Aachen and Trier. It became an Augustinian monastic order in 1469; the patronage of the ascetic St Alexius of Edessa (legendarily fourth–fifth century) dates from the 1480s. The Alexians' mission was to the poor, the sick and the marginalized, with the nursing of plague victims a specialty.[21] In Cologne, the situation of their house on the Longengasse, named after St Longinus, gave them the familiar name of 'Longenbrüder' or 'Lungenbrüder'. They were also known as 'Cellites' or 'Zellbrüder', from 'cella' in the sense of 'grave', and in Cologne they had a general responsibility

---

[18] *Alte Un.*, pp. 177–89; Lassotta, *Formen der Armut*, II, pp. 410–11; Helmstaedter, 'Pestprävention', p. 88; Creutz, 'Pest und Pestabwehr', passim; *BW*, I, pp. 150, 156–58; II, pp. 131–34.
[19] Gotzen, 'Ein kirchliches Bittlied', p. 81; *De novo [...] morbo* (1529), passim; *BW*, II, pp. 63–64.
[20] Hegendorff, *Dialogi*, 2, sig. C8ʳ.
[21] *NCE*, I, p. 275; *KL*, I, cols 532–33; Crusenius, *Monasticon Augustinianum*, p. 146.

for arranging funerals.[22] The colloquy says that female victims are cared for by nuns (l. 30). This almost certainly means the Cologne Beguines, who were particularly associated with tending the dying, including plague victims.[23] In ll. 32–40 the talk turns to the demoralising impact of so many burials, as many as twenty in a single day (l. 35). This too was familiar in Cologne, where some parish churches had supplementary graveyards for times of plague and other epidemics.[24]

Most colloquies which describe Cologne, however, refer to happier customs and traditions. The majority, dealing with calendar customs, are loosely grouped by Schotten (colloquies 31, 32, 34, 36, 40). In colloquy 31, 'De festo Sancti Galli', Nicolaus and Vinandus talk of the 'prosternatio galli', the grisly medieval sport of throwing missiles or shooting arrows at a cock or goose buried in the ground with only its head showing. In the Cologne region the sport was popular at fairs, and still known in the twentieth century. By the sixteenth century the Rhineland 'cock' seems to have been wooden.[25] The sport is usually associated with Pentecost,[26] but Weinsberg records it in proximity to St Gall's Day (16 October): a nephew of his 'killed the cock' on 19 October 1568.[27]

---

[22] 'Die Longbroder, wilche der kranken warten und doeten begraben', *BW*, V, p. 145; Winheim, *Sacrarium Agrippinae*, pp. 160–61; [*Funeral directive, Cologne 1578*], ll. 6–8; *Erneuerte Funeral [...] Ordnung* 1688, §§ 5, 6, 11, 12, 13–14; von Mering and Reischert, *Die Bischöfe und Erzbischöfe von Köln*, I, pp. 301–17.

[23] *BW*, II, pp. 131–34, 257, 278.

[24] E.g. St Alban and St Kolumba: *Topogr.*, I, p. 146*.

[25] Orme, *Medieval Children*, pp. 179, 185; Zender, 'Das Kölnische "Niederland"', pp. 256 (map), 257; Wrede, *Rheinischer Volksbrauch*, pp. 54, 66–67.

[26] *BW*, e.g. II, p. 76; Herborn, 'Fast-, Fest- und Feiertage', p. 43; Wrede, *Rheinischer Volksbrauch*, pp. 54–55.

[27] 'A. 1568 den 19. oct. hat mins broder Christians kind Herman die gans zu s. Georgen abgeworpen. Mir sint uff sinem gans-

Weinsberg uses the standard Rhineland term 'konink' for the boy who 'killed the cock'.[28] He also describes a celebratory meal with wine. Schotten mentions both details: Nicolaus assumes that Vinandus aims to become the 'king', 'rex' (ll. 22–23). If Nicolaus shoots the cock, he will provide a meal of spit-roasted chicken and wine (ll. 33–37).

In colloquy 34, 'De eligendo rege', the boys talk about choosing a 'king' and his 'court' on Epiphany Eve, 5 January. Choosing a 'Hauskonink' was a Cologne family custom; the method used – drawing lots – may have originated in the Netherlands.[29] Weinsberg frequently describes being made king of the house 'in the company of the women and the servants, as is the custom in all houses in Cologne'.[30] However, Weinsberg first mentions the custom in 1552, and it is not positively documented in Cologne burgher circles earlier in the century, so Schotten's description is valuable evidence that it was practised there.[31] The custom was adopted by the students; in 1510 Count Wilhelm von Waldeck was made king in what was probably a University festivity.[32]

Schotten's description tallies precisely with what Weinsberg reports several decades later. The royal titles

---

koninksessen frolich gewest und im den wein geschenkt.': *BW*, V, p. 69; cf. Herborn, 'Fast-, Fest- und Feiertage', p. 55.

[28] Wrede, *Rheinischer Volksbrauch*, p. 66; also 'Hahnenkönig' or 'Ganskonink'.

[29] Klersch, I, p. 88; Herborn, 'Fast-, Fest- und Feiertage', pp. 36–37; cf. *Kulturströmungen*, ed. by Aubin, p. 219; Zender, 'Eigenart und Entwicklung', p. 149.

[30] 'Under der frauwen und gesinde durch das loss koninck im haus worden, wie in allen heusern in Coln sulchs pleicht zu geschein', *BW*, II, p. 1; cf. pp. 268, 272, 343; III, p. 80; V, pp. 12–13, 41, 44, 85, 88, 220–21, 350–52.

[31] Herborn, 'Fast-, Fest- und Feiertage', pp. 36–37.

[32] *Alte Un.*, p. 153; 'Obseruatur [...] per Academias et urbes a studiosis et ciuibus', Hospinianus, *Festa Christianorum*, fol. 35ᵛ; Huyskens, 'Junggraf Wilhelm von Waldeck', p. 100.

are drawn from a hat (l. 21); if a man draws 'queen', the title is sold to the mother or one of the maids (l. 25). Weinsberg's family drew paper slips marked with court titles, as well as mottos, from a hat in order of age. The servants were included; sometimes the maid became queen.[33] Schotten's guests provide the 'king's' wine in exactly the way that Weinsberg's guests did.[34] At a later date, the king treats the other guests to a meal (l. 28). This is the 'Koninksessen', typically held in Shrovetide, a custom which Weinsberg records in both monasteries and private homes.[35] Schotten's 'Regium conuiuium post ferias Epiphaniae' (no. 6), depicts such a 'Koninksessen'.

Colloquy 40, 'De festo Sancti Martini', discusses another important Cologne holiday, the eve of the feast of the affectionately regarded St Martin of Tours (10 November), a family celebration linked to the beginning of winter.[36] In Cologne the new wine was tapped and drunk; family and friends exchanged presents; and, as elsewhere in north-western Germany and the Netherlands, children held a *Heischegang*, that is, they went round the houses singing songs for gifts in cash or kind.[37]

---

[33] *BW*, V, pp. 220–21. 'Rex', 'Cantzlar', 'Hoffmeister', 'Schenk', 'Narr' and consorts.

[34] 'Potu omni nos alii regem donamus', Schotten, *Confabulationes*, ed. by Macardle, colloquy 34, l. 29. 'Ein firdel weins': *BW*, V, pp. 350–51.

[35] 'Darumb hilt ich folgens den 24. Jan. min koninksessen und waren frolich' (*BW*, II, p. 1); cf. *BW*, V, pp. 13, 41, 51, 73, 350–51; cf. Beemelmans, 'Bilder aus dem Kölner Volksleben', p. 149.

[36] Herborn, 'Fast-, Fest- und Feiertage', pp. 53–55; Clemen, 'Der Ursprung des Martinsfestes', esp. p. 14; *BW*, II, pp. 225, 265; V, p. 179.

[37] New wine: *BW*, e.g. II, pp. 44, 201, 265; V, pp. 105, 241, 477; Herborn, 'Fast-, Fest- und Feiertage', pp. 53–55. Presents: *BW*, II, pp. 44, 62, 181; V, p. 241. Children: *KL*, IV, cols 1424–27 (col. 1425); Bahlmann, 'Die Lambertus-Feier zu Münster i. W.', p. 177; Clemen, 'Der Ursprung des Martinsfestes', esp. p. 14; Weingärtner, *Das Kind und seine Poesie in plattdeut-*

This is the scenario in colloquy 40, 'De festo Sancti Martini', where Hieronymus and Hermannus plan to spend the evening singing for food at rich people's doors. The evidence of this colloquy is important, since it contradicts Herborn's assertion that a St Martin's Day *Heischegang* is not recorded in the sixteenth century.[38] The colloquy is unspecific about food. Hieronymus says only that people will be eating meat on St Martin's eve (l. 12). Later in the sixteenth century roast goose was the traditional Cologne fare,[39] but it is unclear whether it was in the first third of the century. Had it been, Schotten, a meticulous recorder of everyday life, would surely have mentioned it. Herborn's suggestion that in the earlier part of the century goose was a dish for St George's Day (23 April) may be the explanation.[40]

In colloquy 41, 'De xeniis mittendis', discussing New Year's presents, Kilianus says he does not want a 'strena farinacea' (l. 12), a gift made of flour: he means a cake, biscuit or pretzel, a common New Year present ('newjar' or 'fruntschaft') in the Rhineland: Weinsberg sent 'scheffenkoichen' in 1579.[41]

Separated from this sequence, colloquy 102 treats another important Cologne holiday, St Blasius's Day, 3 February. Paschasius explains the tradition of children going round the houses, 'ostiatim cursitare' (l. 12) begging

---

scher Mundart, pp. 37, 41; Siuts, *Die Ansingelieder zu den Kalenderfesten*, pp. 410–30. Cf. Schotten, *Confabulationes*, ed. by Macardle, colloquies 11, 15, 20. Dekker, 'Three Unknown "Cantilenae Martinianae" by Georgius Macropedius', passim.

[38] Herborn, 'Fast-, Fest- und Feiertage', p. 55.
[39] *BW*, V, p. 477; Clemen, 'Der Ursprung des Martinsfestes', p. 1; *KL*, IV, col. 1424; Wrede, *Rheinischer Volksbrauch*, p. 69.
[40] 'Fast-, Fest- und Feiertage', p. 55; cf. *BW*, V, p. 69.
[41] *KL*, IV, col. 1397; cf. von Reinsberg-Düringsfeld, *Das festliche Jahr*, pp. 2–3; Keussen, 'Die drei Reisen', II, p. 111; Klersch, I, p. 82; cf. 'Strenas quoque vltrò citròque mittimus, et Dulciariis nos mutuò honoramus', Hospinianus, *Festa Christianorum*, fol. 32ʳ. Weinsberg: *BW*, V, p. 186.

for a gift. This is standard Cologne custom. The fourth-century Armenian martyr bishop Blasius, in Cologne 'Blesy', 'Blesgen', or 'Blyssen',[42] was one of the most popular saints in the Middle Ages. His legend recorded his miraculous cure of a boy with a fishbone stuck in his throat, and how he restored an old woman's pig which a wolf had taken; the woman later brought Blasius the pig's head and feet, bread and a candle. This explains why the pig, or pig's head, is a standard part of the saint's iconography, and why on his feast throats were blessed with crossed candles.[43] In Cologne the day was one for visiting friends, as Weinsberg often mentions.[44] There was also a children's *Heischegang*: Weinsberg records that of over 100 children of St Jakob's parish in 1570.[45] Schotten's colloquy includes two intriguing details: children are usually given a small amount of pork or bread (l. 16); Paschasius is preparing a pointed stick (l. 3), which is presumably to spear them on. Neither detail is recorded in any other sources. Schotten may be the only writer to record them; again the detail is so specific that it seems unlikely to be fictive.

Schotten also mentions several non-calendrical usages. Weddings are discussed in colloquy 86, 'De nuptiis'. The wedding service in the Cologne diocesan use showed a number of interesting ritual peculiarities,[46] but it is with the reception that this colloquy is concerned. The late

---

[42] Wrede, *Rheinischer Volksbrauch*, p. 19.
[43] *Legenda aurea*, XXXVIII, pp. 167–69; Hospinianus, *Festa Christianorum*, fol. 43^{r-v}; *LCI*, V, cols 416–19; Klersch, I, p. 93; ÖH.
[44] E.g. 'Blasii fest zu Cronenberch gehalten und frolich gewest', *BW*, V, p. 59; cf. p. 96; cf. Herborn, 'Fast-, Fest- und Feiertage', pp. 54–55.
[45] *BW*, II, p. 204; V, pp. 59, 96, 143; Klersch, I, p. 93; Herborn, 'Fast-, Fest- und Feiertage', pp. 54–55. St Jakob, 1570: *BW*, V, p. 73.
[46] *GEK*, II,2, pp. 172–73; Vollmer, *Agenda Coloniensis*, pp. 392–408.

medieval and early modern Cologne burgher wedding reception (*bruloft* or *hoichzit*), restricted by sumptuary law, was usually modest in scale, held in a private house, and attended only by close relatives and friends: Weinsberg's account of the wedding of his sister Sibille in 1588 shows the identical pattern and restricted scale of events as a century previously.[47] This is precisely the kind of festivity that Herebertus describes for his sister's wedding. It will take place at his family's house (l. 5); later there will be dancing to the pipe and drum (l. 27). This is exactly the Cologne pattern: a small meal (*middaigsessen, zop, kneildranck*) followed the ceremony, but dancing began only in the evening, when a (legally restricted) number of pipers were permitted to play.[48]

Other details, too, accord with Cologne custom. The bridegroom has pledged 2000 Gulden as a marriage settlement, and his sister an unknown sum (ll. 14–19). In Cologne both spouses commonly pledged an agreed amount; if either died the survivor kept the whole sum. Sibille von Weinsberg and her husband each pledged approximately 1500 Gulden.[49] Herebertus will lead his sister to the church (l. 20). This also reflects usage in Cologne and elsewhere, where the bride was led to church by her family, often with music. Weinsberg describes a 'kirchgank' in 1580, with candles and torches: the bride was preceded by a young boy, and her brother and nephew led her to the church in exactly the way Herebertus plans to do.[50]

---

[47] Stein, II, pp. 485–88, no. 309. *BW*, V, pp. 305–14. Weinsberg describes many weddings, e.g. *BW*, I, pp. 231, 257, 278, 285; III, p. 75; IV, p. 126; V, pp. 59–60, 76, 120, 313–14.

[48] 'Eyn gesetz pijffer': Stein, II, no. 309, §§ 4, 5; cf. *BW*, V, pp. 313–14.

[49] *BW*, V, p. 307 (500 Reichstaler, allowing for inflation a good deal less than Schotten's 2000 Gulden).

[50] 'Mit brutkerzen, tortzen, schonem jongling vor der braut. Und ir broder [...] und neif [...] leiten sie in die kirch', *BW*, III,

Not absolutely exclusive to Cologne, but strongly characteristic of the city with its large and powerful clerical caste, is colloquy 98, 'De conuiuio uicissitudinario, quod sacerdotes inter se agunt'. The boys discuss a meal which the priests of the city take it in turns to organize and pay for. Meals like this were held in individual parishes, such as St Jakob, whose dinners Weinsberg frequently attended,[51] and by the 'Fraternitas Pastorum Coloniensium', the 'brotherhood' of the city's nineteen parish priests.[52] The censures of the 1536 Cologne Provincial Synod on clergy participating in 'immoderatis commessationibus' were probably directed in part against such large and expensive meals.[53] For the dinner described here is expensive: at ten Gulden (l. 21) it represents almost two months' earnings for many skilled workers in the 1520s.[54] But it is probably realistic: in 1571 a lavish 'banneressen' for twenty-one guests cost Weinsberg sixty-four Gulden, about twenty-two Gulden at 1520s food prices.[55]

Most of Schotten's 'local colour' is of a positive kind; yet he finds room for characteristic aspects of Cologne life which reveal the anxieties and dissatisfactions of the early modern citizen.

In colloquy 10 Valterus explains that his parents refuse supper invitations at other houses, because they are afraid to walk the streets at night. Petrus suggests their fears are exaggerated, but Valterus emphatically disagrees: night, he says, brings only bad things, like violence (ll. 25–29).

---

p. 75. Cf. Stein, II, no. 309, §4; *BW*, V, p. 313; Klersch, II, pp. 107–08.

[51] *BW*, IV, p. 75; V, pp. 90, 94, 395.
[52] Dorn, 'Der Ursprung der Pfarreien', pp. 144–50. HAStK, 295 (GA), 209: fraternity membership lists and liturgical details, fourteenth–fifteenth century; 209a, 209b: revised statutes (1668). In 1569 Weinsberg attended a dinner of that 'broderschaft der sementlicher pastorn in Coln': *BW*, V, p. 332.
[53] *Canones concilii prouincialis Coloniensis [...] 1536*, sig. B4r.
[54] Lassotta, *Formen der Armut*, I, p. 415.
[55] *BW*, V, p. 223; Lassotta, *Formen der Armut*, I, p. 407.

Valterus's reply may have some proverbial echoes,[56] but it may well refer to the objective dangers of early modern Cologne, as may a similar remark in colloquy 123, ll. 28–29, that the streets are unsafe at night. For throughout the fifteenth and sixteenth centuries, nightly violence, often fatal, seemed ineradicable in Cologne, despite a curfew, a ban on weapons, and a city patrol.[57] The 'unseemly disputes and quarrels on the street at night, the shrieking, roaring, cursing, beating and stabbing' recorded in 1478 are all too typical, both of their time and of Schotten's.[58] Modern scholars, notably Gerd Schwerhoff, have revealed Cologne's internal policing as underfunded and inadequate. Crimes of violence were common, representting about a fifth of recorded cases. Cologne's annual homicide rate compared with that of many twenty-first-century North American cities.[59] Two of Schwerhoff's findings chime with Schotten's dialogue. The streets were definitely dangerous: the trigger for violence was very often an encounter on the streets, and though some city areas, including the Laurentiana vicinity, were particularly louche, almost nowhere was free from the danger of violence.[60] And night-time was indeed the peak of violent

---

[56] Cf. 'Nox nemini amica', Walther, 39038a1.
[57] Breuer, 'Burgbann und Burgmeile', pp. 22–25; Kemp, 'Die Wohlfahrtspflege des Kölner Rates [...]' esp. pp. 16–25; cf. Schotten, *Confabulationes*, ed. by Macardle, note to colloquy 11, l. 18.
[58] 'Die onfuechlichen sachen ind handell [...] bynnen nachtz [...] up der straissen [...] mit gekrisch, geruchte, oevelsprechen, slaen ind stechen': Stein, II, p. 564, no. 411; cf. I, no. 193; II, nos 224, 265, 436, 402, 494. Cf. incidents recorded in *BRStK*, III, pp. 15, 37, 58, 84, 91, 143; Breuer, 'Burgbann und Burgmeile', p. 25, n. 108.
[59] Approximately ten per 100 000 inhabitants: Schwerhoff, 'Insel des Friedens', p. 147; cf. id., *Köln im Kreuzverhör*, esp. pp. 49–65, 275–86.
[60] Schwerhoff, *Köln im Kreuzverhör*, pp. 297–99; Irsigler and Lassotta, *Bettler und Gaukler*, pp. 40–41.

crime: over three quarters took place after 5 pm, with 20% perpetrated after 10 pm, when the curfew was supposed to have emptied the streets.[61] Schwerhoff concludes that this endemic violence seems not to have produced a widespread sense of insecurity amongst the citizens; indeed that they seem if anything to have underestimated the dangers.[62] Schotten's colloquy, however, suggests a certain level of anxiety which has not been expressed in other sources. It is perhaps significant that he made the brief exchange about the dangers of the streets longer and more explicit in the second edition of the *Confabulationes*. The first edition simply read:

> PETRVS. Quamobrem recusant?
> VALTERVS. Timent noctu plateas emetiri.
>
> (colloquy 10, ll. 25–26)

In the second edition, Schotten added two more lines:

> PETRVS. Vane timent.
> VALTERVS. Nequaquam, nescis noctem nihil boni, sed saepe pugnos afferre.[63]

A much greater level of dissatisfaction, even grievance, is revealed in colloquies 89 and 90, which describe death and burial: the 'exequiae' or requiem, known in Cologne as the 'begencknis', and the burial, 'sepultura'.[64] Schotten does not directly allude to the 'memoria' or 'Totengedächtnis', the customary memorial masses held respectively a week, a month and a year after death, the 'septimus/um', 'tricesimus/um' and 'anniversarium', or 'sevent', 'maintdrissich' and 'jairgezit'.[65]

---

[61] Schwerhoff, *Köln im Kreuzverhör*, pp. 300–01 and table 29, p. 301.
[62] Schwerhoff, 'Insel des Friedens', p. 150.
[63] Schotten, *Confabulationes*, ed. by Macardle, colloquy 10, ll. 27–29 and apparatus.
[64] *GEK*, II,2, p. 196.
[65] Stein, II, e.g. nos 76–77; *GEK*, II,2, pp. 196–97.

Again there are Cologne ritual specifics. In colloquy 90, 'De sepultura', Eberhardus notices that a deceased person's house has candles protruding from its windows, a custom unknown in his home region, where the door is left open (ll. 3–8). This was indeed a usage long prescribed in Cologne, to avoid clandestine burials, which could have covered up murder, or simply avoided expense.[66] Funeral regulations of 1592 describe the rule as a longstanding custom, both laudable and mandatory.[67] Other regulations of the sixteenth century specify that candles were to be put out of the window as soon as anyone died, and to be displayed for at least a day.[68] Arnold Buchelius from Utrecht observed the practice in 1587, noting that the number of candles reflected the deceased's status.[69] The colloquies say that the candles, later carried in front of the corpse, are not bought but hired (colloquies 89, l. 24; 90, l. 14). This too was Cologne practice: processional candles with long wooden shafts were hired from the parish, as was still the case in the late seventeenth century.[70]

But both colloquies push beyond local colour to deal with the perceived abuses surrounding death and burial

---

[66] Klersch, II, pp. 163–64; burials early in the morning, late in the evening and even at night are noted, and condemned, in [*Funeral directive, Cologne, 1578*], ll. 3–6.
[67] 'Alte[r] alhier herbrachte[r] löblicher brauch/ und mehrmalen erwiderte[r] befelch': [*Funeral directive, Cologne, 1592*], ll. 6–9; 'von alters breuchlich und herbracht', ibid., l. 26.
[68] '[...] daß so baldt einig Mensch jung oder alt verstorben/ solchs mit außstechung kertzen [...] wie breuchlich angezeygt werde': [*Funeral directive, Cologne, 1578*], ll. 14–16. 'Auch [soll ein jedweder] dieselb zum wenigsten einen gantzen Tag also außgestochen bleiben lassen.' [*Funeral directive, Cologne, 1592*], ll. 26–27.
[69] Keussen, 'Die drei Reisen', I, p. 80; *BW*, V, p. 259.
[70] E.g. 'die lange höltzerne Kertzen', [*Erneuerte Funeral [...] Ordnung*, 1688], § 12; 'ligne[ae] candel[ae]': *Kurkölnische Begräbnisordnung*, 1688, l. 43.

in early modern Cologne. The city's parish churches had the exclusive, and very lucrative, right to bury parishioners, but did not always exercise it in an edifying manner.[71] The exorbitant fees for everything connected with burial were a constant source of complaint, as was the compulsion on the mourners to make generous offerings in cash and kind to the officiating clergy.[72] Like many city councils in the later Middle Ages, that of Cologne attempted to set some limit to the number and expense of funeral and memorial services.[73] As early as 1372 it restricted attendance at funerals, and thus the number liable to make offerings; in 1390 it tried to reduce the traditional three *memoriae* to a single requiem Mass.[74] In 1419 the council forbade the celebration of *sevent* and *maintdrissich*, to save citizens' time and money.[75] The powerful clergy 'brotherhood', however, vigorously resisted this attack on clerical prerogative and income, and seemingly with success: a council decree of 1470 merely states that *begencknis*, *sevent* and *maintdrissich* may be celebrated together if desired.[76] The council also attempted to ban other costly funeral trappings, such as the (paid) involvement of the mendicant orders.[77] Dissatisfaction with funeral and memorial practice played a major part in a Cologne citizens' revolt in April–June 1525, shortly after the appearance of the *Confabulationes*. This revolt was in the long Cologne tradition of civic protest: its anticlericalism (including assaults on and theft

---

[71] *KiM*, p. 146; Schäfer, 'Inventare', II, esp. pp. 10, 13, 17; *GEK*, II,2, pp. 188–99 (esp. 192–93), 486–99; Vollmer, *Agenda Coloniensis*, pp. 339–52.
[72] von Looz-Corswarem, 'Die Kölner Artikelserie', pp. 128–34: arts 35, 36, 37, 39, 76; *GEK*, II,2, p. 198.
[73] *GEK*, II,2, p. 199.
[74] Stein, I, pp. 78, 103; II, nos 76–77; *GEK*, II,2, p. 198.
[75] *GEK*, II,2, p. 495.
[76] Stein, II, p. 487, no. 309, § 12; cf. Gescher, *Der Kölner Stadtdechant*, pp. 234–35. Cf. colloquy 98.
[77] *BRStK*, II, p. 517, 1520, no. 275.

from clerics) was fuelled not by Lutheran sympathies but by long-standing resentments about the economic and fiscal privileges of the clergy.[78] 184 articles which the citizens handed to the council in June included demands to limit the expense of funerals and memorials; some the council endorsed; to others its response was diplomatically evasive.[79] All in all, it had limited success in changing practice. Even late in the century, generous offerings in money and kind, and pious practices such as paying beguines to lie on graves, which the 1525 articles had demanded be abolished, were still widespread, as Weinsberg attests.[80] The *Confabulationes* just predate the uprising, and the dissatisfactions expressed in these two colloquies are very similar to those which would a few months later find powerful expression in the articles.

In colloquy 89, Bernardus's remark that at the funeral he will have to offer 'Tres [nummos], in tribus altaribus' (l. 20) makes it clear that three offerings are still mandatory. Possibly the *begencknis*, *sevent* and *maintdrissich* are being conflated here, as the council intended;[81] but a triple offering is still being collected, against the spirit and the letter of the council's intentions. Colloquy 90 is more critically pointed. Iodocus explains that burial in Cologne costs a lot, 'Certe maximo aere' (l. 20). Eberhardus denies that the clergy have any right to sell places in the cemetery, which belongs not to them but to God: as the Psalm says, 'The Lord's is the earth and its fulness' (l. 30). Schotten makes Iodocus produce a partial defence of the status quo (ll. 32–37), but there is

---

[78] HAStK, 56, 385, esp. fols 76ʳ–88ᵛ; von Looz-Corswarem, 'Die Kölner Artikelserie', esp. pp. 70–71, 91–97, 100.
[79] HAStK, 30, V 108, esp. fols 17ʳ–19ʳ; von Looz-Corswarem, 'Die Kölner Artikelserie', pp. 128–34, arts 36, 37, 39, 76.
[80] Klersch, II, p. 174; von Looz-Corswarem, 'Die Kölner Artikelserie', p. 129, art. 39; *BW*, II, pp. 93, 277–79; V, pp. 237–38, 366.
[81] Stein, II, p. 487, no. 309, § 12.

no mistaking the underlying animus. It too is typical of widely shared resentments: the 1525 articles demanded an end to the selling of 'the sacraments and the earth'.[82]

Colloquy 80, 'De balneis ingrediendis', treats a phenomenon much in evidence in Cologne. Hermannus assiduously avoids bathhouses: many visitors come out with diseases (ll. 8–15). Public baths were immensely popular in Cologne in the fifteenth century, as elsewhere. The sexual services often offered in bathhouses had long earned them a louche reputation;[83] but the advent of syphilis in the sixteenth century added a new, dangerous edge, and sapped public confidence in baths. Erasmus's colloquy 'Diversoria' (1523) talks of how syphilis, the 'scabies noua', has largely killed off public baths, which had been so popular at the turn of the century.[84] Cologne had eleven bathhouses in 1438, and probably still in 1531, and even in the later sixteenth century figures like Weinsberg visited, often for treatments such as cupping.[85] But there is no doubt that a massive decline in confidence had begun in the early sixteenth century, and by 1631 only four remained; one proprietor also ran a makeshift syphilis 'clinic'.[86] It is interesting that Walther's collection of proverbial phrases contains over forty concerning baths, twenty-seven of them negative or cautionary.[87] Schotten's juxtaposition of this colloquy with nos 81–83, on plague, war and famine, speaks volumes.

---

[82] 'Die sacramenten und die erde nit zo verkoufen', von Looz-Corswarem, 'Die Kölner Artikelserie', p. 134, art. 76.
[83] Albala, *Eating Right in the Renaissance*, p. 134; Irsigler and Lassotta, *Bettler und Gaukler*, pp. 189–90.
[84] 'Thermae publicae [...] nunc frigent vbique. Scabies enim noua docuit nos abstinere': Erasmus, *Colloquia*, p. 336, ll. 100–02.
[85] *Topogr.*, I, pp. 133*–34*; *BW*, V, pp. 11, 65, 92, 101.
[86] Irsigler and Lassotta, *Bettler und Gaukler*, pp. 97–109, esp. p. 105.
[87] Walther, 1909a, 1910, 1913–19, 1923–25, 2383a, 4231, 16155, 16944, 22038, 23506, 26869, 35113a, 38256m.

Where Schotten's descriptions can be checked against known Cologne practice, he is found to be entirely reliable; in cases where he is the only author to mention Cologne details, then, he must at least be taken seriously as a source. Two dialogues are particularly intriguing in this respect. 'Conuiuium nuptiale' (no. 9), mentions the custom of punching the bridegroom in church, to prepare him for nagging and beating at the hands of his new wife (ll. 49–59). It also offers a comic interpretation of the candle carried before the bride on her way to church: marrying a woman means bringing home fire and constant torment (ll. 61–65). Neither of these details is recorded elsewhere; it would seem that they are a piece of Cologne lore now lost. Similarly with colloquy 32, where Paulus says that on St Lambert's Day (17 September) he must take a gift of money for his schoolmaster (l. 11). No other known source mentions a teachers' gratuity on St Lambert's Day, yet it is hard to imagine why Schotten, who is always meticulously accurate in recording Cologne usage, would have invented a non-existent tradition. Oediger's study of schools on the Lower Rhine goes too far in simply citing Schotten as a primary historical source for the custom,[88] but the colloquy must be taken as a serious indication that this custom, like the pointed stick for St Blasius's Day, was known, at least in Cologne.

It is unfortunate, though probably inevitable, that Schotten, even when depicting known Cologne cultural practice, does not always supply as much detail as the modern reader would like. In colloquy 36 two boys discuss Shrovetide, and colloquy 123 depicts a burgher Shrove Tuesday evening party. It is regrettable that neither offers any concrete detail on Cologne Shrovetide customs, because the modern Cologne *Karneval*, like those elsewhere, is a romanticized and sanitized re-

---

[88] Oediger, 'Die niederrheinischen Schulen', pp. 369–71 and ns 82, 83, 91.

creation of the early nineteenth century, and comparatively little is known of the late-medieval and early modern celebrations.[89] About the only detail which emerges is an ambivalent attitude to masking: the wife in colloquy 123 absolutely refuses to admit masked guests (l. 17). Shrovetide in Cologne certainly included masking, *Mommen* or *Mommengehen*; the account of a magnificent masked party in the Wasservas house in 1535 is well known.[90] But masking was not universal, and seems to have been frowned on in some bourgeois circles. This probably reflected its origin amongst the artisans, who still helped to set the sometimes rowdy tone of the celebrations in the sixteenth century.[91] Masking may also have been connected with *Heischegänge*, when money was demanded, sometimes with menace, and which the council repeatedly forbade.[92] Masks were eventually forbidden to clerics and religious in the seventeenth century.[93]

Schotten's coverage of Cologne culture is so full and detailed as to make some practices not mentioned in the *Confabulationes* distinctly conspicuous by their absence. Most obvious are the two greatest Cologne popular

---

[89] Mezger, 'Rückwärts in die Zukunft', passim; Klersch, I, pp. 93–151; Klersch, *Die Kölnische Fastnacht*, pp. 37–39; Herborn, 'Fast-, Fest- und Feiertage', pp. 37–42.

[90] E.g. *BW*, V, pp. 20, 64, 124; Kemp, 'Die Wohlfahrtspflege des Kölner Rates [...]', passim, esp. p. 35; Stein, II, nos 94, §§ 5–6; 156; 214, § 30a; 249. Wasservas party: von Zimmern, *Die Chronik der Grafen von Zimmern*, III, p. 94; cf. Herborn, 'Fast-, Fest- und Feiertage', pp. 37–38.

[91] E.g. *BW*, I, p. 122; IV, pp. 10, 185. In Mosellanus, *Paedologia*, 27, 'De Bacchanalibus Christianorum', a schoolmaster forbids the boys to wear masks 'opificum istorum manuariorum exemplo' (p. 34, ll. 27–28). Cf. Beemelmans, 'Bilder aus dem Kölner Volksleben', p. 150.

[92] Klersch, *Die Kölnische Fastnacht*, p. 29; Hofmann, 'Hermann von Weinsberg und die kölnische Fastnacht', p. 98.

[93] *Decreta* [...] *synodi Coloniensis* 1662 [1667], I, V, IX, § IV, p. 36).

festivals. On *Holzfahr(t)tag*, the Thursday after Pentecost, the *Gaffeln*, the trade guilds which were also representtative political groupings, marched to the Ossendorf Wood, where bonfires were lit. After an evening march back to the city, drinking continued till late at night. *Petrivinkelstag*, the feast 'ad vincula Petri' (1 August), saw a kind of street party lit by bonfires and burning tar-barrels.[94]

Absent too are the three most important religious processions in medieval Cologne, the *Gottestracht* and the processions of St Sylvester and St Boniface. The *Gottestracht*, on the second Friday after Easter, followed the thirteenth-century city walls. It eclipsed the Corpus Christi procession, which ironically had originated in Cologne. The following Friday saw the St Sylvester procession, the oldest in the city, when the saint's head was carried along the course of the Roman wall. The St Boniface procession on 5 June went to the saint's chapel on the Severinstraße.[95]

The absence of both classes of holiday is probably explained by Schotten's social position and cultural terms of reference. *Holzfahrttag* and *Petrivinkelstag* were festivities of the people, with a certain artisan bias, whereas Schotten is concerned with the customs and practices which impinge on the world of the schoolboy or student; and he cannot entirely conceal a degree of bourgeois-humanist condescension towards the populace at large.

---

[94] *Holzfahrttag*: Herborn, 'Fast-, Fest- und Feiertage' p. 44; L. Ennen, 'Kölner Holzfahrttag', 641–42. *Petrivinkelstag*: Herborn, 'Fast-, Fest- und Feiertage', pp. 52–53; *BW*, II, p. 56; III, pp. 46, 246, 287; V, pp. 46, 305, 425.

[95] *Gottestracht*: Schwerhoff, 'Köln rüstet sich zur Gottestracht', passim; id., 'Das rituelle Leben der mittelalterlichen Stadt', p. 54; Herborn, 'Fast-, Fest- und Feiertage', pp. 46–50; Klersch, I, p. 214. St Sylvester: Schwerhoff, 'Das rituelle Leben der mittelalterlichen Stadt', p. 55; Herborn, 'Fast-, Fest- und Feiertage', pp. 46–50. St Boniface: Herborn, 'Fast-, Fest- und Feiertage', p. 49.

This perhaps explains why in his references to Christmas in colloquy 35 Schotten does not mention the typical Cologne family customs of 'rocking the Christ-child' ('das kintgin wiegen') and carol-singing described by Weinsberg.[96] The three processions had been introduced for reasons of municipal politics. The *Gottestracht* was tightly controlled by the council as an expression of civic power and pride; the St Sylvester procession commemorated the city's victory over the archbishop at the Battle of Worringen in 1288. They were never genuinely popular festivals, and were already on the wane by the early sixteenth century.[97]

The other prominent element of Cologne life and mentality conspicuously missing from the *Confabulationes* is the 'Colonia sancta' tradition, in which Cologne saw itself as a kind of second Rome or Jerusalem, crowded with churches and monasteries, and under the powerful protection of saints like St Ursula, or the Three Kings, whose bones were reputed to lie in the Cathedral. One city history was called the *Chronicle of the Holy City of Cologne*.[98] Local saints, too, were central to this vision, especially the early bishops of Cologne like Maternus, Severinus, Evergislus, Cunibertus, Agilolphus, and Heribertus.[99] Yet for all the local bias in the naming of the boys, several of the most eminent Cologne saints' names, Agilolphus, Cunibertus and Maternus, are conspicuous by their absence from the *Confabulationes*. Schotten seems

---

[96] E.g. *BW*, V, pp. 32, 202.
[97] Herborn, 'Fast-, Fest- und Feiertage', pp. 57–58. These processions are not mentioned by Weinsberg (*BW*, V, p. 49).
[98] *Cronica van der hilliger stat van Coellen* (also known as *Koelhoffsche Chronik*), ed. by Cardauns; Militzer, 'Collen eyn kroyn', passim, esp. pp. 19–20.
[99] E.g. surrounding the arms of the city in Hermann van Beeck, *Agrippina* (*ca.* 1470), HAStK, 7030, 20, fol. 55r, repr. in Militzer, 'Collen eyn kroyn', p. 15; guarding Cologne in *Koelhoffsche Chronik*, fol. 228r; See Militzer, 'Collen eyn kroyn', p. 20; *SEECO*, V,1, pp. 7–17.

distanced, perhaps by his humanism, from this essentially medieval local Catholicism.

Missing too is any reference to the legend of the virtual foundation of Cologne by fifteen Roman senatorial families who had been sent to Colonia Agrippina by Trajan and had settled there.[100] This, first mentioned by Vincent of Beauvais, was by the fifteenth century a very widespread assumption. The leading Cologne families, too, had developed legends tracing their origins back to Roman times.[101] By the sixteenth century however, these legends, discredited by humanists, were no longer generally believed; and some Cologne humanists were mocking those still naïve enough to give them credence, so their absence from the *Confabulationes* is not unduly surprising.[102] More remarkable, however, is the fact that Schotten also makes no reference to the Roman origin of the city, which was of course entirely authentic.

The degree to which Schotten integrates Cologne life of the 1520s into the *Confabulationes* is considerable: no other colloquy author gives anything approaching the palpable sense of locality and culture which the *Confabulationes* deliver. This is clearly linked with Schotten's mode of composition. He originally wrote his dialogues not for a general schoolboy readership, but specifically for his own pupils, 'in eorum usum qui sub mea agunt ferula'.[103] He did not initially conceive them as

---

[100] Militzer, 'Collen eyn kroyn', pp. 23–25. Seen in Hermann van Beeck, *Agrippina*, HAStK, 7030, 20, fol. 14ᵛ; *Cronica van der hilliger stat van Coellen*, ed. by Cardauns, p. 317. See Hiestand, 'Civis Romanus sum', pp. 91–109.

[101] Herborn, 'Bürgerliches Selbstverständnis', p. 504. E.g. Werner Overstolz, family chronicle of 1446, HAStK, 7657, 67, fol. 22a.

[102] Höhlbaum, 'Zur Geschichte der sogenannten Koelhoffschen Chronik', esp pp. 105–8; Militzer, 'Collen eyn kroyn', pp. 25, 27.

[103] Schotten, *Confabulationes*, ed. by Macardle, 'Hermannus Schottennius Hessus candido lectori', l. 3; cf. 'in meorum discipulorum usum composui': ibid., l. 25.

a collection but produced them singly, and only afterwards brought them together into a single volume.[104] Is is clear that he constructed his dialogues on the basis of the lived experience of his schoolboys: colloquies which treat particular events, feasts and seasons, for example, will have been written for the relevant occasion. But more than this, Schotten designed the dialogues as faithful depictions of his boys' way of life, social circumstances, attitudes and feelings, and was prepared to include details which were pedagogically less than ideal simply because they were true. The similarity with modern methods of language teaching, with their stress on 'authenticity' of language and cultural reference, is striking.

Dates

The detail and precision of the Cologne references, and the way in which this relates to their composition by Schotten, suggests another line of enquiry. Some colloquies mention or imply dates. Might these help to date Schotten's period of schoolteaching, which the University documents cannot pinpoint (see Chapter 1)? *A priori*, it is fairly certain that Schotten will not have begun teaching before gaining his MA in 1520, given that he took a perfectly normal length of time to attain that degree. He will also probably not have begun before being elected to the Arts Faculty 'consilium' in April 1522, for the required university exercises would have left little or no

---

[104] 'Latinas locutiones, quas hactenus satis abunde tibi tuisque commilitonibus litterariis dictaui, in unum hunc confabulationum libellum congessi': Schotten, *Confabulationes*, ed. by Macardle, 'Et genere et moribus adolescenti ingenuo Gisberto Sterckenberg [...]', ll. 9–11.

time for schoolmastering (see pp. 42–43). Also, as will be argued in Chapter 3, the *Confabulationes* avowedly imitate Erasmus, and were almost certainly based on the March 1522 edition of the *Colloquia*, suggesting that composition began in late 1522 at the earliest. The text was complete by mid-February 1525, the date of dedication.[105] The dates mentioned or implied in the colloquies do indeed fit into the period 1522–1525; but as will be seen, do not answer all questions of dating.

The most definite reference to dates is in colloquy 91, 'De Anno Iubilaeo': Raimundus is preparing for a pilgrimage to Rome, for a papal decree promises a special indulgence to all penitents journeying to Rome that year (ll. 16–17). He must mean the Holy Year of 1525, which began at Christmas 1524: since he says he is going to prepare himself 'this winter' (l. 3), he must be speaking from the perspective of mid-to-late 1524.

In colloquy 40, two boys plan an evening's singing at burghers' doors on St Martin's Eve (see pp. 111–12). The holiday itself, 11 November, falls on Friday, a fast day, but the eve will be a day of feasting, and the boys look forward to presents of food or money for their songs. The days of the week fit the year 1524.[106]

1524 would also fit colloquy 33, 'De eligendo episcopo', a rare reference in humanist literature to the custom of choosing a schoolboy 'bishop', one of the many medieval ceremonies of misrule. The chosen boy presided, episcopally vested, over the services of a defined period, often preaching a mock sermon (see notes to colloquy 33). Neither the colloquy nor any sixteenth-century documents offer specifics on Boy Bishop ceremonies in

---

[105] Schotten, *Confabulationes [...]* (Augsburg: S. Ruff, 1525), fol. A2ᵛ.
[106] All dates are calculated from the calendars in Grotefend, *Taschenbuch der Zeitrechnung des deutschen Mittelalters*, and Grotefend online. Page- and URL references are not given in the footnotes.

Cologne. It is for example uncertain how many schools in Cologne elected their own 'bishop': Weinsberg mentions St Aposteln and possibly St Jakob,[107] but presumably there were others. By the later Middle Ages the Boy Bishop's rule in Cologne, as all over western Europe, lasted from the feast of St Nicholas till the Holy Innocents (6–28 December).[108] Major saints' days began liturgically at First Vespers on the vigil of the feast, and some sources show the Boy Bishop starting his rule at First Vespers of St Nicholas.[109] This would fit perfectly with Schotten's colloquy, where the boys speak of electing the 'bishop' on the following Monday (ll. 3–5), for 5 December fell on a Monday in 1524.

The fit is perhaps too good to be true. A good deal of evidence from Cologne and region documents the Boy Bishop being chosen on St Nicholas's Day itself, but not appearing in choir till Holy Innocents' Day.[110] Then too, records speak of the 'bishop' taking up office immediately he is elected. The draft of the 1662 Cologne Diocesan Synod resolutions speak of the 'bishop', episcopally vested and accompanied by a band of 'retainers', riding round the streets on the day of his election.[111] If the 'bishop' did

---

[107] *BW*, II, pp. 157, 210.

[108] Meisen, *Nikolauskult und Nikolausbrauch*, pp. 317–28. *Decreta [...] synodi Coloniensis* (1667), I, V, IX, § II, p. 36: 'pueri à die S. Nicolai, usque ad festum SS. Innocentium, personatum Episcopum colunt'; cf. *KL*, IV, cols 1399–1401.

[109] E.g. Geldern, fifteenth and sixteenth centuries: Meisen, *Nikolauskult und Nikolausbrauch*, p. 327.

[110] E.g. chapter of Xanten, 1526. Cf. municipality of Wesel, 1526: 'bishop' chosen on 6 December; date of choir presence unspecified: Meisen, *Nikolauskult und Nikolausbrauch*, pp. 327–28.

[111] 'Neve puerilis aetatis Episcopus, *die, quo eligitur*, vel munere suo defungitur, ad se ostendandum, vel colligendam pecuniam Mitratus, Baculo, et ornamentis caeteris Pontificalibus decoratus, cum personatis aliquot militibus per plateas equitet', *Decreta [...] synodi Coloniensis* (1661), I, V, IX, § III, p. 52, emphasis supplied).

start his term of office on 6 December rather than on the vigil, and began on the day he was elected, then the election would have been held on 6 December; and that date did not fall on a Monday in any of the years when the *Confabulationes* could have been written (1522: Saturday; 1523: Sunday; 1524: Tuesday). The mention of Monday, then, could be fictive. But if it does refer to actual time, then 1524 still seems the most plausible. In some schools the 'bishop' may have assisted at First Vespers of St Nicholas; or it may in some places have been found more practical to hold the election a day in advance of a 6 December start. But a gap of more than a day or so seems unlikely; and in the other years in question, 1522 and 1523, St Nicholas's Day fell on days (Saturday and Sunday respectively) which make a Monday election less probable.

All these dates, however, fall towards the end of the period in which the *Confabulationes* must on external evidence have been composed. And unfortunately other, possibly earlier, dates implied by the colloquies prove too imprecise to establish when composition might have begun.

In colloquy 83, David and Lucas talk of the shortage of wheat, presently selling for one Goldgulden, a price tolerable only to the rich (ll. 19–22). Similarly in colloquy 107: a dinner-party is dominated by the talk of profiteering grain-merchants; prices are unlikely to fall before the next harvest (ll. 18–19). This reflects the climatic realities of the time, as the European 'Little Ice Age' brought colder and rainier summers, poorer harvests and frequent shortages. The harvest of 1523 was disastrous in much of Germany, including Cologne, where it was followed by an unusually hard winter. Records show that in 1523–1524 grain was indeed scarce and expensive. A contemporary chronicle records famine conditions in

Cologne and elsewhere:[112] many starved to death, and surrogate bread was baked from beans and even acorns till the good harvest of 1524 ended the crisis.

Both colloquies clearly allude to the situation between the 1523 and 1524 harvests. But, though cereal prices were recorded very fully in early modern Cologne, where the council intervened to stabilize prices in times of famine, no greater precision seems possible. Since 1512 mixed wheat/rye bread-grain had cost between about 3.5 and 5.25 Marks per Malter (164 litres), and at the 1522 harvest had been cheap, at 3.96 Marks: at harvest 1523 it rose to 7.33 Marks.[113] In May 1524 the council intervened, selling grain from its stores below harvest prices, initially at five Marks for rye and six for wheat, but these prices were driven up during 1524: by late September rye was selling for seven Marks, wheat at over eight, and until harvest 1524 the council was constantly discussing and regulating grain supply, and trying to prevent speculation.[114]

By comparison with these recorded prices, however, the one Gulden quoted in the colloquy as worryingly high seems distinctly low: it would equate to the 1522 figure of 3.96 Marks, but that was a cheap price after a normal harvest. Even the council's reduced selling price of six Marks shortly after the 1523 harvest equals 1.4 Gulden; the later price of over eight Marks would be nearer two Gulden.[115] What could explain this disparity?

---

[112] 'Dat koirn ind die fruicht [was] sere qualich bÿkomen ind geraiden, ind wart derhaluen tzo Coellen ind in vÿll landen sere duyr tzÿdt': HAStK, 8830, 12, *Kleine Kölnische Chronik*, 1528, p. 9. Cf. *Die Mirakelbücher des Klosters Eberhardshausen*, ed. by Hoffmann and Dohms, no. 680, pp. 320–21. Isenmann, p. 39.

[113] Irsigler, 'Getreide- und Brotpreise', p. 521; Ebeling and Irsigler, *Getreideumsatz*, I, pp. LIII–LV.

[114] BRStK, III, nos 378, 411, 435, 454, 497, 619, 646, 678, 679, 772, 830, 839; Ebeling and Irsigler, *Getreideumsatz*, I, p. LV.

[115] Ebeling and Irsigler, *Getreideumsatz*, I, p. LV and p. XXXV,

Is Schotten's price of one Gulden simply a mistake – understandable in someone who probably had little practical experience of buying groceries? No unit of measurement is specified in the colloquy: might it refer to the Zentner, roughly half a Malter? In this case it would be roughly right for the harvest 1523 price. Might it reflect rising prices shortly after the 1523 harvest but before the unheard-of levels of winter 1523 and spring 1524? There is no way of deciding; and records of weekly prices do not exist for the 1520s. It is impossible to improve on the rough dating autumn 1523 to autumn 1524.

Similarly ambivalent is colloquy 36, 'De tempore bacchanali', which begins with an explicit statement that Shrovetide will this year be unusually long: there will be nine weeks 'inter ferias natales Christianas et Quadragesimam' (ll. 3–4). But from when exactly are the boys calculating? The plural 'feriae natales Christianae' may mean Christmas Day: 'feriae' denoting a single day, correct classical usage, is frequent in the *Confabulationes*.[116] It may however mean the period of the school holiday, which lasts from the day before St Thomas's Day to the day after the Circumcision, 20 December to 2 January (colloquy 35, ll. 15–16). From the Circumcision to Ash Wednesday inclusive, Shrovetide varies from five weeks (Easter 22 March; normal year) to ten weeks (Easter 25 April; leap year): counting from Christmas adds a week. In two of the years in which the *Confabulationes* could have been written, 1523 and 1524, Shrovetide was short (seven weeks and five weeks three days respectively, counted from the Circumcision). Only 1522 and 1525 fit the description, but it is impossible to know which is meant. 'Nine weeks' could equally well refer to 1522 (9 weeks 1 day counting from the Circumcision) and

---

Tabelle 1. 1 Gulden = 4 Marks.
[116] E.g. colloquies 32, l. 13; 40, l. 4; 93, l. 5; 102, l. 1.

to 1525 (9 weeks 4 days counting from Christmas). Thus the most pointed reference to dates in the entire text is ambivalent. On external evidence 1525 is much the more probable year, for a reference to Shrovetide 1522 would have had to be written in late 1521 or very early in 1522, when Schotten, still working towards membership of the Arts Faculty *consilium*, was far less likely to have been a full-time schoolmaster; and this was before the 1522 Erasmus edition, a crucial source for the *Confabulationes*, appeared.

The dates mentioned in the *Confabulationes*, like so much of the detail relating to Schotten, do not go beyond the helpfully corroborative. They all point to the same limited period between mid-1524 and early 1525, when we in any case know that Schotten must have been schoolteaching. They cannot determine how early the composition of the dialogues began, or prove that Schotten had begun in the classroom before mid-1524.

Time

As well as locality, culture and dates, the *Confabulationes* are profoundly concerned with the time of day. 'Quota est hora?' asks Valterus in colloquy 5, l. 3, beginning a revealing exchange with Adrianus:

> ADRIANVS. Octaua.
> VALTERVS. Quotam horam sonuit?
> ADRIANVS. Octauam.
> VALTERVS. Quota est audita hora?
> ADRIANVS. Octaua, et nona imminet.
>
> (colloquy 5, ll. 4–8)

This is the first of the numerous references in the *Confabulationes* to the time, and ('sonuit'; 'audita') to the use of mechanical clocks as the standard way of measuring it.

By the early sixteenth century public mechanical clocks were of course long established in northern European cities, and were displacing other methods of telling the time:[117] it is evident that the boys in the *Confabulationes* do not measure time in any other way, such as by the sun or church bells. Schotten also uses the modern twelve-hour terminology, whereas Heyden, for instance, who also refers to clocks striking, uses the classical Roman method of counting the hours of day from 6 am and those of night from 6 pm.[118]

The daily timetable which Schotten describes is comparable with that known from other early modern Cologne sources. In colloquy 6, the boys get up at 6 am, 'hora sexta' (l. 10). In colloquy 21, however, they speak of having to be at school by six (l. 7). 6 am is certainly a common time to begin the school day, and boys would have to be up well beforehand if they were to reach school at that hour. 5 am is mentioned in colloquy 72, but this is a particularly early start, so as to go to Mass before school (ll. 13–18). However Weinsberg gives 5 am as a standard time for getting up and for boys to go to school.[119] These may reflect different times for summer and winter: 6 am is mentioned in colloquy 6, which seems to be set in winter, as a reference to the shortening days implies (l. 11).

The hour for breakfast, 'ientaculum', is not specified (colloquy 13); but if it divides the time between the start of school and lunch, it must be at about 7.30 or 8 am. Lunch ('prandium') is eaten at either 10 or 11 am: 'Sonat decimam?' (colloquy 67, l. 8); 'decima postquam sonuerit' (colloquy 14, l. 23); 'undecima hora accumbimus mensae'

---

[117] Dohrn-van Rossum, *The History of the Hour. Clocks and Modern Temporal Orders*, Chapter 5 (esp. pp. 153–54 on Germany) and pp. 96–98, 232–36 on Cologne.

[118] E.g. 'Iam imminet prima' on waking in the morning: Heyden, *Formulae*, VII, sig. G6^r.

[119] *BW*, V, pp. 120–21.

(colloquy 13, l. 21); 'Expecta, iam audies horam undecimam' (colloquy 8, l. 13). 10 am was perhaps the more usual time: hence Michael is surprised that Crato eats at 11 (colloquy 13, l. 21); but 11 am was by no means unknown; it was for instance Weinsberg's normal time.[120] The boys mention an afternoon snack, 'uictus pomeridianus' or 'cibus merendinarius' (colloquy 9), but again no time is given. No hour is specified for dinner, 'cena', but in colloquy 40, Hieronymus and Hermannus plan to start singing round the doors on St Martin's eve 'Postquam octaua sonuerit' (l. 27), at the end of the evening's rich meal (ll. 30–31). This would put dinner at about 7 pm, which is certainly a standard time recorded elsewhere.[121]

Beyond these minutiae, Schotten's discourse of time points to an interesting wider problem. Recently, Max Engammare has developed a thesis on time and punctuality: that Calvin's insistence that Christians were accountable to God for the use of every minute allotted them made sixteenth-century Calvinists, particularly in Geneva, develop a new relationship to time, a new ethic governing its employment, and a new virtue, punctuality, effectively unknown in Antiquity and the Middle Ages. The works of Erasmus, Vives, Montaigne and the Jesuits rarely mention the time; by contrast, Mathurin Cordier's colloquies (1564), written in Geneva, do so frequently, and consciously inculcate an ethic of punctuality.[122] Engammare's thesis perhaps underestimates the extent to which there may have been a culture of time and punctuality before Calvin, and in other confessional

---

[120] 10 am: Kluppel, *Konrad Kluppels Chronik*, ed. by Jürges, p. 154. 11 am: *BW*, II, pp. 265–67; V, p. 119.
[121] *BW*, II, pp. 265–67.
[122] Engammare, *L'ordre du temps. L'invention de la ponctualité au XVIe siècle*, passim, esp. pp. 110, 117–25. See Mathurin Cordier, *Colloquiorum scholasticorum libri IIII [...]* (Lyon: T. Straton, 1564).

milieux. Schotten certainly shows a good deal more concern (in both senses of the word) with the passing of time, with its precise measurement, and with the consequences, than Engammare sees as typical for early-sixteenth-century Catholic humanists. As well as the numerous references to the times when things happen, a level of concern, sometimes even a slight anxiety, about time and punctuality is visible.

The boys in colloquy 21 are appalled to find they have overslept and will be late for school. In colloquy 67, 'De modo sternendi mensam', they are galvanized into double-quick laying of the lunch table when one of them realises that the clock has just struck ten, and that lunch is due (ll. 3–10). In colloquy 5, Valterus asks Adrianus for the time in three different formulations: 'Quota est hora?'; 'Quotam horam sonuit?'; 'Quota est audita hora?' (ll. 3, 5, 7). This is of course partly linguistic schooling, an Erasmus-inspired demonstration of different phrasings of the same question, but as so often, Schotten gives it a realistic edge. Valterus seems to have lost track of the time: his repeated questions suggest he mistrusts Adrianus's assurance that it is 8 pm: 'Id non credo' (l. 9). When he does accept this, his immediate reaction is to say it is bedtime: 'Tunc eundi cubitum tempus est' (l. 11) and to go off to sleep. He is very sleepy ('Me autem somnus oppido urget', l. 13), but the fact that the clock is telling the 'proper' time for bed seems the decisive factor. Adrianus calls Valterus an 'Endymion', a sleepy-head; Valterus counters that this really applies to Adrianus, who normally goes to bed before him (l. 21). The argument appeals to a 'proper' bedtime, regulated by the clock rather than by physical need. Similarly, in colloquy 6, Georgius is confused by the fact that it is still dark at 6 am (ll. 9–10); the prissily superior Volfgangus, however, knows that the days are shortening, but that the clock shows the right time – 'surgendi tempus', time to get up (l. 7).

Once again Schotten the recorder of ordinary life is to the fore. The specialized literature on time has established that by the early sixteenth century mechanical time-measurement had firmly established itself and had made an impact on the public and private consciousness of time.[123] Dohrn-van Rossum, for instance, traces the gradual establishment of a clock-based temporal order in Cologne between the late fourteenth century and the fifteenth.[124] But he notes that concrete traces of this are sparse, and almost entirely confined to lapidary remarks in civic regulations; he stresses that 'contemporaries were rarely aware of the largely anonymous process of change in time-consciousness.'[125] As with so many areas of Cologne life, it is Schotten who is amongst the first actually to document that changing consciousness in the real lives and the real discourse of ordinary people.

---

[123] Dohrn-van Rossum, *The History of the Hour*, esp. Chapter 8, 'The Ordering of Time'.
[124] Ibid., pp. 232–36, based mainly on data in Stein and in von Loesch, *Die Kölner Zunfturkunden*: see p. 234, n. 46.
[125] Ibid., pp. 232–33.

CHAPTER 3

The *Confabulationes* and other Humanist Colloquies

The genesis of texts involves the confrontation of authors not solely with external reality, but also with other texts. This is especially true of sixteenth-century humanist Latin texts, which avowedly reflect, emulate and directly imitate previous texts. It is unlikely that Schotten composed the *Confabulationes* in complete ignorance of other examples of school colloquies, nor did he claim to have done so.

Erasmus, Colloquia familiaria

The titlepage advertises the *Confabulationes* as imitations of Erasmus, 'ad amussim Colloquiorum Erasmi Roterodami', and Schotten's preface pays reverent tribute to Erasmus as his literary model.[1]

Erasmus's *Colloquia*, the premier colloquy collection of the sixteenth century, first appeared in 1518.[2] By the time

---

1   Schotten, *Confabulationes*, ed. by Macardle, 'Hermannus Schottennius Hessus candido lectori', esp. ll. 6–8.
2   *Familiarium colloquiorum formulae, et alia quaedam, per Des. Erasmum* Roterodamum [...] (Basel: J. Froben, November 1518): edition A (Erasmus, *Colloquia*, pp. 27–70); *VD 16*, E 2301. Cf. Erasmus, *Colloquia*, pp. 3–7; *CWE*, XXXIX, pp. xx–xxi.

Erasmus died in 1536 he had supervised a further fourteen progressively enlarged editions; about 100 editions of the complete text, and a still uncounted number of selections for the use of schools, had been printed all over Europe.³

Erasmus had originally designed the *Colloquia* for schoolboys, and the earliest editions contained material suitable for that age-group and featured boys as speakers. Much was formulaic: lists of alternative ways of expressing certain facts and sentiments, some set in a rudimentary, discontinuous dialogic framework.⁴ Only towards the end of the collection did texts approaching genuine conversations appear, and these were still very much in the service of the formulae.⁵ It was the Basel edition of March 1522, the edition that really established the shape and tone of the *Colloquia*, which contained real dialogues as well, texts with developed plot, structure and characterization.⁶ The fame of the *Colloquia* rests on several of these, such as 'De votis temere susceptis', 'Confessio militis', 'Lusus pueriles', 'Pietas puerilis' and 'Conuiuium profanum'.⁷ The 1522 edition was also the first to insist on the colloquies' moral as well as linguistic

---

3   Editions B (Louvain: T. Martens, March 1519): Erasmus, *Colloquia*, p. 25, pp. 71–111; to P (Basel: H. Froben and N. Episcopius, March 1533): Erasmus, *Colloquia*, p. 25, pp. 711–33). Other printings: see Erasmus, *Colloquia*, p. 15.
4   E.g. 'Valetudinis', 'Responsoria', etc., Erasmus, *Colloquia*, pp. 33–39.
5   E.g. 'Consecratio coenae', 'Si cognoscerem quid te oblecteret, tibi seruirem', Erasmus, *Colloquia*, pp. 46–47, 49–61.
6   Edition D (Basel: J. Froben, March 1522); *VD 16*, E 2334: Erasmus, *Colloquia*, pp. 25, 121–222; cf. pp. 7–8.
7   Erasmus, *Colloquia*, pp. 147–50; 154–58; 163–71; 196–215. Most were given these titles only in edition H (Basel: J. Froben, August–September 1524): Erasmus, *Colloquia*, pp. 25, 409–49.

value: they were useful not only 'ad linguam puerilem expoliendam', but also 'ad uitam instituendam'.⁸

The possibilities of the dialogue genre led Erasmus to use the colloquies increasingly as a vehicle for the critical and often satirical and polemical discussion of the major preoccupations of his age, moral and religious topics far beyond the horizon of the classroom. The March 1522 edition had already set the trend. 'De votis temere susceptis' is a swingeing critique of pilgrimage; 'De captandis sacerdotiis' exposes simony and other corruptions of the ecclesiastical benefice business.⁹ Even the edifying 'Pietas puerilis' expounds a devotion critically distanced from conventional Catholic forms: fasting is only for boys of over seventeen; confession is made daily directly to Christ, but to a priest only in the case of serious sin; there are reservations about the monastic life.¹⁰ Every new edition Erasmus oversaw would add several dialogues, and these were increasingly concerned with such burning contemporary issues of morality and religion.¹¹

Literature's gain, however, was the classroom's loss. Such issues of theology and religious praxis were of interest to (some) adults, but far too advanced for youths; even Vives thought so.¹² In his defence, Erasmus began by asserting that boys nowadays did discuss topics like this; but then changed tack, admitting that his pen had run away with him.¹³ Erasmus probably had been seduced by his creative urges. In his dedication to Erasmius Froben in

---

8   Edition D, titlepage: Erasmus, *Colloquia*, p. 122 (facsimile).
9   Erasmus, *Colloquia*, pp. 147–50; 150–54.
10 Erasmus, *Colloquia*, pp. 171–81, especially p. 177, ll. 1707–12; p. 177, l. 1725; p. 179, l. 1761; p. 179, l. 1778–p. 180, l. 1791. Originally called 'Confabulatio pia'.
11 Erasmus, *Colloquia*, pp. 8–9.
12 'Alienissima videtur mihi et loco et personis illis dissertio', Erasmus, *Epistolae*, 1732, ll. 29–39 (l. 33).
13 Erasmus, *Epistolae*, 1830, ll. 5–10, especially ll. 9–10.

the March 1522 Basel edition, he described how he had had to 'become a boy again', 'repuerascere', to produce material suitable for Erasmius's tender years.[14] Now he had once again put away childish things, as shown by dialogues like 'Coniugium' (later called 'Υxor μεμπσίγαμος'), in the August 1523 edition, where Eulalia and Xanthippe discuss how to manage a husband's drinking, violence and philandering, and Xanthippe describes getting pregnant as the result of non-consensual sex with her fiancé.[15] How suitable as class reading was this? Like many of the *Colloquia* it shows remarkable practical wisdom and social, psychological and literary realism; but considerations of propriety aside, it transcends the experience and understanding of schoolboys.

In 1523 or 1524, then, Schotten may well have thought that there was room in the world for more colloquies in the Erasmian mould, but pitched, as the earlier *Colloquia* had been, at the schoolboy level. Then too, Erasmus's ideas were not merely adult; they were doctrinally suspect. Almost from their appearance, the *Colloquia* had been under theological attack.[16] As early as 1522 the Louvain Carmelite Nicholas Baechem alleged heresy in the *Colloquia* on topics such as fasting, confession, indulgences and vows.[17] The subsequent exchange between Erasmus and the Louvain Theological Faculty was brief but bitter.[18] 1525, when the *Confabulationes* appear-

---

[14] 'Visum est enim nobis tua causa dies aliquot repuerascere, dum stilum ac sententias ad tuam aetatulam attemperamus', Erasmus, *Colloquia*, p. 123, ll. 13–14; also Erasmus, *Epistolae*, 1262.

[15] Edition F, Erasmus, *Colloquia*, pp. 301–13, especially p. 311, ll. 342–59.

[16] Bierlaire, *Les Colloques D'Erasme*, pp. 201–303; Gutmann, *Die Colloquia familiaria des Erasmus von Rotterdam*, pp. 23–128; Barth, 'Desiderius Erasmus, *Colloquia familiaria*', col. 407.

[17] Erasmus, *Colloquia*, pp. 9–10; Erasmus, *Epistolae*, 1254, l. 13; 1296, ll. 23–25; *CWE*, XXXIX, p. xxxvii.

[18] Bierlaire, 'Le *Libellus Colloquiorum* de mars 1522 et Nicolas

ed, saw accusations of heresy in the *Colloquia* by Vincent
Dierckx, OP and Jacobus Latomus at Louvain; in 1526
there would follow the higher-profile assault by the Paris
Theological Faculty led by Noël Bédier.[19] In 1531 the
Sorbonne issued its condemnation: four more were to
follow by 1556.[20] Erasmus's opponent Alberto Pio was
largely provoked by passages in the *Colloquia*.[21] In 1557
and 1559 the *Colloquia* were condemned by Pope Paul
VI, and in 1564 by the Council of Trent.[22] When the
Confabulationes appeared, this chapter had only opened,
but the early Louvain controversies would have been

Baechem'; Crahay, 'Les censeurs louvanistes d'Erasme', esp.
pp. 227–28; Barth, 'Desiderius Erasmus, *Colloquia familiaria*',
cols 402–03; Erasmus, *Colloquia*, p. 10. Erasmus, *Epistolae*,
1296, ll. 8–30, 54–71; 1300, 1301 (to the Louvain theologians).

[19] Crahay, 'Les censeurs louvanistes d'Erasme', pp. 227–28; Gutmann, *Die Colloquia familiaria des Erasmus von Rotterdam*, p. 35. Halkin, *Erasmus*, p. 206; Barth, 'Desiderius Erasmus, *Colloquia familiaria*', cols 403–05; *Annotationes Natalis Bedae [...] in Desiderium Erasmum [...]* (Paris: J. Bade, 1526); Erasmus, *Epistolae*, 1723, to the Paris Theological Faculty, ll. 41–45.

[20] *Determinatio [...] super quamplurimis assertionibus D. Erasmi Roterodami*. Erasmus, *Colloquia*, p. 15. Erasmus's reply: *Declarationes ad censuras Facultatis Theologiae Parisiensis. LB*, IX, 928–54. Further condemnations in 1544, 1547, 1551, 1556: Bierlaire, *Les Colloques d'Erasme*, pp. 201–303; *CWE*, XXXIX, p. xxxix.

[21] E.g. Alberto Pio, *Ad Erasmi Roterodami expostulationem responsio accurata et paraenetica [...]* (Paris: J. Bade, 1529). Erasmus, *Responsio ad epistolam paraeneticam [...] Alberti Pii [...]* (Basel: J. Froben, 1529); *LB*, IX, 1095B–122E; *CWE*, LXXXIV, pp. 1–103. Alberto Pio, *Tres et viginti libri in locos [...] Desiderii Erasmi* (Paris: J. Bade, 1531). Erasmus, *Apologia adversus rhapsodias [...] Alberti Pii* (Basel: J. Froben, 1531); *LB*, IX, 1123A–96D; *CWE*, LXXXIV, pp. 105–360; Gilmore, 'Erasmus and Alberto Pio'; id., 'Italian Reactions to Erasmian Humanism'.

[22] *CWE*, XXXIX, p. xxxix; Crahay, 'Les censeurs louvanistes d'Erasme', pp. 221–22; *Index des livres interdits*, ed. by de Bujanda and others, passim.

known in Cologne, where the Franciscans were accusing Erasmus of having 'laid the egg which Luther had hatched'.[23] In his defence Erasmus protested that he was teaching eloquence, not theology.[24] Schotten may have felt moved to produce colloquies of his own of which this could be said without the suspicion of disingenuousness which Erasmus could never entirely escape.

The *Colloquia* are the source from which much of the *Confabulationes* was quarried. This is clear from the Erasmian lexis and phraseology which Schotten imitates, from the breezy Terentian tone of the language, from the fast-moving exchange in the shorter dialogues, and from the subject-matter. Since Schotten's Erasmian borrowings are recorded in detail in the notes to the colloquies in Schotten, *Confabulationes*, edited by Macardle, only a few particularly telling examples are discussed here.

Some of Schotten's characteristic lexical uses are Erasmian. One is 'nidus' for 'bed', seemingly otherwise unknown in Classical, Late and Medieval Latin; the normal figurative sense is one's home. It is however frequent in Erasmus's *Colloquia*.[25] Schotten's frequent 'bolus' for 'morsel, mouthful' is Medieval Latin, deplored as such by Massebieau, and indeed avoided by some humanists, such as Vives; but it is Erasmian.[26] Erasmian,

---

[23] The only known source of the gibe is 'Ego peperi ouum, Lutherus exclusit', Erasmus, *Epistolae*, 1528, l. 11; cf. ll. 12–17.

[24] 'In eo libello doceo loqui Latine, non trado articulos fidei', Erasmus, *Epistolae*, 1300, l. 14; cf. 1301, ll. 10–11.

[25] E.g. 'Mature me confero ad nidum', Erasmus, *Colloquia*, p. 175, l. 1622; cf. p. 338, l. 168; p. 359, l. 498. See Schotten, *Confabulationes*, ed. by Macardle, note to colloquy 6, l. 22, and index of non-classical words.

[26] See Schotten, *Confabulationes*, ed. by Macardle, note to colloquy 11, l. 25, and index of non-classical words. Massebieau, *Les colloques scolaires du seizième siècle*, p. 128; not used in Vives's *Exercitatio*. Erasmus, *Adagia*, 2650, 'Tribus bolis', *ASD*, II-6, p. 451, ll. 472–73. Also Hegendorff, *Dialogi*, sig. D2^r.

too, is Schotten's frequent retort 'quidni?' (literally 'why not?') in the sense 'of course'.[27] A great many of Schotten's other words and phrases have almost certainly been taken in the first instance from the *Colloquia*; they are discussed in the notes to the individual colloquies in Schotten, *Confabulationes*, ed. by Macardle.

Even in the case of items which Schotten could have found in a variety of sources, details of placing and context often point to Erasmus. In colloquy 17, for instance, Schotten uses two formulations, 'Nunc naso me suspendis' and 'ex animo loquor' (ll. 18, 19) which Erasmus places within a few lines of each other in a single colloquy in the 1522 edition.[28]

The subject-matter of many of Schotten's colloquies is also clearly indebted to Erasmus. Again, details of this are recorded in the notes in Schotten, *Confabulationes*, ed. by Macardle; but a few telling examples deserve detailed discussion. Colloquy 111, 'De fertili sacerdotio', is obviously inspired by Erasmus's 'De captandis sacerdotiis', as is some of its language, such as the image of 'fishing with a golden hook', 'aureo hamo' (l. 10). Here again Schotten is closely dependent on Erasmus. 'Fishing with a golden hook', a phrase coined by Suetonius, means to risk losing tackle worth more than the likely catch, as Erasmus explains in the *Adagia*.[29] However, in 'De captandis sacerdotiis', Pamphagus says 'Complures illic piscantur hamo, quod dici solet, aureo', and though

---

[27] Colloquies no. 8, l. 5; 21, l. 5; 32, l. 9; 33, l. 32; 53, l. 7; 58, l. 34; 90, l. 26; 93, l. 29. Frequent in Erasmus, *Colloquia*, e.g. p. 180, l. 1821; p. 367, l. 112; p. 369, l. 206; p. 370, l. 237; p. 401, l. 443.

[28] Cf. 'Naso me suspendis adunco' and 'Emoriar, ni loquor ex animo', Erasmus, 'Alia', *Colloquia*, p. 143, l. 609; p. 144, ll. 614–15. Cf. 'Ex animo loquor', ibid., p. 154, l. 926. See Schotten, *Confabulationes*, ed. by Macardle, notes to colloquy 17, ll. 18, 19.

[29] Suetonius, *Augustus*, 25; Otto, 783. Erasmus, *Adagia*, 1160, 'Aureo piscari hamo'.

Cocles's reply 'Stultum piscandi genus' alludes to the risk involved, the main meaning seems to be simply using bribery in the pursuit of benefices.[30] It is this restricted and untypical sense which Schotten apparently took from the *Colloquia*.

In colloquy 123, the host accuses his guests, who are picking at their food, of 'acting like Chrysippus': 'Vt ita Chrysippum agitis? Non delectat uos cibus?' (l. 73). This imitates Christianus's accusation 'Tu nunc Chrysippum agis' in Erasmus's 'Conuiuium profanum';[31] a phrase which Erasmus coined under a slight misapprehension. Christianus explains that Chrysippus, preoccupied by logical problems, would have eaten nothing at dinners had his slave Melissa not fed him.[32] This story is told by Valerius Maximus – not however about Chrysippus, but about his contemporary Carneades.[33] Erasmus, probably quoting, as so often, from memory, has misremembered the passage. He may have been confused by the fact that Valerius also mentions Carneades's disputations with Chrysippus.[34] He may even have recalled that Diogenes Laertius describes Chrysippus's behaviour at parties, but forgotten that the sage habitually got tipsy.[35] Schotten has not gone to the classical sources, but has taken Erasmus at face value.

It is, above all, obvious borrowings of subject-matter which make it clear that Schotten was using the March 1522 edition of the *Colloquia*, since the colloquies from which he was borrowing had not been in earlier editions.

---

[30] Erasmus, *Colloquia*, p. 152, ll. 866–68.
[31] Ibid., p. 199, l. 2415.
[32] Ibid., ll. 2417–19.
[33] Valerius Maximus, *Facta et dicta*, 8.7.ext.5.
[34] 'Idem cum Chrysippo disputaturus elleboro se ante purgabat ad expromendum ingenium suum adtentius [...]', Valerius Maximus, *Facta et dicta*, 8.7.ext.5.
[35] Diogenes Laertius, *Lives*, 7.183: Chrysippus was 'unsteady on his legs' at parties.

As dating evidence this is clear, but unfortunately not helpful. It means only that the bulk of the *Confabulationes* were written after mid-1522; but it is already evident from the chronology of Schotten's studies that he can hardly have begun schoolmastering before then (see pp. 42–43).

Schotten's dependence on other writings of Erasmus, notably the *Adagia*, is evident. In colloquy 84, Adelarius condemns town-dwellers who squander their money, when they have it, on food and drink: 'Ipsi super choenice non sedent' (1. 34). This obviously reflects Erasmus, *Adagia*, 2, iii, 'Choenici ne insideas', 'Don't sit down on your bushel'; but it just as obviously reflects misunderstandings which Erasmus introduces. 'Choenix' ('χοῖνιξ'), was a Greek dry measure. One *choenix* of corn was a day's ration, so the Pythagorean dictum 'Μὴ 'ἐπὶ χοίνικος καθίζαι', 'Don't sit on your grain-measure', meant 'don't be content with the day's rations; have a care for the future'.[36] However, Erasmus begins his discussion of the adage by citing precisely the opposite sense, 'don't worry about food for the morrow', which he wrongly attributes to St Jerome – probably remembering that in *Contra Rufinum* Jerome deals with some of the 'symbola Pythagorica', but forgetting that this is not one of them.[37] Much of Erasmus's treatment of the proverb is similarly confused: he wrongly ascribes 'Jerome's' interpretation to Suidas and Diogenes Laertius, even though both of them give the proverb in its original sense.[38] Erasmus does not in fact accept the first interpretation he

---

[36] Plutarch, *Moralia*, 12E, cf. 354F; cf. Diogenes Laertius, *Lives*, 8.18; Suidas, *Πυθαγόρας*, 3124; Apostolios, *Proverbia*, 8.89.

[37] 'De uictu ne fueris solicitus in diem crastinum', *ASD*, II–1, p. 90, ll. 797–99; cf. Jerome, *Contra Rufinum*, 3.39, *PL*, XXIII, cols 484B–86C.

[38] *ASD*, II–1, p. 90, l. 803. See the detailed discussion of Erasmus's sources and errors in *ASD*, II–1, notes to p. 90, ll. 796–856.

cites; he eventually opts for the correct meaning: people should not be parasitical but work to provide for themselves.[39] Schotten, however, has obviously taken the first meaning, possibly from a cursory reading of the *Adagia*.

Yet for all the obvious verbal and thematic imitation of Erasmus, Schotten's collection of colloquies does strike notes distinctively different from the *Colloquia*. One of these is in the matter of literary realism. In his earlier colloquies, Erasmus was always ready to sacrifice realism to linguistic content. Typical is the question 'Rectene vales?', which triggers not a plausible reply but a catalogue of eleven ways of describing one's health:

> Vellem quidem. Non admodum ex sententia. Equidem vtcunque valeo. Sic satis. Valeo vt possum, quando vt volo non licet [etc.].[40]

Schotten, however, completely rejects this pattern. A question always triggers a single response which is plausible in context. To present formulaic catalogues, Schotten devises a scenario where they are deliberately used. Thus in colloquy 66 Emmericus asks Chrysantus to help him learn some phrases and responses for serving wine. Chrysantus produces a string of such phrases, and Emmericus replies appropriately to each one. Similar arrangements are found elsewhere.[41]

Schotten also differs sharply from Erasmus in the treatment of religious and ecclesiastical themes. His occasional persiflage of monks and some (ignorant) priests in the *Confabulationes* is a good deal more limited than

---

[39] 'Non oportere per inertiam ocium et cibum alienum sectari, sed sua quenque industria sibi parare facultates, quibus mundiciem vitae sustineat', *ASD*, II–1, p. 90, ll. 820–22.
[40] Erasmus: 'Valetudinis', *Colloquia*, p. 132, ll. 218–22.
[41] E.g. colloquy 2, 'De salutatione matutina'; 3, 'De salutatione pomeridiana'; 4, 'De salutatione uespertina'; and cf. 5, 'De uerbis dum cubitum itur', discussed pp. 124–26.

Erasmus's astringent and systematic critique. Indeed on several occasions Schotten's religious attitude contrasts quite pointedly with that of Erasmus. Schotten's colloquy 123, 'Conuiuium Bacchanale, siue ultima cena dierum Lupercalium', is set on Shrove Tuesday, with the guests departing as Lent begins at midnight (ll. 139–47). This almost certainly imitates the situation in Erasmus's 'Conuiuium profanum';[42] but Schotten does not use this as a stepping-stone to a critical discussion of the Church's imposition of fasting, as Erasmus does.[43]

In Erasmus's colloquy 'Pietas puerilis' Gaspar insists that daily Mass is not an absolute devotional priority: it is very well for those with plenty of free time; but to think that you are not a Christian unless you hear Mass daily, or that a day not begun with Mass will be inauspicious, is mere superstition.[44] In Schotten's colloquy 72, 'De missa indies audienda', Conradus, a daily Mass-goer, rebukes Bernardus for going only on Sundays and major feasts, insisting that this is why he is making poor academic progress. He urges him to attend more often, so as to do better at school (ll. 22–36). Whilst Conrad does not exactly say that a day without a Mass is unlucky, this is effectively his implication; Schotten's colloquy is an 'orthodox' counterpart to Erasmus's heartfelt, but still unconventional, piety.

A similar orthodoxy is expressed in colloquy 95, describing buying expensive wax candles for the feast of the Purification of the Blessed Virgin ('Candlemas', 2 February), a pious practice hallowed by medieval com-

---

[42] Erasmus, *Colloquia*, p. 227, ll. 2–5; cf. p. 206, ll. 2656–p. 207, l. 2659.
[43] Ibid., p. 227, l. 6–p. 230, l. 119; cf. p. 207, l. 2660–p. 208, l. 2706.
[44] 'Illos non approbo, qui superstitiose sibi persuaserunt eum diem fore parum faustum, nisi fuerint eum auspicati a missa', Erasmus, *Colloquia*, p. 176, ll. 1664–66; cf. ll. 1661–68.

mentators.[45] The superstitious aspects of the ritual were an obvious target not only for reformers,[46] but for humanists too. In Mosellanus's colloquy on the same topic, which clearly inspired Schotten's, Nicolaus mounts quite an astringent attack. He will not be carrying a candle, he says, but this does not make him a heretic, especially since he has no money to buy one; in any case, Christ would surely prefer money spent on candles to be given to the poor.[47] Schotten's treatment is more ambiguous. The conventional Germanus plans to conform to custom by carrying a large wax candle. Theophilus teasingly criticizes the outward pomp of the ceremony; but Germanus insists that he does everything with a sincere heart and to the honour of the Blessed Virgin, not for show (ll. 20–21). Theophilus says he would rather please God than humans, backing this up with Galatians 1.10, 'If I were to please men I would not be the servant of Christ' (ll. 35–36); but this does not work, as it would in Erasmus, as a decisive scriptural knock-down, for Germanus retorts that Paul is referring to bad actions, not good ones. He has the last word; the colloquy ends here. This is far from a victory for Theophilus; indeed Germanus even manages to suggest that Theophilus's motives cover up a desire to save money. The argument is more evenly and ambiguously balanced than in many of Erasmus's colloquies, where an obviously right (Erasmian) speaker enjoys an authorially endorsed logical and rhetorical victory. Schotten's colloquy allows the articulation of a moderate humanist, indeed broadly Erasmian, piety, and puts it in the mouth of someone whose name, 'he who loves God', at first sight hints that he represents true piety, and still at the end of the discussion suggests

---

[45] E.g. Durandus, *Rationale divinorum officiorum*, VII, vii, 12–16; *Legenda aurea*, XXXVII, pp. 158–67.
[46] E.g. Luther, *Vermahnung an die Geistlichen*, WA, XXX,2, p. 253; Hospinianus, *Festa Christianorum*, fols 41^r–43^r.
[47] Mosellanus, *Paedologia*, 26 (p. 33, ll. 23–27).

that he is not evil or perverse. But this reforming position does not by any means emerge as simply right, and time-hallowed Catholic custom is not rejected as misguided or antipathetic to true faith or inner devotion.

Here, perhaps, is another factor which motivated Schotten to produce his own colloquies. Tewes depicts Schotten as a straightforward Erasmian, the exception that proves the rule of the Cologne Albertists' opposition to Erasmus's vision of a reformed Christianity.[48] But a more detailed analysis of Schotten's writing suggests that he knew and expressed something of the ambiguities felt by many who were sincere humanists and sincere Catholics: that he could wholeheartedly follow Erasmus only as a literary mentor, not as a religious guide. This would square with his friendship with theologically conservative humanists like Georg Lauer and Johann and Hermann Rinck (discussed in Chapter 5), and with the fact that he is not recorded as ever having made any statement remotely critical of the religious status quo in Cologne. It would explain why he produced a colloquy collection closely conformed to Erasmian diction and composition, but discreetly avoiding, and at times implicitly questioning, Erasmian theology.

Schotten's creative dialogue with Erasmus, however, is almost entirely confined to the March 1522 edition of the *Colloquia*. Very little in Schotten's subject-matter or expression reflects later editions. One reason for this, of course, was timing. The last edition of the *Colloquia* which Schotten could possibly have consulted before the publication of the princeps of the *Confabulationes* was edition H of August–September 1524; for the next appeared only in February 1526.[49] Even that would have

---

[48] Tewes, *Bursen*, pp. 794–95.
[49] Basel: J. Froben, August–September 1524, edition H (Erasmus, *Colloquia*, pp. 409–49). Basel: J. Froben, February 1526, edition I (Erasmus, *Colloquia*, pp. 451–551).

been very tight timing, since the latest *Confabulationes* seem to have been composed in late 1524 to early 1525 (see Chapter 2). The only editions after edition D of March 1522 which Schotten is realistically likely to have seen were editions E of July–August 1522, F of August 1523 and G of March 1524.[50]

Just as important as timing, however, must have been content. The new material in all these editions was controversial: 'Apotheosis Capnionis' in praise of Reuchlin in edition E; in editions F and G 'adult' dialogues such as 'Proci et puellae' and 'Υxor μεμπσίγαμος', and critiques of traditional piety like 'Naufragium' and 'Inquisitio'.[51] If Schotten did intend the *Confabulationes* to represent a more orthodox piety than that of Erasmus, he would have found little in these editions that he would have wanted to imitate.

Several data suggest that content was a stronger constraint than timing. There are some indications that Schotten had seen editions E, F and G. In his colloquy 77, for example, the guests refuse the host's offers to stoke up the stove because the room is already warm enough:

HOSPES. Ipse nequeo ferre dum nimio calore aestuat.
CONVIVAE. Insalubre etiam est. (ll. 13–14).

This is remarkably like an exchange in Erasmus's 'Diuersoria' in edition F of August 1523, where Bertulphus complains that German innkeepers grossly overheat their rooms; Gulielmus finds this unhealthy.[52] An aversion to the heat and fumes of stoves, especially German ones, was a hobby-horse which Erasmus had ridden in several letters which Schotten could have read, since they were published in 1522.[53] But the probability of

---

50   Erasmus, *Colloquia*, pp. 223–73 (E); 275–359 (F); 361–408 (G).
51   Ibid., pp. 267–73, 277–88, 301–13, 325–32, 363–74.
52   Ibid., p. 335, l. 82–p. 336, l. 95.
53   Erasmus, *Epistolae*, e.g. 1248 (December 1521), ll. 9–11 and note to l. 10; printed in Erasmus, *Paraphrasis in [...]*

'Diuersoria' as source is supported by what looks like a further Schotten borrowing from a few lines later in 'Diuersoria', where Erasmus shifts the conversation to fear of the 'scabies nova', syphilis, which has made public baths extremely unpopular in recent years.[54] This resembles the exchange in Schotten's 'De balneis ingrediendis' (80), where Hermannus worries about the diseases picked up in baths: 'Multi ingressi mundi exeunt ulcerosi' (l. 15). In neither case is there great linguistic similarity between Erasmus and Schotten, but these two close content parallels side by side in one colloquy of Erasmus strongly suggest that colloquy as Schotten's source.

In colloquy 106, 'De nouis indumentis', Carolus announces that he is about to change; Daniel wonders if this means a change 'in aliud animal' (l. 4), but is assured that it is just a new suit of clothes. This is similar to a passage in Erasmus's 'Γεροντολογία siue 'ὄχημα', in edition G of March 1524, where Glycion uses the same phrase to describe how Pampirus has played many different roles in life: he has changed costumes as though turning into a 'different kind of animal'.[55] Some details in Schotten's thirty 'conuiuia', added to the 1526 second edition of the *Confabulationes*, could have been suggested by editions of the *Colloquia*: an 'Epicurean' dinner from edition E of July–August 1522;[56] the names Crassus and Codrus

---

    Matthaeum (Basel: H. Froben, March 1522; repr. 1523 and 1524).

[54] 'Atqui ante annos viginti quinque nihil receptius erat apud nos, quam thermae publicae. Eae nunc frigent vbique. Scabies enim noua docuit nos abstinere', Erasmus, *Colloquia*, p. 336, ll. 100–02.

[55] 'Quum tam subinde nouam vestem sumeres ac velut in aliud animal transformareris', Erasmus, *Colloquia*, p. 386, ll. 397–98; Schotten, *Confabulationes*, ed. by Macardle, colloquy 106, ll. 3–5.

[56] From the revised version of 'Conuiuium religiosum', Erasmus, *Colloquia*, p. 248, l. 517. Schotten, *Confabulationes*, ed. by Macardle, 'Conuiuium Epicureum' (no. 10).

perhaps from edition F of August 1523.[57] These few details, however, are very much exceptions. There are several other words and phrases which Schotten could have borrowed from these editions, but he could have found them elsewhere in Erasmus, pre-eminently the *Adagia*, of which progressively enlarged editions had been available since 1508,[58] in other humanist writers, or in the classical originals.

In writing his own colloquy collection Schotten was doing something very similar to the numerous printers who produced editions of Erasmus's *Colloquia* which were in fact selections, restricted to dialogues deemed suitable for school use.[59] These selections, too, tended to favour the earlier editions, with their shorter, more pedagogically practical colloquies which generally avoided controversial subject-matter and attitudes. Even if Schotten did read editions later than 1522, they seem to have had remarkably little influence on the *Confabulationes*. Whilst the most obvious factor in this is timing, the evidence adduced above strongly suggests that Schotten avoided imitating the potentially controversial subject-matter and theological positions of Erasmus's later *Colloquia*.

---

[57] Erasmus, *Colloquia*, p. 347, l. 87; Schotten, *Confabulationes*, ed. by Macardle, 'Conuiuium diuitum' (no. 13), l. 2; 'Conuiuium caninum' (no. 11), l. 2.

[58] Editions A (1508) to E (1523): *ASD*, II–1, pp. 5–8.

[59] E.g. Antwerp: W. Vorsterman, 1530; Antwerp: M. Hillen van Hoochstraten, 1534; Madgeburg: M. Lotther, 1534; Strasbourg: J. Frölich, 1537 and 1542; Zurich: C. Froschauer, 1579; listed in Barth, 'Erasmus, *Colloquia familiaria*', col. 409.

Petrus Mosellanus, Paedologia

Erasmus was not however the only model whom Schotten emulated. One of the most successful colloquy collections of the sixteenth century had appeared a few years before the *Confabulationes*: Petrus Mosellanus's *Paedologia*.[60] The author, Peter Schade (1493–1524) from Bruttig on the Mosel (hence 'Mosellanus'), had studied briefly at Cologne from 1512 to 1514, only a few years before Schotten's arrival. There he had made considerable progress in Greek, which he perfected at Leipzig University from 1515, in 1517 succeeding his teacher there, Richard Croke, as professor of Greek. A passionate Erasmian, he corresponded with Erasmus and numerous other humanists. Chronic illness led to his very premature death in 1524.[61]

The *Paedologia* first appeared in 1518, but was most frequently reprinted in the expanded edition of 1520, containing thirty-seven dialogues.[62] The first eighteen deal with general topics of school life; the rest are largely devoted to the customs associated with the holidays of the church calendar. The dialogues are short (very few of

---

[60] Petrus Mosellanus, *Paedologia Petri Mosellani Protegensis in puerorum vsum conscripta [...]* ([Leipzig: Melchior Lotter, 1518]); *VD 16*, S 2136. All references to the *Paedologia* are to Mosellanus, *Paedologia*, ed. by Michel; see Barth, 'Petrus Mosellanus, *Paedologia*'.

[61] Mosellanus: *NDB*, XVIII, pp. 170–71; *CoE*, II, pp. 466–67; *Matrikel*, 493,2; *Die Matrikel der Universität Leipzig*, ed. by Erler, I, p. 452; II, pp. 25–26, 543–44; Schmidt, *Petrus Mosellanus*, passim; Krafft and Krafft, 'Über Petrus Mosellanus' Studium in Köln 1512–1514'; Kremer, 'Mosellanus, Humanist zwischen Kirche und Reformation'.

[62] *Editio princeps* (see n. 1), containing 35 dialogues: see *Paedologia*, pp. XLIV–XLVIII. *Petri Mosellani Protegensis, Paedologia, iam iterum, vna cum scholijs in loco appositis, edita. adiectis insuper dialogis duobus [...]* (Leipzig: M. Lotter, 1520); *VD 16*, S 2144; *Paedologia*, p. XLII.

more than two pages) and most involve only two boys. Mosellanus aimed to offer reliable models of Latin speech, to ensure that, when beginning to speak continuous Latin, schoolboys did not produce what would today be called an interlanguage, heavily influenced by the vernacular.[63] Though the Latinity reflects a variety of ages and authors, the 'proprietas' of Terence and the 'facilitas' of Cicero are dominant.[64]

The *Paedologia* is also an important cultural document, recording early sixteenth-century school life at Leipzig.[65] Much of what Mosellanus describes is hard: schoolboys live in poor accommodation (7), and their general penury often forces them to beg (18, p. 25, ll. 4–7). But there are happier sides, too, such as games (15), and the colourful round of church and school holidays with their associated customs: the Boy Bishop (21); electing a 'King' at Epiphany (25, p. 32, ll. 10–15); Shrovetide (27); St Gregory's Day (28, p. 35, l. 27–p. 36, l. 6); Corpus Christi (31). Many of these reappear in the *Confabulationes*. Mosellanus's approach is to an extent adapted to the schoolboy readers' actual situation and tastes, but he remains an academically and morally serious writer, whose aim is to correct boys' behaviour 'ad Christianam regulam' (p. 3, ll. 12–13), and his dialogues often treat subjects like fasting on the eve of the feast of St Katherine, the patron saint of scholars and students, going to confession, or receiving the Eucharist (19, 28, 30). The acceptability of this (Catholic) Christian humanist pedagogy is testified by over seventy editions of

---

[63] 'Novam quandam loquendi rationem plane barbaram et per vernaculi sermonis vestigia ingredientem', Mosellanus, *Paedologia*, p. 1, ll. 10–13; cf. ll. 6–15.
[64] Barth, 'Petrus Mosellanus, *Paedologia*', cols 415, 417;
[65] Ibid., cols 414, 420–23; Kaemmel, *Geschichte des deutschen Schulwesens*, p. 391.

the *Paedologia* before 1570, and by the number of schools which prescribed them as a set text.⁶⁶

Though Schotten nowhere mentions the *Paedologia*, the close parallels of content between some of his dialogues and some of Mosellanus's clearly show that he had read it and been impressed by it. Some of the basic – and self-evident – similarities of content have been noted by Michel and Barth;⁶⁷ and the comparisons below show that there are also many telling parallels of detail and ductus. But what also emerges is the freedom and individuality of Schotten's use of Mosellanus, and the distinctiveness of his adaptation.

In Mosellanus, 1, 'De nundinis', Caspar and Modestus look forward to the holidays at the upcoming fair; Schotten's colloquy 54, 'De nundinis et munerum nundinariorum emptione', presents a similar situation. The colloquies differ in one interesting respect, however. Mosellanus's boys describe the fair bringing many merchants to their city from elsewhere. Caspar wants news, letters and most importantly money, which he sorely needs; Modestus's father has promised to send him cloth for a suit (p. 4, ll. 11–13). In the next colloquy, 'De natali celebrando', Michael describes how he was to have been sent money by the hand of a merchant visiting the fair, but that the fair was too busy and crowded for him to have the time to count out the cash (p. 5, ll. 14–17). In Schotten's colloquy, however, there is no sense at all of outsiders descending on the city in number. Seuerinus, a local boy, is hoping for fair-gifts from relatives, but Balthasar, who is from another region, expects nothing (ll. 16–19). This does indeed reflect the particular status of fairs in early modern Cologne. The permanent market

---

66   Barth, 'Petrus Mosellanus, *Paedologia*', cols 427–28, citing further literature, instances schools in eleven German localities.
67   *Paedologia*, p. XL; Barth, 'Petrus Mosellanus, *Paedologia*', col. 426.

activity in the city, and the influence of the great Frankfurt fairs (described in Schotten's colloquy 55) meant that Cologne fairs had begun to decline as early as the thirteenth century, leaving only the week-long 'Jahrmarkt' at the *Gottestracht*, in the second week after Easter.[68] This did not attract the multitudes of outside traders that Frankfurt did, and would not have presented the opportunity for parents of boys from outside Cologne to communicate with their sons as in the scenario sketched by Mosellanus. Schotten has given his adaptation a distinct Cologne twist.

In Mosellanus, 8, 'De vindemia et aucupio', Andreas and Philippus discuss the imminent vintage. Andreas longs for a break from school to help his parents (p. 14, ll. 18–26); he describes grape-picking and tasting the new 'mustum' with a rapture and a grasp of detail which reminds us that Mosellanus himself grew up in a wine-growing region; Philippus, however, rejects this as a distraction from study: 'me certe non habebis huius tuae stultitiae comitem' (p. 15, ll. 7–8; cf. p. 14, ll. 16–17, 27–28). Schotten's colloquy 69, 'De uuis carpendis', is similar, but only superficially. It describes the grape-harvest taking place locally, as was indeed the case in Cologne in the 1520s, where small vineyards were numerous in outlying suburbs.[69] Neither of Schotten's boys sees grape-picking as anything but a delightful opportunity to eat their fill of grapes (e.g. ll. 7–26), a perspective probably much closer to that of real boys than was Mosellanus's higher-minded approach.

In Mosellanus, 12, 'De nuptiis, balneis ac viscerationibus', Burchardus sees a forthcoming wedding as a chance to acquire some good food (p. 19, ll. 12–16); so do

---

[68] Irsigler, 'Kölner Wirtschaft im Spätmittelalter', p. 273; cf. Klersch, I, pp. 66, 174–79.

[69] See Chapter 2, and Schotten, *Confabulationes*, ed. by Macardle, notes to colloquy 69.

Herebertus and Hilgerus in Schotten's colloquy 86, 'De nuptiis'. But there the resemblance ends. Whereas Mosellanus's boys pass quickly on to the competing attractions of a theatrical performance, a free visit to the baths and a handout of food (p. 19, ll. 17–31), Schotten's colloquy develops the description of the wedding of Herebertus's sister.

In Mosellanus, 14, 'De signo tintinnabulorum deque immodico somno', Servius wakes Sulpicius, who has overslept: the bell for morning Mass is ringing (p. 21, ll. 4–8). Schotten's colloquy 21 presents a similar situation: Vinandus and Sebastianus are woken by the clock striking six (ll. 3–7). In both colloquies, one boy, to avoid punishment, goes off to school quickly, making much the same remark to his companion:

> Servius: Ego hinc abeo; tu, quando lubet, sequere aut tuo periculo dormi.
> (Mosellanus, 14, p. 21, ll. 15–16)

> Sebastianus: Abeo, tu in medium dormias diem.
> (Schotten, colloquy 21, l. 30).

In Mosellanus, Sulpicius decides to get up as well; in Schotten, Vinandus opts to stay in bed for a while; he asks Sebastianus to tell the teacher he is doing jobs for his mother. (ll. 20–22).

Mosellanus, 16, 'De quaestionibus commissorum, quae die Veneris in ludis exercentur', describes how schoolmasters secretly instruct one of the pupils to report his classmates' errors and misdemeanours for punishment at the end of the week. He calls this spy a 'Corycaeus' (p. 23, l. 19). Schotten uses the same term in colloquy 20, 'De Corycaei metu auscultantis in eos qui non Romano utuntur sermone' (see note to l. 1). Apart from the term, however, the two colloquies are not very similar. Schotten's simpler and less rhetorical presentation gives a much more convincing sense of the boys' perspective, their real fear of being caught and punished, than does Mosellanus's more poised and rounded diction.

In both Mosellanus, 18, 'De canticis deque feriis divi Martini', and Schotten, colloquy 40, 'De festo Sancti Martini', boys describe the custom of singing at citizens' doors on St Martin's Eve (10 November) for gifts of food and money:

> Georgius: [...] in eius diei vespera [...] stipem egenis dari ostiatim est receptum.
> (Mosellanus, p. 25, ll. 18–21).

> Hieronymus: Quicquid iusculi uel carnis a mensis leuarint nobis ad fores cantantibus impartient.
> (Schotten, ll. 16–17)

In both cases, the boys hope for good pickings: Schotten's Hieronymus says that the previous year he was given enough food for a week (ll. 32–33); Mosellanus's Conradus hopes to make enough money to help see him through the winter (p. 25, ll. 22–24).

Schotten's colloquy 41, 'De xeniis mittendis', has clearly been affected by Mosellanus, 25, 'De novi anni ingressu [...] deque missitandis strenulis'. A striking similarity is that in both colloquies one boy (Brutus in Mosellanus, Kilianus in Schotten) follows up a New Year greeting to a friend with an importunate demand for a New Year gift:

> Brutus: Tametsi mallem strenulam mihi potius dares quam magnificam illam et sollemnem imprecationem
> (Mosellanus, p. 31, ll. 27–29).

> Kilianus: Xenium fac mihi praebeas
> (Schotten, colloquy 41, l. 5).

In both cases, the other boy claims he has little to give. Apart from his books, Mosellanus's Petrucius has 'plane nihil' (p. 31, ll. 31–32); Theodoricus can offer nothing better than a cake (Schotten, l. 13). In neither case is this accepted as an excuse. Brutus retorts that a book would make an acceptable gift; Kilianus suggests that handkerchiefs are cheap to make (Mosellanus, p. 32, ll. 1–3; Schotten, l. 21). The two colloquies then take rather different directions, but the start is so similar in dynamics, if not in the details of formulation, that there can be no doubt that Mosellanus provided the basis for Schotten.

Mosellanus, 27, 'De Bacchanalibus Christianorum' (pp. 34–35), begins with Fabianus asking Franciscus why he was off school the previous day. Franciscus has had a serious headache: 'Graviter ex capite laborabam, ut lucem ferre non possem' (Mosellanus, p. 34, ll. 11–12). Fabianus then deplores the way that schoolboys invent illnesses to escape work or punishment, making 'scholasticus morbus' a synonym for fake illness. Franciscus assures him that, whatever other boys may do, he does not 'throw sickies' like that. The ductus of Schotten, colloquy 22, 'De morbo socordiae quem scholasticis ascribunt', is very similar. Petrus, asked why he has not been in school for some time, replies that he has had 'Dolor [...] capitis et uentris' (ll. 4–8). Valterus guesses the disease: 'Eam quae ascribunt scholasticis, scilicet desidiam' (l. 16). Petrus denies this stoutly (ll. 17–19); Valterus says that many boys who are off school have succumbed to that illness (ll. 20–21); Petrus replies, 'Assentio, sed istius cohortis non sum' (l. 22). Though the two colloquies develop rather differently, it is clear that Schotten's beginning closely imitates Mosellanus's.

In Mosellanus, 29, Antonius asks Marcellus if he will come with him to the countryside to beg eggs from the peasants: 'Quaero, qui mecum rus eat mihique in emendicandis ex more ovis sit socius' (p. 36, ll. 26–27). This is strikingly similar to the situation in Schotten's colloquy 120, 'De ouis colligendis circa Paschatis ferias', where Buttubatta explains to Aristophorus how he always visits the countryside after Easter, to beg food, including eggs, from the peasants (ll. 15–26). In both cases the boys claim the trip is worthwhile, even necessary. Antonius asks: 'Sed unde famem pellam, si non cibos undecumque conquirere licet?'; Buttubatta makes enough to live off for a month.[70] The characteristic differences between Schotten and his model emerge clearly, however. Mosellanus's Marcellus finds the idea *infra dig.* for a serious scholar:[71] but Schotten's boys agree that the stratagem is excellent, and Antonius asks to accompany Buttubatta. Schotten also has much more circumstantial detail: Buttubatta begs his eggs by singing the popular Lenten hymn 'Christe, qui lux es et dies' (l. 29); and he uses flattery to wheedle eggs out of unwilling peasants (ll. 30–33).[72] Both were probably part of the actual approach of boys to this task.

Mosellanus, 33, 'De coronis gestandis', deals with the custom of wearing wreaths of flowers on the head, though it does not relate this to any particular day or season. Schotten, colloquy 96, 'De sertis in die celebri ferendis', mentions the same custom for an unspecified 'dies celebris'. Both colloquies mention the relative cheapness of crowns, or the flowers to make them.[73]

Schotten thus definitely did read and imitate Mosellanus. This is hardly surprising in an age which saw emulation as the highest tribute to a literary model, especially when much of what that literary model described was the common experience of the early modern schoolboy. But it is Schotten who has the wish, and the ability, to enter into the world of that schoolboy, whereas Mosellanus stays at a somewhat idealistic remove. Mosellanus, moving only reluctantly beyond the confines of the classroom, makes only a brief reference to ball and

---

[70] Mosellanus, *Paedologia*, p. 37, ll. 1–2; Schotten, *Confabulationes*, ed. by Macardle, colloquy 120, l. 19.

[71] 'Quid enim servilius quam decem ovorum gratia agrestium caulas ostiatim obambulare atque interim domi lectionum iacturam facere?', Mosellanus, *Paedologia*, p. 36, ll. 28–32.

[72] See Schotten, *Confabulationes*, ed. by Macardle, notes to colloquy 120, l. 29.

[73] Mosellanus, *Paedologia*, p. 40, ll. 18–19; Schotten, *Confabulationes*, ed. by Macardle, colloquy 96, ll. 24–26.

marbles in *Paedologia,* no. 15, 'De ludendi ratione' (pp. 21–22). Schotten devotes a series of colloquies to relatively detailed accounts of a variety of popular games: 44, 'Quem ludum debeant iuuenes exercere'; 46, 'De ludo pilae'; 47, 'De ludo globorum missilium [...]'; 48, 'De ludo globorum qui torquentur per annulum'; 49, 'De ludo saltus'; 50, 'De certamine cursus'.

There is a reference to confession in Mosellanus, 28, 'De ieiunio deque confessione, quam vocant'. Both Vitus and Severus see the obligation to make a confession in preparation for Easter as onerous. Severus, who suggests getting the ordeal over by St Gregory's day, now ten days off, knows a diligent confessor, but Vitus would prefer some dozy priest ('oscitans') who will not make the experience too demanding.[74]

Schotten's colloquy 57, 'De confessione', may have been inspired by Mosellanus: it begins with a similar discussion about the desirability of getting the ordeal of confession over; but as so often it develops differently, with some very revealing insights into boys' anxieties surrounding the experience. Iodocus says he was afraid of confession when he was younger, though not now (l. 20). This was surely a widespread fear: certainly Hermann von Weinsberg was so frightened of confession as a young boy that he would rather have walked through fire.[75] Iodocus also recalls one cause of his fear: a story going the rounds that a confessor had hammered a nail into a penitent's forehead.[76] This story sounds bizarre enough to have come from the German *Schwank* tradition of vernacular comic literature, but no source has been identified. Yet even a conventionally conformist Catholic like Weins-

---

[74] Mosellanus, *Paedologia,* p. 35, ll. 27–31; p. 36, ll. 8–17.
[75] 'Ich wolt lieber durch ein fur sin gangen, dan gebicht haben', *BW,* I, p. 40.
[76] 'Dicebatur passim, quod uni a confessore fronti clauus infigeretur', Schotten, *Confabulationes,* ed. by Macardle, colloquy 57, ll. 22–23.

berg regarded the confessional as a place of weird goings-on: 'I have heard and read strange things about [confession]; if anyone were to say much about it, he might be thought un-Catholic.'[77] Unfortunately, Weinsberg does not specify what he had heard; but given the general reliability with which Schotten records details of real life, the possibility must be considered that this story, whatever its precise origins, was an 'urban legend' current in early-sixteenth-century Cologne, or at the very least representative of the horror-stories that haunted the youngest children's imagination. From Schotten's colloquy we also learn that some boys were in the habit of using a written list of their sins: Thomas makes one because otherwise his fear would make him forget everything (ll. 26–27). This is interesting, since such clear evidence of practice in this area is very rare indeed. Writing lists of one's sins was never formally prohibited, indeed some penitential manuals of the period suggest it;[78] but concerns about the consequences of losing such lists meant that pastoral practice fairly strongly discouraged it.[79] The glimpse into how real penitents disregarded such guidelines is very valuable. Another fascinating piece of evidence is in the boys' judgement on a confessor who refuses to hear confessions in Latin: they suspect he does not understand it (ll. 34–37). In his study of late-medieval and early modern penitential manuals, Thomas Tentler notes that some manuals considered the possibility of penitents doubting their confessor's intellectual competence, and wonders whether this ever actually

---

[77] 'Ich hab wol seltzam dingen dar von gehoirt und gelesen, sult emans davon vil sagen, der mogt vor uncatholischs gehalten werden' (*BW*, V, p. 303).

[78] E.g. *Manipulus curatorum*, 1509, sig. J5ʳ; see Tentler, *Sin and Confession on the Eve of the Reformation*, p. 86.

[79] Lea, *A History of Auricular Confession and Indulgences in the Latin Church*, II, p. 283.

happened.[80] The colloquy strongly suggests that at least sometimes it did. All this fascinating circumstantial detail is a world away from Mosellanus's generalized, edifying treatment of the same subject.

Mosellanus, 24, 'De feriis nataliciis Christi' (pp. 30–31) has clearly influenced Schotten's colloquy 35, 'De festo natali Christi'. Mosellanus opens with a lengthy statement by Penius:

> Et gaudeo et doleo, mi Francisce, festa haec natalicia appetere. Gaudeo quidem, quod hae feriae omnia laeta et festiva secum apportant; doleo autem, quod scholasticis nobis in addiscendis horum festorum cantionibus grandis est exhauriendus labor. Praeterea totis diebus in templis algendum. Postremo et illud vereor, ne, si matutina sacra alto nimis sopore detentus neglexero, et plagas mihi lucrifaciam. [...] Certe plus satis delicati essemus, si non tantum molestiae vel pro solo Christo devoraremus, [...]
> (p. 30, ll. 20–28; p. 31, ll. 4–6).

Penius's ability to see both sides of the question is admirable, but no more typical of a schoolboy than is his ponderous rhetorical sweep. His friend Franciscus can only agree (p. 30, l. 29–p. 31, l. 4).

Schotten's approach is quite different. Applying a technique frequently seen in the *Confabulationes*, he atomizes the balanced synthesis 'Et gaudeo et doleo' of Mosellanus's Penius into the two opposing takes on Christmas of Georgius ('gaudeo') and Gisbertus ('doleo'), a tension which generates a quick-fire debate:

> GEORGIVS. Ego nunquam toto anno plus gaudeo quam nunc temporis.
> GISBERTVS. Ego uero nunquam magis doleo.
> GEORGIVS. Doles tu, tempore adeo laeto?
> GISBERTVS. Non dolerem, in tanto frigore?

---

[80] Tentler, *Sin and Confession on the Eve of the Reformation*, p. 128.

> GEORGIVS. Ipse totus laetor ob festorum dierum aduentum et copiam. [...]
> Plurimum laetor quod nunc temporis adeo mitis est aër, et non acerbum frigus.
> GISBERTVS. Et ego gaudeo, alias in matutinis precibus frigore perirem.
> GEORGIVS. In lecto me continerem si frigus saeuiret.
> GISBERTVS. Ah, propter nouum regem natum nihil uelis pati?
> GEORGIVS. Durum est a tepido nido discedere.
>
> (ll. 3–9, 31–37)

The difference between the techniques, and the effects, of the two similar dialogues is emblematic of the difference between Mosellanus and Schotten.

At every turn two things are evident. First, that the *Paedologia* had made a profound impression on Schotten, much more profound, indeed, than scholarship has so far noticed: it had influenced not only much of the content of the *Confabulationes*, but even their treatment of their topics. Second, that Schotten, though taking many of his impulses from Mosellanus, was technically, rhetorically and imaginatively independent of the better-known humanist. Hermann Michel, Mosellanus's early-twentieth-century editor, conceded that Schotten was livelier than Mosellanus, but felt that this had come at the cost of overly informal language and excessive closeness to reality and to the perspective of schoolboys.[81] It is ironic that the changes in attitude and expectations over the last century have made Schotten's realism precisely what a current readership is likely to consider his major strength to be.

---

[81] Mosellanus, *Paedologia*, p. XL.

Christoph Hegendorff, Dialogi pueriles

Another collection of humanist school colloquies which Schotten almost certainly came across were the *Dialogi pueriles* of Christoph Hegendorff.[82] A native of Leipzig, Hegendorff (1500–1540) began as a schoolmaster, then lectured in theology, law and classics, initially at Leipzig University, then in various other universities and towns; when he died of the plague he was Lutheran superintendent of Lüneburg.[83] His publications in classics, law and theology include several dealing with, or inspired by, Erasmus, for whose writings Hegendorff, though a Lutheran, always retained the greatest respect.[84]

Hegendorff's *Dialogi pueriles*, a slim collection of twelve short dialogues, appeared first in early 1520 in Leipzig and Nuremberg.[85] Later that year it was printed at the end of an edition of Mosellanus's *Paedologia*.[86] This

---

[82] See Bömer, *Die lateinischen Schülergespräche*, I, pp. 108–12; Barth, 'Mosellanus, *Paedologia*', cols 424–25; Bierlaire, 'Les "Dialogi pueriles" de Christophe Hegendorff'; Günther, *Plautuserneuerungen*, pp. 78–91.

[83] *NDB*, VIII, pp. 227–28; *CoE*, II, pp. 171–72, both citing further literature.

[84] *VD 16*, H 1103–246 (144 entries); *CoE*, II, p. 172. E.g. *Explicatio locorum implicatissimorum in Colloquiis Erasmi* (Hagenau: J. Setzer, 1526) (*VD 16*, H 1194); Erasmus, *De Copia [...] Cum scholiis marginalibus Christophori Hegendorphini* (Hagenau: J. Setzer, 1528) (*VD 16*, E 2669); *Methodus conscribendi epistolas* (Hagenau: J. Setzer, 1526), based on Erasmus, *De conscribendis epistolis* (*VD 16*, H 1203).

[85] Hegendorff, *Dialogi pueriles [...]* (Leipzig: V. Schumann, 1520); Bierlaire, 'Un livre du maître au XVIe siècle', p. 200, n. 5. *Dialogi pueriles Christophori Hegendorffini* (Nuremberg: F. Peypus for J. Rostock, 6 April 1520), *VD 16*, H 1160; Bierlaire, 'Les "Dialogi pueriles" de Christophe Hegendorff', p. 393. References to Hegendorff, *Dialogi*, here are to the edition of Strasbourg: J. Knobloch, 1523.

[86] Petrus Mosellanus, *Paedologia Petri Mosellani Protegensis in puerorum usum conscripta et aucta. Dialogi XXXVII. Dialogi*

proved a winning combination, and numerous reprints were made in this format,[87] entirely eclipsing two extended editions of the *Dialogi*, printed by Schumann in 1520 and 1521.[88]

It is clear that Hegendorff's dialogues are thematically influenced by Mosellanus. Many of the same feast days and seasons are discussed: Epiphany, Shrovetide, St Katharine's day and Christmas, à propos of which both authors refer to the drudgery of learning and singing much music.[89] Both collections have dialogues on how best to repeat lessons, and both enthusiastically recommend schools and the university in Leipzig.[90] Hegendorff's work is not designed for the least advanced learners: it offers a large diet of Latin constructions and a broad vocabulary. The tone is also not overtly moral in the manner of Mosellanus. Other particularities of

---

pueriles Christophori Hegendorphini XII. lepidi æque, ac docti (Strasbourg: J. Knobloch, 1520); (*VD 16*, S 2149); Bierlaire, 'Les "Dialogi pueriles" de Christophe Hegendorff', p. 398, n. 21; id., 'Un livre du maître au XVIᵉ siècle', p. 200, n. 5; Barth, 'Petrus Mosellanus, *Paedologia*', col. 424.

[87] *VD 16 online* records 28 surviving editions in German-speaking countries to 1579.

[88] Hegendorff, *Dialogi pueriles [...]* (Leipzig: V. Schumann, 1.5.1520); Bierlaire, 'Les "Dialogi pueriles" de Christophe Hegendorff', p. 393. Hegendorff, *Dialogi pueriles [...] tercio in graciam puerorum recogniti* (Leipzig: V. Schumann, 1521) (*VD 16*, H 1161); see Bierlaire, 'Les "Dialogi pueriles" de Christophe Hegendorff', p. 393; Barth, 'Petrus Mosellanus, *Paedologia*', col. 424.

[89] Epiphany: Mosellanus, *Paedologia*, 25; Hegendorff, *Dialogi pueriles*, 5, sig. D3ʳ–D4ʳ. Shrovetide: Mosellanus, *Paedologia*, 27; Hegendorff, *Dialogi*, 6, sig. D4ʳ⁻ᵛ. St Katharine: Mosellanus, *Paedologia*, 19; Hegendorff, *Dialogi*, sig. D2ᵛ. Christmas: Mosellanus, *Paedologia*, 24; Hegendorff, *Dialogi*, sig. D3ʳ. Bierlaire, 'Les "Dialogi pueriles" de Christophe Hegendorff', pp. 389–401.

[90] Mosellanus, *Paedologia*, 10 (1520), pp. 44–46; Hegendorff, *Dialogi*, sig. C8ʳ. Mosellanus, *Paedologia*, 37, p. 48, ll. 16–20; Hegendorff, *Dialogi*, sig. D7ʳ⁻ᵛ.

Hegendorff's style include the enthusiastic use of Greek expressions (one or more on nearly every page) and proverbial phrases (over sixty in nineteen brief pages).

Schotten almost certainly read Hegendorff when he read Mosellanus, since the *Paedologia* nearly always came with the *Dialogi*. But it is extremely difficult to assess what use may have made of the *Dialogi*. Superficial similarities in subject-matter, style and tone there most certainly are, but many of these could reflect shared experience of school life and similar stylistic aims. Hegendorff's frequent use of proverbial phrases is an interesting similarity with Schotten; but Hegendorff's repertoire of proverbial utterances is slightly different from Schotten's, and is almost entirely classical, whereas Schotten has a good many from medieval Latin and vernacular sources. The dozen common phrases do not suggest that Hegendorff was Schotten's source. Nearly all are adages of Erasmus;[91] one is a well-known proverb and one a common classical tag.[92]

---

[91] 'Rem acu tetigisti', Hegendorff, *Dialogi*, sig. C6ᵛ; Schotten, *Confabulationes*, ed. by Macardle, colloquy 9, l. 6, etc.; Erasmus, *Adagia*, 1393; 'Nec obolus restat, quo restim emamus', Hegendorff, *Dialogi*, sig. C7ʳ; Schotten, *Confabulationes*, ed. by Macardle, *conuiuium* 27, l. 15; Erasmus, *Adagia*, 248; 'Colophonem imponere', Hegendorff, *Dialogi*, sig. D1ʳ; Schotten, *Confabulationes*, ed. by Macardle, colloquy 93, ll. 1–2; cf. Erasmus, *Adagia*, 1245; 'Ex tripode pronuntiare', Hegendorff, *Dialogi*, sig. D1ʳ; Schotten, *Confabulationes*, ed. by Macardle, colloquy 101, l. 5; Erasmus, *Adagia*, 690; 'Ego non manum uerterim', Hegendorff, *Dialogi*, sig. D1ᵛ; Schotten, *Confabulationes*, ed. by Macardle, colloquy 20, l. 21; Erasmus, *Adagia*, 221; 'Sanguinem flerem', Hegendorff, *Dialogi*, sig. D2ʳ; Schotten, *Confabulationes*, ed. by Macardle, colloquy 121, l. 4; Erasmus, *Adagia*, 1365; 'Optat ephippia bos piger, optat arare caballus', Hegendorff, *Dialogi*, sig. D2ᵛ; Schotten, *Confabulationes*, ed. by Macardle, colloquy 112, ll. 26–27; Erasmus, *Adagia*, 571; 'Quid distent aera lupinis', Hegendorff, *Dialogi*, sig. D6ᵛ; Schotten, *Confabulationes*, ed. by Macardle, *conuiuium* 21, l. 38; Erasmus,

Hegendorff's Latin is lighter and more fluid than Mosellanus's, with an easy Terentian ductus more along Schotten's lines, though Hegendorff's dialogic turns are considerably longer and more convoluted than Schotten's pregnant one-liners. Since both authors emulate Terence as seen through the lens of Erasmus, it is hard to see any definite instances of imitation of Hegendorff by Schotten. Even a few close textual similarities may have other explanations.

Schotten's 'Hui, tam cito?' (colloquy 41, l. 6) might imitate an identical phrase in Hegendorff, but it could have been taken directly from Erasmus.[93] It is also ordinary enough to have been composed by Schotten independently. A very few other similarities could easily be examples of shared non-standard usage rather than imitation of Hegendorff by Schotten.[94] Only one verbal parallel, in Schotten's colloquy 121, suggests that he was imitating formulations of Hegendorff:

> Petrus: Quid eiulas, o Bartholomæe?
> Bartholomæus: Cur non eiularem uel sanguinem, ut dicitur, flerem [...?]
>
> (Hegendorff, *Dialogi*, 4, sig. D2r)
>
> IODOCVS. Lamentarisne?
> MATTHAEVS. Non lamentarer? Sanguinem paene flerem.
>
> (*Confabulationes*, 121, ll. 3–4)

Adagia, 279.

[92] 'Omnium rerum satietas est', Hegendorff, *Dialogi*, sig. C8v; Schotten, *Confabulationes*, ed. by Macardle, colloquy 69, l. 27; Walther, 39294; cf. 39279. 'Apollinis oraculum', Hegendorff, *Dialogi*, sig. D2r; Schotten, *Confabulationes*, ed. by Macardle, colloquy 81, l. 51.

[93] 'Hui, tam cito?': Hegendorff, *Dialogi*, sig. D1r; Erasmus, *Colloquia*, p. 343, l. 139.

[94] E.g. 'ecquid?' synonymous with 'quid?' (Plautus, Terence): Hegendorff, *Dialogi*, e.g. sig. C6v, D1r, D4v; Schotten, *Confabulationes*, ed. by Macardle, colloquies 34, l. 16 and note; 102, l. 15; 118, l. 5.

Here there is first of all the phrase 'sanguinem flere'. This is of course in Erasmus's *Adagia*, 1365. But Erasmus consistently uses the ablative 'sanguine'[95] whereas Schotten has the accusative 'sanguinem' like Hegendorff. And whilst for Erasmus 'weeping blood' means going to the utmost lengths in the attempt to soften someone's feelings,[96] both Hegendorff and Schotten use it as a simple hyperbole for lamenting. Schotten's Matthaeus will not be receiving a large sum of money promised to him; Hegendorff's Bartholomaeus cannot beg enough food to supply his master, and fears punishment.[97] Added to these two striking similarities of morphology and meaning there are the parallel structures and forms, the questions 'Lamentarisne?' and 'Quid eiulas?' and the replies 'Non lamentarer?' and 'Cur non eiularem?'. Here Schotten was either consciously or unconsciously imitating Hegendorff.

There is clear evidence, then, that Schotten had read Hegendorff (which would be inevitable given that the *Dialogi* were routinely printed together with Mosellanus); but there is little sense that he had been particularly influenced by Hegendorff's techniques or approaches, by contrast with the demonstrably powerful influence of Mosellanus and, *a fortiori*, Erasmus.

---

[95] Erasmus, *Adagia*, 1365, imitating the dative of "αἵματι κλαίειν', *LB*, II, 544B.
[96] '*Sanguine flere*, proverbialis hyperbole significans nihil non fieri, quod [sic] flectatur aliquis. [...] *Haud flectes illum, ne si sanguine quidem fleveris*', *LB*, II, 544B.
[97] Schotten, *Confabulationes*, ed. by Macardle, colloquy 121, ll. 12–14; Hegendorff, *Dialogi*, 4, sig. D2^r.

Sebald Heyden, Formulae puerilium colloquiorum

In his relations to contemporary colloquy collections, Schotten was not always the taker, as is clearly shown by the *Formulae puerilium colloquiorum* of the Nuremberg humanist Sebald Heyden.

The first surviving edition of the *Formulae* (Erfurt 1527)[98] is probably not the actual princeps, for Heyden, who produced his dialogues for the school in Nuremberg where he was working, had no conceivable reason to go to Erfurt to get his work printed.[99] A recently rediscovered edition of the *Formulae* with Polish, German and Hungarian translations provides further evidence: it was printed in Craców in 1527, and so is unlikely to have been copied from an Erfurt edition of the same year.[100] But other factors limit how early Heyden's text could have appeared. Heyden (1499–1561) was appointed rector of the St Sebaldus school in Nuremberg in January 1525; in August the city council officially charged him with the task of more effectively 'encouraging and inducing' the school's pupils to learning.[101] The *Formulae* were almost certainly Heyden's response to this charge, and so cannot have appeared before very late 1525, or more likely 1526.

---

[98] *Formulae puerilium colloquiorum pro primis Tyronibus Sebaldinae Scholae Norimbergae* (Erfurt, M. Sachse [I], 1527): *VD 16 online*, ZV 24475; Zwickau, Ratsschulbibliothek, 2.7.22,5. This edition was first noted by Riecke, 'Sebald Heydens "Formulae puerilium colloquiorum"', especially p. 100.

[99] Heyden, *Nomenclatura rerum domesticarum*, ed. by Müller and van der Elst, p. 7*; Riecke, 'Sebald Heydens "Formulae puerilium colloquiorum"', p. 101.

[100] (Craców: H. Vietor, 1527): Riecke, 'Sebald Heydens "Formulae puerilium colloquiorum"', pp. 102–03.

[101] Council decree of 1 August 1525, Nuremberg, Staatsarchiv, Rep. 60a, cit. Riecke, 'Sebald Heydens "Formulae puerilium colloquiorum"', pp. 103–04.

The final factor which makes such a dating certain is the very evident fact that Heyden composed his *Formulae* largely by imitating Schotten's *Confabulationes*. Comparison shows very numerous instances of Heyden using sections of Schotten's text, in a shortened and simplified form.

One characteristic example must suffice: Heyden's fifth dialogue, 'Dum itur cubitum':

FELIX. Quotta [sic] est hora?
GASPAR. Sonuit tertiam.
FELIX. Eundum est cubitum.
GASPAR. Nondum dormiturio.
FELIX. At ego oppido.   5
GASPAR. Tu eas cubitum.
FELIX. Quid tu autem ages ?
GASPAR. Legam ulterius.
FELIX. Malo quiescere.
GASPAR. Facesse hinc Endimion.   10
FELIX. Haud te impediuero.[102]

It will be seen at once that this little dialogue is a drastically pruned version of part of Schotten's colloquy 5, 'De uerbis dum cubitum itur':

VALTERVS. Quota est hora?
ADRIANVS. Octaua.
VALTERVS. Quotam horam sonuit?   5
ADRIANVS. Octauam.
VALTERVS. Quota est audita hora?
ADRIANVS. Octaua, et nona imminet.
VALTERVS. Id non credo.
ADRIANVS. Verum est per Herculem.   10
VALTERVS. Tunc eundi cubitum tempus est.
ADRIANVS. Ego nondum dormiturio.
VALTERVS. Me autem somnus oppido urget.
ADRIANVS. Ipse adhuc horam aut alteram uigilarem.

---

[102] Heyden, *Formulae*, sig. G5ʳ⁻ᵛ.

> VALTERVS. Vigila tu quoad placuerit, ego cubitum ibo. 15
> ADRIANVS. Abi tu Endymion.
> VALTERVS. Ita me appellas, sed id nominis rectius tibi conuenit.[103]

Heyden's ll. 1–2 and 3–10 are cut-down versions of Schotten's ll. 3–8 and 11–16 respectively, with Heyden using the Roman method of counting the hours and Schotten the modern European one: hence Schotten's 'hora nona' (l. 8) is Heyden's 'hora tertia' (l. 2).[104] Everything in Heyden, the vocabulary, phraseology, and the general ductus of the exchange, mirrors Schotten closely. The same applies to a large percentage of Heyden's dialogues.[105]

It is more usual for authors to imitate simple texts and embellish them than to simplify more complex texts, and one might almost think that Schotten had based himself on Heyden and not *vice versa*, if the other evidence did not virtually guarantee that Heyden's *Formulae* did not exist before 1525.

Heyden's use of Schotten, so far unnoticed by scholarship, demands a detailed study, but since Schotten was the passive object of imitation, it is a study of Heyden, not of Schotten, and so must be conducted elsewhere. One reflection, however, is rather intriguing. The 1527 Craców edition of the *Formulae*, and a number of reprints, were used as phrase-books which facilitated communication between the German-, Polish- and Hungarian-speaking students at the University of Craców, and helped the non-Poles to cope with vernacular conversation in the city. Riecke reflects that Heyden thus

---

[103] Schotten, *Confabulationes*, ed. by Macardle, colloquy 5, ll. 3–18.
[104] This is characteristic of Heyden: see p. 87.
[105] Detailed references to the similarities of Heyden's dialogues with those of Schotten are given in the notes to the colloquies in Schotten, *Confabulationes*, ed. by Macardle.

played a not unimportant role in the development of a 'common Central European cultural area'.[106] Since so much of Heyden was taken straight from Schotten, it is also true to say that Schotten shared this role. Riecke remarks that Heyden had no idea that he was playing this part; one can only add that Schotten was just as unwitting, and that his role has till now also remained concealed from scholarship in general.

One would not expect a new colloquy collection of the early sixteenth century to have been produced in complete independence from preceding collections; and this is predictably not the case with the *Confabulationes*. It is clear that Schotten knew and used the three major collections of his day. But it is clear too that Schotten had his own voice and his own vision, and that, for all the obvious stimuli which he received from Erasmus, Mosellanus and Hegendorff, the *Confabulationes* are far from mere clones of these earlier texts. Schotten produced something very individual indeed, which, as the frequent reprintings show, for many decades played a much appreciated part in the teaching and learning of Latin in Germany and beyond.

---

[106] Riecke, 'Sebald Heydens "Formulae puerilium colloquiorum"', p. 109 and ns 44 and 45.

Master and scholars, titlepage of the *Manuale scholarium* (Cologne: H. Quentel, *ca.* 1490).

CHAPTER 4

Schotten's Latinity

To produce a schoolbook aimed at initiating boys into speaking Latin was automatically to situate oneself somewhere on the map of Latinity. Every colloquy collection presented an image of the kind of Latin which the author wanted to inculcate into his charges. An exact situation of Schotten, however, must remain brief and provisional. Scholarship on humanist Latin is still in its infancy. There is as yet no full-scale investigation of the Latinity of any major humanist figure, though recent years have seen the beginnings of such study.[1] And real progress will not be possible until a large selection of humanist writings, beginning with those of Erasmus, are available in electronically searchable format.[2]

---

[1] E.g. Thomson, 'The Latinity of Erasmus'; Wolff, 'Mots rares et mots nouveaux dans les Colloques d'Erasme'; Tunberg, 'The Latinity of Lorenzo Valla's *Gesta Fernandi Regis Aragonum*'; id., 'Further Remarks on the Language of Lorenzo Valla's *Gesta Fernandi* and on *De reciprocatione "sui" et "suus"*'; id., 'The Latinity of Lorenzo Valla's Letters'.

[2] For the moment the most helpful works include: Stotz, I, 67; IJsewijn, 'Mittelalterliches Latein und Humanistenlatein'; Claes, 'De lexicografie in de zestiende eeuw'; Schoeck, 'A Step towards a Neo-Latin Lexicon'; Tournoy and Tunberg, 'On the Margins of Latinity? Neo-Latin and the Vernacular Languages'; Tunberg, 'De locutionibus nonnullis humanisticis quae pro vestigis linguarum nationalium habentur'; id., 'Humanistic Latin'; id., 'Quae Latinitas sit moderna?'; id., 'The Latinity of Erasmus and Medieval Latin: Continuities and Discontinuities'. See also the other literature cited by Tunberg, 'Humanistic Latin', pp. 134–36.

The *Confabulationes* aim to teach a 'classical' Latin, and they are certainly in many ways prescriptive. The boys are constantly correcting one another: 'Sic ego non loquerer'; 'Inconcinna est locutio'; 'Barbarum est, et doctis displicet'.³ Medieval usages like the rhyming greeting 'Bonum mane – Semper sane' (colloquy 2, ll. 3–4) are excoriated. In condemning the typically medieval greeting 'Bonum serum', because 'serum' in Classical Latin is exclusively an adjective, not a noun, Schotten was in fact more punctilious than some good sixteenth-century Latinists, like the lexicographer Petrus Dasypodius, Heyden and even Vives.⁴ And yet, other strata of Latinity – Late, Medieval, and Neo-Latin – are clearly visible in the text. Features of this kind were enough for a late-nineteenth-century scholar like Louis Massebieau to condemn Schotten as a 'pédant' rather than a real 'érudit' like Mosellanus. Massebieau, unaware of Schotten's university career, assumes he was 'un simple maître d'école', in a Cologne which was the capital of obscurantism.⁵ His overall verdict on Schotten's Latinity is the dismissive 'on voit, il est loin d'être pur' (p. 130).

Massebieau's standard of purity, however, is grossly anachronistic on two counts. It presupposes a detailed historical overview of Latin writing which could only be reached centuries after Schotten. And even more significantly, the 'purity' which nineteenth-century scholars invoked was that of a dead language, used only for literary purposes and for its cultural prestige – the purity of a bloodless corpse. Schotten, however, was trying to forge

---

3   Schotten, *Confabulationes*, ed. by Macardle, colloquies 4, l. 6; 33, l. 8; 2, l. 7. Cf. 'Sic ipse non responderem' (ibid., colloquy 2, l. 5); 'Verbum istud barbarum [...] maxime impolitum' (ibid., colloquy 36, ll. 11–14; cf. colloquy 47, l. 11), etc.
4   See Schotten, *Confabulationes*, ed. by Macardle, note to colloquy 4, ll. 5–9.
5   Massebieau, *Les colloques scolaires*, pp. 113–116 (p. 116).

and hand on a living Latin for a wide range of contemporary cultural and intellectual purposes, a language for learned discourse and civilized intercourse. If the classical language did not contain suitable terminology or conceptual material, then new forms had to be minted somehow. The most obvious area was the Christian religion, whose praxis, concepts and vocabulary had been formed after, sometimes long after, the end of the classical period, in many cases using classical lexis but giving it meanings quite different from those which it originally had.

Schotten was also operating in a world of scholarship and knowledge entirely different from that of the nineteenth century. There were as yet no comprehensive dictionaries (in 1525 indeed hardly any dictionaries at all), nor, beyond a general acknowledgement of Cicero as a paragon of correctness and elegance, any agreed and clearly formulated prescription of correctness and purity of the kind which nineteenth- and early twentieth-century schoolmasters were able to invoke.[6] Mario Nizolio's *Observationes in Ciceronem*, the handbook of Ciceronian usage, would not appear till ten years after the *Confabulationes*.[7] And these were but the beginnings: much of what humanists concluded about Classical usage has since been refined and corrected by several centuries of systematic scholarship.[8]

Nonetheless, it would be wrong to patronize Schotten and humanists like him as hapless victims of their era's

---

[6] And indeed such prescriptions were often unjustifiably restrictive, proscribing usages found in impeccably classical authors: see Tunberg, 'Quae Latinitas sit moderna?', ns 8–10.

[7] Mario Nizolio, *Observationes in M.T. Ciceronem* (Brescia: G.F. Gambara, 1535); much revised and reprinted into the nineteenth century.

[8] Tunberg, 'Humanistic Latin', p. 131; id., 'Ciceronian Latin', pp. 44–60; id., 'The Latinity of Erasmus and Medieval Latin', pp. 164–66.

ignorance. In many cases humanists' deviations from 'pure' Latinity represent deliberate and well-informed choices. The Ciceronianism of Pietro Bembo, Budé, Scaliger or Christophorus Longolius was never as popular in Germany as in Italy.[9] Many leading humanists took a much broader view of what constituted good Latin. Lorenzo Valla, whose *Elegantiae linguae latinae* (1449) was the first major humanist investigation of Latin stylistics, argued that it was preferable to invent new words, or adapt Late or Medieval Latin ones, than to misuse classical words or produce irritating periphrasis.[10] This was also the view of Schotten's model Erasmus, whom Thomson very fittingly describes as 'prepared to exploit the entire resources of the language as it has historically been developed, in any save barbarous hands'.[11]

Classical Latin

Overall, it is clear that Schotten aims to present and teach a Classical Latin. This is apparent even at the level of orthography: with few exceptions, the spelling and other features of written representation are those of Classical Latin as we now recognize it, not those of the medieval

---

[9] Stotz, I, 67.5; Tondini, 'De Ciceronianae imitationis ortu et progressione'; Tunberg, 'Ciceronian Latin: Longolius and Others'; id., 'Humanistic Latin' p. 130; Thomson, 'The Latinity of Erasmus', p. 116.
[10] See S. Rizzo, 'Il Latino nell'Umanesimo', pp. 382–83; Tunberg, 'The Latinity of Lorenzo Valla's *Gesta Fernandi Regis Aragonum*', p. 52, ns 85, 86; p. 53, ns 91–93.
[11] Thomson, 'The Latinity of Erasmus', p. 122; cf. Tunberg, 'The Latinity of Erasmus and Medieval Latin', pp. 13–14.

language.[12] Here of course the role of printers is an imponderable.

In diction and style, the *Confabulationes* are close to Roman comedy, particularly to Terence, the humanist model for easy elegance in colloquial language. As Hegendorff put it, 'Terence is pure and polished, and close to our own everyday way of speaking; and I doubt you could express anything you had to say speedily, but without being reduced to babbling, unless you had Terence's comedies constantly in your hands'.[13] Erasmus's *Colloquia* transmitted a Latin that was heavily based on Terence; so did the new Neo-Latin theatre in Germany, much of it written to be played by schoolboys.[14]

The language of the *Confabulationes* is replete with direct and indirect quotations, and complete phrases lifted from Terence.[15] There is even a tendency towards Terentian lexical specialities. In *conuiuium* 11, l. 55, Schotten uses the verb 'pytisso', from Greek 'πυτίζω', literally 'spit out'. Since one did this to wine after tasting it, the verb took on the sense of 'taste or sip wine'. The form is unique to Terence.[16] When Schotten writes 'Facile *emergi* eos, qui opulenti sunt' rather than 'emergere' (colloquy 85, l. 1) he is probably imitating the 'middle passive' use of the verb by Terence rather than mistaking the

---

[12] See the discussion of the closeness of Schotten's orthography to standard 'classical' norms in Schotten, *Confabulationes*, ed. by Macardle, II, 'Editorial Principles and Conventions'.

[13] Hegendorff, *Dialogi pueriles*, sig. D7ᵛ.

[14] Seminal was Gulielmus Gnapheus's *Acolastus* (1529), a dramatization of the parable of the Prodigal Son. See Macardle, *The Allegory of Acolastus* (Durham: Centre for Medieval and Renaissance Studies, 2007).

[15] See the large number of Terentian references in the notes to individual colloquies in Schotten, *Confabulationes*, ed. by Macardle.

[16] 'Pytissando modo mihi | quid uini absumpsit', Terence, *Heautontimorumenos*, 457–58.

verb for a deponent.¹⁷ A great many of these Terentianisms had been transmitted by Erasmus, but by no means all.¹⁸

Schotten goes further than his many Terentianizing contemporaries in the overall pace and ductus of his dialogues. His quick-fire, one-liner exchanges are much more in the spirit of Terence's dialogue than the longer and more ponderous utterances in Mosellanus's *Paedologia* (or indeed even in Erasmus's *Colloquia*). They are also brilliantly suited to the dialogic situation of the *Confabulationes*, with their discussions not between adults but young schoolboys, who cannot realistically be expected to produce long conversational turns.

But as many humanists, including Erasmus, did, Schotten used other strata of Latin: Late Latin, often of Christian origin; Medieval Latin; and Neo-Latin, in the sense of lexis and sometimes syntax which is unknown in both the classical and the medieval language.

Post-classical forms are often seen in nominal forms of words, and so are a legitimate, even desirable, complement to the other forms in the same word-family which existed in Classical Latin. Examples are 'allisio', 'hitting' (colloquy 93, l. 31) and 'assuefactio', 'habituation' (colloquy 74, l. 35). In 'merendinarius' Schotten provides an otherwise unrecorded adjectival form corresponding to the Late Latin 'merendinare' and the Medieval Latin 'merendina', both developed from the Classical Latin 'merenda', 'afternoon meal'.¹⁹ Extending the classical lexis in this way can hardly be regarded as barbarous.

---

17   'Tot res repente circumuallant se unde emergi non potest', Terence, *Adelphoe*, 302; see *TLL*, V,2, col. 473, ll. 28–39.
18   See the large number of Erasmian references in the notes to individual colloquies in Schotten, *Confabulationes*, ed. by Macardle.
19   'Merendinare': *DMLBS*; DuC, V, p. 353. 'Merendina': DuC, V, p. 353; *LLMA*. See Schotten, *Confabulationes*, ed. by Macar-

Late and Medieval Latin is particularly evident in religious vocabulary. This was of course the realm *par excellence* in which Late Latin lexis had developed, and humanists did not separate the pagan authors of the Classical period from the largely Christian writers of the centuries immediately following to the extent that nineteenth-century classicists did.[20]

It is in this religious realm that Schotten's lexis is the most traditional. There are some pointedly humanist terms like 'aedituus' for 'sacristan, parish clerk' (colloquy 90, l. 24) or 'diuus' for 'saint' (colloquy 58, l. 25, etc.); but for the most part Schotten is content with long-established vocabulary, most of it Late and Medieval Latin. Hence 'church building' may be the humanist 'aedes sacra' (colloquy 72, l. 29) or frequently 'templum' (colloquy 35, l. 20); but also the long-standard 'ecclesia' (colloquy 51, l. 6). The Mass or Eucharist may be 'eucharistia' (colloquy 59, l. 1) or 'Sacra Synaxis' (colloquy 39, l. 18); but more often it is simply 'missa' (colloquy 72, ll. 1, 19). Schotten makes no attempt at all to use alternatives for the word-group 'confiteor/confessio' for sacramental confession (colloquy 39, l. 24; and see notes to colloquy 57). There are only a few humanist equivalents for religious holidays, such as 'feriae natales Christianae' for Christmas (colloquy 36, l. 3). For the most part Schotten simply uses the standard liturgical and calendrical terms: 'dies Dominicus', 'dies Circumcisionis', 'Epiphania', 'Quadragesima', and so on. This includes much that is distinctly medieval, either in itself or in its specific ecclesiastical meaning: 'decimae', 'tithes' (colloquy 45, l. 5); 'dies macra', 'fast day' (colloquy 40, l. 7); 'hostia', 'host, Eucha-

---

dle, note to colloquy 9, l. 15.
[20] Tournoy and Tunberg, 'On the Margins of Latinity?', p. 173.

ristic wafer' (colloquy 59, l. 25); 'pastor' and 'plebanus', 'parish priest' (colloquies 51, l. 6; 90, l. 36).[21]

Given that authors like Mosellanus are often concerned to find more humanistically acceptable equivalents for these traditional terms, or at least to flag them up as non-classical,[22] Schotten's easy acceptance of a received religious vocabulary interestingly reflects his apparent conformity to received Catholic custom, discussed in Chapter 3.

The other area where Schotten seems happy to accept the standard terminology is that of school and university: 'gradus' for 'university degree' (colloquy 60, l. 41); 'gymnasium triuiale' for 'grammar school' (colloquy 60, ll. 1, 22); 'beanus' for 'freshman' (colloquy 61, l. 12) and its abstract noun 'beanitas' (colloquy 61, l. 2); 'bursa' for 'university hall or college' (colloquy 60, ll. 2, 24). This too seems consistent with the generally non-militant and non-oppositional ways in which he operated in the university (see Chapter 1).

Medieval Latin

The most obvious way in which medieval forms emerge is in spelling. Despite the overwhelmingly 'classical' orthography, there are a few tellingly medieval forms: 'cimiterium' for 'coemiterium' (colloquy 90, ll. 22, 36); 'cyphus' for 'scyphus' (e.g. colloquy 123, ll. 71, 81) and 'uendico'

---

[21] Also 'coenobium'; 'eleemosyna'; 'monachus'; 'monasterium'; 'monialis'; 'paroecianus', etc. See the notes on these in Schotten, *Confabulationes*, ed. by Macardle: locations, ibid., Section III, 'Non-Classical Latin Vocabulary'.

[22] E.g. 'Ipse mihi oricularium sacrum (sic enim vocant nonnulli eruditi) quaeram', Mosellanus, *Paedologia*, p. 26, ll. 9–11 (rather than 'confessor').

for 'uindico' (e.g. colloquy 42, l. 30); though of course, as with 'classical' orthography, these may reflect the choice of the printers as well as, or rather than, that of Schotten.

There is also a broad selection of distinctly medieval vocabulary. Some is unknown to the classical language, such as 'deplumo', 'fleece' (colloquy 116, l. 30); 'opitulamen', 'help' (colloquy 59, l. 21); 'prosternatio', 'knocking down' (colloquy 31, l. 14). Some is classical vocabulary used in distinctively medieval senses: 'diplois' for 'doublet' (colloquy 20, l. 29); 'halec' for 'herring' (e.g. colloquy 8, l. 19); 'officium' for 'craft, skilled trade' (colloquy 112, l. 1); 'decoquo' for 'digest' (colloquy 59, l. 30).[23] But lexis like this, though writers like Massebieau predictably deplore it, does not make Schotten unusually barbaric by the standards of his time. Much of it is simply necessary to express early modern reality: 'chirothecae', 'gloves' (colloquy 29, l. 10) or 'charta lusoria', 'playing card' (colloquy 44, l. 26). Even the occasional blunder in this area is not untypical: Schotten's use of the quintessentially medieval intensifying adverb 'fortiter' is paralleled by Hegendorff.[24]

There are admittedly some medieval usages which a humanist pedagogue ought to have avoided. In 'Crepidae me calere faciunt' (colloquy 29, l. 8), the quite unclassical causative use of 'facere' is probably influenced by Biblical Latin.[25] 'Consuetudini non satages' is almost certainly a medievalism, with the verb 'satagere' used in a medieval

---

[23] See Schotten, *Confabulationes*, ed. by Macardle, notes to all colloquies mentioned here.
[24] 'Fac edas fortiter' (Schotten, *Confabulationes*, ed. by Macardle, colloquy 16, l. 28); 'fortiter esurio' (ibid., colloquy 8, l. 6); Massebieau, *Les colloques scolaires*, p. 128. Cf. 'fortiter esuriturus', Hegendorff, *Dialogi*, 6, sig. D4^v.
[25] E.g. Vulgate, Matthew 21.17: Sheerin, 'Christian and Biblical Latin', p. 147. Criticized by Massebieau, *Les colloques scolaires*, p. 130.

sense to mean 'satisfy, fulfil', whereas the classical sense is 'busy oneself'. Other words which betray a medieval background include 'deuotio': in Classical Latin it means 'consecration' or 'curse', but Schotten understands it in the medieval sense as 'devotion'; similarly 'captio' (classically 'trickery' or 'sophistry') is taken by Schotten for 'capturing'.[26]

On numerous occasions Schotten uses the pronoun 'se' where classical usage requires 'is', and the related adjective 'suus' for 'eius', a common Medieval Latin tendency.[27] Valla had researched this distinction, which had escaped medieval authors,[28] and an early sixteenth-century humanist like Schotten ought to have been more clearly aware of the nuance. Yet classical usage was not absolutely consistent or unambiguous, and humanists took some time to master this complex topic.[29] Schotten uses 'consulo', which in Classical Latin means 'take counsel', in the frequent medieval sense of 'give counsel, advise'. This also remains common amongst humanists, however, so Schotten is not guilty of a major barbarism.[30]

In some cases, too, Schotten's 'guilt' is less than has been alleged. Massebieau accuses Schotten of medievalism in using 'manere' (rather than 'exspectare') in the sense of 'wait for': 'Nunc ingrediemur, ne coquinae ministra ien-

---

[26] Schotten, *Confabulationes*, ed. by Macardle, notes to colloquies 95, l. 31 ('satagere'); 57, l. 16 ('deuotio'); 23, l. 22 ('captio').

[27] Stotz, IX, 38. See Schotten, *Confabulationes*, ed. by Macardle, notes to 'Et genere et moribus adolescenti ingenuo Gisberto Sterckenberg', l. 24, and to colloquy 53, l. 27.

[28] Tunberg, 'Further Remarks on the Language of Lorenzo Valla's *Gesta Fernandi* and on *De reciprocatione "sui" et "suus"*'.

[29] Tunberg, 'Further Remarks on the Language of Lorenzo Valla's *Gesta Fernandi*', pp. 49–49 and n. 75; pp. 50–53 (p. 52).

[30] Tournoy and Tunberg, 'On the Margins of Latinity', p. 153; see Schotten, *Confabulationes*, ed. by Macardle, note to colloquy 23, l. 22.

taculo nos maneat'.³¹ Yet 'maneo' is used in this sense in the classical language: it is particularly common in Plautus and Terence, but is found in Livy, Statius and other classical authors.³²

The same applies to the 'quod' constructions of which Schotten makes frequent use. They appear in indirect speech, where Classical Latin uses an accusative and infinitive: 'Quintilianus inquit quod et corporis et animi neruos omnes corrumpit mollis illa educatio'.³³ They follow verbs of believing, fearing, hoping, etc.: 'Credebant quod ab ouibus pelleret lupos' (colloquy 36, ll. 36–37); 'Vereor quod non' (colloquy 29, l. 27).³⁴ They are used instead of Classical Latin 'ut' or 'ita ut' in final and consecutive clauses: 'Dentes comprimo, quod ictus non sentio' (colloquy 20, ll. 26–27).³⁵ And they appear in several other uses.³⁶ This is certainly a common feature in Medieval Latin, where 'quod' was a kind of 'universal conjunction', pressed into service in a vast range of contexts; it remained frequent in earlier humanist usage.³⁷ But, though

---

31 Schotten, *Confabulationes*, ed. by Macardle, colloquy 13, l. 28. Cf. 'Hic [...] te manebo' (ibid., colloquy 80, l. 34); 'Ad portam te manebimus' (ibid., *conuiuium* 16, l. 60), etc. Massebieau, *Les colloques scolaires*, p. 130.

32 *TLL*, VIII, col. 291, l. 11–col. 292, l. 37; *OLD*, 'maneo', 3b: e.g. 'Nox, quae me mansisti' (Plautus, *Amphitruo*, 546); 'Mansurus patruom pater est' (Terence, *Phormio*, 480); 'Qui [...] hostem maneat' (Livy, *Ab urbe condita*, 10.35.10); 'Quem [...] manet Bellum' (Statius, *Achilleis*, 2.34).

33 Schotten, *Confabulationes*, ed. by Macardle, colloquy 114, l. 31; cf. colloquies 57, l. 22; 74, l. 27; 104, l. 28, etc.

34 Cf. ibid., colloquies 1, l. 21; 9, l. 5; 29, l. 27; 79, l. 33, etc.

35 Cf. ibid., colloquies 13, l. 25; 43, l. 9; 117, l. 32.

36 E.g 'Pinguis Mineruae homo es, quod ista non capis' (ibid., colloquy 45, l. 12); 'Quod macer appareo mirum non est' (ibid., colloquy 83, l. 4); 'Fertur, sed certum est quod false' (ibid., colloquy 108, l. 23).

37 *Medieval Latin*, ed. by Harrington, p. 38; cf. Stotz, IX, 111.35. Hofmann, *Lateinische Syntax*, pp. 579–82; Tunberg, 'Huma-

its development began in earnest in Late Latin, it was not foreign to the classical language. 'Quod' constructions for indirect speech, and after verbs of saying and verbs expressing emotion, had existed in parallel with the more elevated accusative and infinitive form in all periods of Classical Latin.[38] They are found, for instance, in Plautus, one of Schotten's explicit models.[39] And Schotten is perfectly capable of using the accusative and infinitive constructions when he wishes: there are about fifty instances in the colloquies alone.

The same applies to Schotten's (infrequent) 'quando' rather than the 'correct' 'cum' as a temporal conjunction: 'Quando corrigor, dentes comprimo' (colloquy 20, l. 26); 'Quando lubet accubitum ite' (*conuiuium* 24, l. 22).[40] This too is certainly a medieval feature, but not exclusively: it began as a colloquial or informal usage in the classical period.[41] Again it is particularly common in Plautus,[42] but also in a wide range of other authors. Schotten, who does use 'cum' as a temporal conjunction,[43] almost certainly

---

nistic Latin', p. 132.

[38] *Medieval Latin*, ed. by Harrington, p. 48; Stotz, IX, 103, and n. 1, citing further literature. See ibid., IX, 104.1–7 for a nuanced discussion of the construction. Hofmann, *Lateinische Syntax*, pp. 576–79.

[39] Lodge, *Lexicon Plautinum*, II, p. 521. E.g. 'Rem narraui uobis, quod uostra opera mihi opus siet' (*Poenulus*, 547); 'Scio iam filius quod amet meus istanc meretricem' (*Asinaria*, 52); 'Ne mirere mulieres quod eum sequuntur' (*Poenulus*, 1374).

[40] Cf. Schotten, *Confabulationes*, ed. by Macardle, *conuiuia* 5, l. 85; 6, l. 6; 7, l. 27 etc.

[41] *Medieval Latin*, ed. by Harrington, 6.1 (p. 38); Tournoy and Tunberg, 'On the Margins of Latinity?', p. 159; Hofmann, *Lateinische Syntax*, pp. 607–08.

[42] Lodge, *Lexicon Plautinum*, II, pp. 419–20 (C), cites hundreds of examples, e.g. temporal: 'Mensam, quando edo, detergeo' (*Menaechmi*, 78); 'Auceps quando concinnauit aream, offundit cibum' (*Asinaria*, 216). Conditional uses also recorded.

[43] E.g. Schotten, *Confabulationes*, ed. by Macardle, colloquies

imitated such constructions quite deliberately, as examples of colloquial Latin suitable for the conversational register of the *Confabulationes*.

Neo-Latin

Distinctively Neo-Latin lexis and syntax, that is to say items unknown in Medieval Latin, but also in the Classical language, even though they imitate or develop Classical vocabulary, are not greatly in evidence. There are only isolated words like 'procenium', 'hors-d'œuvres, starter' and 'postcenium', 'light collation or dessert after dinner'.[44] The phrase 'glaciem secare', 'break the ice', meaning to make a start on something, was probably coined by Filelfo and popularized by Erasmus: Schotten makes one of his boys explain this relatively recent formula.[45] 'Saepiuscule', 'rather often', is strictly a Late Latin word, but one which became particularly popular in late humanist writing.[46] Schotten uses 'amusus' to mean 'uncultured, uneducated', also a Neo-Latin tendency.[47]

Germanisms

Schotten seems to have been as aware of Mosellanus of the dangers of speaking a German–Latin 'interlanguage', and his Latin shows very few traces indeed of German-

---

19, l. 21; 32, l. 6; *conuiuia* 11, l. 71; 13, l. 72.
[44] See ibid., notes to colloquies 77, l. 19 and 11, l. 1.
[45] See ibid., note to colloquy 18, l. 29.
[46] See ibid., note to colloquy 20, l. 32.
[47] See ibid., note to colloquy 64, l. 14.

ism.[48] A very rare example is when Vilhelmus says that during the winter 'post fornacem latui' (colloquy 29, l. 21). This perhaps imitates German 'hinter dem Ofen', literally 'behind the stove'. However, even Erasmus had used a similar phrase, 'recubans post vaporarium'.[49] In one remarkable instance, Christianus approves of a friend's ruse: 'Istud te sapere arguit, et pituitae (ut uulgo fertur) non esse obnoxium' (colloquy 23, ll. 33–34). 'Pituitae non [es] obxoxius' translates the German 'du kriegst nicht leicht den Schnupfen', 'you don't catch cold easily', a phrase then in use to mean 'you aren't stupid'.[50] It seems a clumsy piece of Germanism, though the possibility that Schotten was using it as a deliberate joke cannot be discounted. Similarly, perhaps, with 'solidus', the equivalent of the coin 'Schilling', which Valterus uses to refer to a caning (probably meaning twelve strokes, like the twelve Pfennigs in a Schilling.[51] The vernacular word is widely attested in this sense, the Latin equivalent not at all: yet this might be a piece of genuine Latin schoolboy slang now lost from record.

Other allusions to German are more controlled and deliberate. Describing a dinner-party which a group of parish priests take it in turn to host, Conradus says, 'Canonici inter se conuiuium agunt, quod a serto capitis uocitant' – a meal 'named after the wreath you wear on your head' (colloquy 98, ll. 9–10). This refers to the German word 'Kränzchen', 'wreath', a standard term for such

---

[48] Note that what may look like vernacular influence is often in fact Medieval Latin: Tunberg, 'De locutionibus nonnullis humanisticis [...]'; and Tournoy and Tunberg, 'On the Margins of Latinity? Neo-Latin and the Vernacular Languages', passim.
[49] Erasmus, *Colloquia*, p. 392, l. 93.
[50] Grimm, 'Schnupfen', 2; Wander, IV, 308–09. See Schotten, *Confabulationes*, ed. by Macardle, note to colloquy 23, l. 33.
[51] See Schotten, *Confabulationes*, ed. by Macardle, note to colloquy 5, l. 28.

'moveable feasts' (originally, the guest who received the wreath had to host the next meal).⁵² Yet in a very real sense this is the opposite of Germanism. Conradus admits he does not know what a party which changes host is called in Latin. His friend Burchardus encourages him to explain it as best he can, and Conradus makes his roundabout allusion to the German word. Burchardus then produces the correct Latin term: 'Scio, conuiuium uicissitudinarium Latine dices' (l. 10). The exchange is a typical piece of Schotten realism, perhaps even based on an actual classroom incident.

A similar, but slightly more complex case is seen in colloquy 47 which deals with the game of marbles. It is mentioned that Cologne schoolboys always call marbles 'omnia'.⁵³ This is quite true: 'omnia' was a Latinized version of the Ripuarian German dialect word 'Ommer', which was (and still is) the local Cologne term for marbles.⁵⁴ Amongst Latin schoolboys at least the Latin form had clearly bled across into the vernacular. Hermann von Weinsberg uses it in a German description of his childhood games.⁵⁵ Schotten's attitude to the word is clearly split. When Iacobus produces it (l. 10), his friend Cornelius condemns it as 'impolitum' (l. 11), and suggests that the correct term would be 'globuli missiles per pollices'

---

52   Grimm, 'Kränzchen', 3a, c; 'Kränzlein', 4. The term is frequent in Weinsberg: *BW*, I, pp. 348, 356; II, pp. 21, 90, 221–24; V, p. 82, etc. See Schotten, *Confabulationes*, ed. by Macardle, note to colloquy 98, l. 9.
53   'De ludo globorum missilium, quos 'omnia' uocant Colonienses tirunculi literarii', colloquy 47, ll. 1–2.
54   *Rheinisches Wörterbuch*, VI, p. 400, 4–20. See Chapter 2, n. 14, and Schotten, *Confabulationes*, ed. by Macardle, note to colloquy 47, l. 1.
55   'A. 1528 [...] do war uns spill [...] mit dem topp, koiten [bone dice], omnian', *BW*, I, p. 57. Cf. 'Zwei kleine jungen mit omrian [sic] gespielt' (HAStK, Turmbuch 29, quoted in Klersch, II, p. 139).

(l. 13). On the face of it, Schotten simply makes Iacobus mention the word so as to expose it as barbarous and correct it: very probably his own boys insisted on using the word, and he wanted to thematize the error in the *Confabulationes*. But on the other hand, this lexical oddity entirely fits into Schotten's depiction and even celebration of Cologne particularities; and he uses the word again two years later in his *Instructio prima puerorum* (sig. f1ʳ). The suspicion must be that while Schotten the Latinist deplored the word, Schotten the cultural chronicler found it intriguing, characteristic of his adopted city, and well worth recording.

Solecisms

Several of Schotten's departures from classical correctness seem to be not so much medievalisms or Germanisms as simple mistakes, though perhaps mistakes more likely to be made by someone familiar with Medieval Latin.

He uses deponent forms for several verbs which are simple actives in classical usage. Whilst 'ientor', rather than 'iento' is a medieval usage,[56] other erroneous deponents seem not to be. These include 'diuinor' for 'diuino', though this is in the first edition only, and so might be a printer's error; and 'exploror' for 'exploro'.[57] Schotten's shakiness in this area may reflect the influence of the medieval language, in which some verbs had taken on deponent forms. But other mistakes are not to be explained in this way, such as the adverb 'dapsilice', a form unknown

---

[56] See Schotten, *Confabulationes*, ed. by Macardle, note to colloquy 7, l. 18.

[57] 'Diuinor': colloquy 22, ll. 13, 14; 'exploror': colloquy 86, l. 13; *conuiuium* 2, l. 11.

in any period of Latin.⁵⁸ Probably the lack of reference works led Schotten into this; though a really well-read Latinist would surely have got this right. A rather odd use of the medieval noun 'ligneolum' ('small piece of wood') may mean that Schotten had confused it with a word for 'band' or 'tie' like 'ligamen', 'ligamentum', 'ligatura' or 'ligaculum'.⁵⁹

Idiolect

Through the heavily Terentian and Erasmian tone there do emerge traces of idiolectal usage, of a distinctly Schottennian voice. Admittedly, some of Schotten's idiolectal terms do seem slightly bizarre. 'Suppactor calcearius' for 'shoemaker' (colloquy 120, l. 7) is otherwise unknown, and surely unnecessary, given the classical terms 'sutor', 'calcearius' and 'calceolarius'. Similar is 'panniculus emunctorius' for 'handkerchief', where the adjective 'emunctorius' is used in a sense ('for blowing the nose') unknown in any period of Latin.⁶⁰ 'Poculorum baratrum' and 'cereuisiae baratrum' for 'heavy (beer-)drinker, toper' also seem otherwise unused.⁶¹

Others are more interesting. 'Raptitius liber' for a notebook or commonplace book (colloquy 122, l. 7) is an imaginative formula based on Classical Latin 'raptito', an alternative form of 'rapto', 'carry off, plunder'. In other cases Schotten coins words for medieval and early modern objects and phenomena unknown in Antiquity. This

---

58 Correctly 'dapsile' or 'dapsiliter': see Schotten, *Confabulationes*, ed. by Macardle, note to *conuiuium* 15, l. 63.
59 See ibid., note to colloquy 70, l. 9.
60 See ibid., note to colloquy 41, l. 21.
61 See ibid., note to *conuiuium* 30, l. 33 and colloquy 97, l. 1.

is evident in the culinary realm: 'halec erutum salsugine' for 'pickled herring' (e.g. colloquy 8, l. 26); 'ouorum sorbitiuncula', probably for 'egg custard' (colloquy 22, l. 30); or 'panis iurulentus', 'soup containing chunks of bread' (e.g. colloquy 7, l. 21).[62]

Humanist excesses?

It is only on a very few occasions that Schotten goes too far in the direction of humanist propriety. Amongst the 'barbaric' words which his schoolboys condemn is 'carnispriuium' for 'Shrovetide': 'uerbum barbarum [...] maxime impolitum' (colloquy 36, ll. 10–14). The word is of course as unknown to Cicero as was Shrovetide itself; but Schotten's suggested equivalent, 'tempus Bacchanale' (colloquies 36, ll. 1, 16; 123, l. 1) is not unproblematical. As recent scholars argue, the origin of Shrovetide is not pagan but profoundly Christian;[63] and the term 'carnisprivium' is well suited to expressing these Christian roots. It is lexically well established, and used by a good many humanist authors.[64] Ironically, then, Schotten's humanist preference for 'tempus Bacchanale' is misleading, and a step on the way to seeing Shrove as essentially a pagan relic: a line of argument taken up by Protestant humanists like Hospinianus who saw virtually all of the 'times and seasons' of the Catholic liturgical year as pagan at heart.[65]

---

[62] See ibid., notes to all lines listed in this paragraph, for detailed discussion and etymology.

[63] E.g. Moser, 'Fastnacht und Fronleichnam', pp. 360–67.

[64] Stotz, VI, 60.2; DuC, II, p. 179; *LLMA*. The word was widely used by Neo-Latin authors: e.g. 'Diebus stultificiis carnisprivii': Bebel, *Facetien*, p. 19; cf. pp. 36, 125; 'De ludo carnispriuiali': Johann Botzheim, in Erasmus, *Epistolae*, 2117, l. 5).

[65] Hospinianus, *Festa Christianorum*, fol. 45ᵛ.

Schotten's classical reading

Massebieau's judgement that, apart from Terence, Schotten knew classical literature not directly but from one of the many fifteenth-century anthologies (such as the *Flores poetarum*) is completely misleading.[66] Schotten's writing repeatedly shows traces of his independent engagement with classical authors, most obviously Terence. It is clear that his engagement with Terence was direct and personal, and not simply mediated by Erasmus and other authors. The same would seem to be true for Plautus: the imitation of Plautine usages such as 'quod' and 'quando' suggest as much, as does the fact that, for example, three quotations from Plautus's *Epidicus* follow one another in *conuiuium* 21.[67]

Other classical authors are much less well represented. There are for instance fewer than a dozen references to Vergil in the whole text; and Schotten is hazy enough to attribute to Vergil the sentiment 'nemo ubique felici ludet dextra', which is actually an approximate version of a line from the *Carmina duodecim sapientium*, a collection of late-classical verse which was frequently reproduced in the Middle Ages.[68] This, though, is hardly the mark of the utter barbarian. The line was still in common use: it was for instance used by Vives in the *Exercitatio*.[69] And in the case of such extremely common

---

[66] Massebieau, *Les colloques scolaires du seizième siècle*, p. 118; cf. [*Flores poetarum de virtutibus et viciis ac donis sancti spiritus*].

[67] See Schotten, *Confabulationes*, ed. by Macardle, notes to *conuiuium* 21, ll. 67, 72, 75.

[68] 'Nullus ubique potest felici ludere dextra': *Anthologia Latina*, I, 2, p. 61, no. 503, line attributed to Vomanius; *Carmina Burana*, I,3, p. 62, no. 213, l. 9. See Schotten, *Confabulationes*, ed. by Macardle, note to colloquy 48, l. 28.

[69] Vives, *Exercitatio linguae Latinae*, VI, p. 21.

sentiments, confusion about their precise origin is understandable. Otherwise, Schotten's Vergilian quotations are correct, and suggest he had a reasonable direct knowledge of the *Aeneid* and the *Eclogues*.[70]

More frequently quoted is Horace. No doubt much was mediated by Erasmus, for many *Adagia* are based on Horatian tags. It is also interesting that on one occasion when Schotten thinks he is quoting Horace, it is in fact Ovid.[71] Still, there are enough examples to suggest that Schotten had made his own reading of Horace, particularly of the *Sermones*. 'Credat hoc Iudaeus Apella' (colloquy 56, l. 28) is probably a direct quotation from Horace (*Sermones*, 1.5.100–01). When he says that Horace says that boys are won over to study by gifts (colloquy 106, l. 28) he is no doubt thinking of the gentle teachers who encourage young schoolboys with biscuits (*Sermones*, 1.1.25–26). When he cites Tarentum as a city of luxury (*conuiuium* 10, l. 55), he is probably thinking directly of Horace's 'molle Tarentum' (*Sermones*, 2.4.34). The phrase 'pedes caeno extrahemus' (*conuiuium* 30, l. 53) varies 'Caeno cupiens euellere plantam' (*Sermones*, 2.7.27).

There are distinct traces, too, of an independent reading of the satirist Persius. Here too some material is mediated by Erasmus: Schotten probably first met such tags as 'intus et in cute' or 'corneae fibrae homo' in the *Adagia*.[72] But there are clear signs of Schotten's own engagement with Persius. He describes himself as a 'semipaganus', using a term Persius coined to describe himself as an undeserving member of the poetic community.[73] In *conuiuium*

---

[70] See Schotten, *Confabulationes*, ed. by Macardle, notes to colloquies 29, ll. 33, 36; 48, l. 25; 81, ll. 14, 49; 108, l. 19; 123, l. 64.

[71] Ibid., colloquy 99, l. 22, quotes Ovid, *Epistulae ex Ponto*, 2.3.8, as 'Horatii uerbum'.

[72] See ibid., notes to colloquies 22, l. 23 and 23, l. 35.

[73] Ibid., 'Hermannus Schottennius Hessus candido lectori', l. 21;

30, l. 32 he quotes directly from the *Satires* (1.30–31); and there are several other quotations of this kind.[74]

Neither of these authors constitutes strong humanist credentials. Horace and Persius were well known in the Middle Ages, and Schotten quotes almost exclusively from Horace's *Epistulae* and *Sermones*, precisely the texts best known then, rather than from the *Odes*.[75] Persius, too, on account of his high moral tone, was a writer who recommended himself to the Church Fathers and was consequently appreciated in the Middle Ages.[76] In other authors, too, Schotten shows himself a rather conservative reader. Valerius Maximus, and Cicero's *De officiis* and *De senectute*, were all well known to medieval readers.

As stated at the outset, it would be premature to reach a definitive judgement on Schotten's Latinity before the tools and materials which allow a proper comparative view of it are in place. But it seems fair to judge it as an honourable attempt at a humanist-Classical Latin. Boys who imitated it would not be lured into barbarism, but would speak a flexible, basically classical Latin, well adapted to the conversational purposes and situations, and for the engagement with the real world around them which Schotten clearly had in mind. There are much worse pedagogical aims.

---

cf. 'Ipse semipaganus | ad sacra uatum carmen adfero nostrum', Persius, *Satires*, prologue, ll. 6–7.

[74] E.g. 'impallescere chartis': see Schotten, *Confabulationes*, ed. by Macardle, note to colloquy 73, l. 28; cf. Persius, *Satires*, 5.62; the reference to the 'ciconia' (ibid., colloquy 112, l. 17; cf. Persius, *Satires*, 1.58).

[75] See Manitius, *Analekten zur Geschichte des Horaz im Mittelalter*.

[76] See particularly Fetkenheuer, *Die Rezeption der Persius-Satiren in der lateinischen Literatur*.

Hans Weiditz, *St Anthony*, woodcut, *ca.* 1522.

CHAPTER 5

Visible Means of Support? Traces of Schotten's Networks

The modern term 'networking' was unknown to the humanists, but the activity was familiar and necessary in a precarious world where changes of regime or intellectual fashion could bring devastating shifts of fortune. Humanists worked not in isolation, but as part of a group, or several overlapping groups, defined by kinship, friendship, regions, institutions, and political, confessional and intellectual allegiances or sympathies. James V. Mehl rightly insists that any attempt to advance our understanding of the Cologne humanists must go beyond their individual accomplishments and examine 'the interrelationship of the humanists with other humanists, as well as others, within the broader intellectual, socio-economic, religious, and institutional life of the community.'[1]

But trying to apply this to Schotten is extremely difficult. The humanist medium of communication, self-representation and networking *par excellence* is the letter; but Schotten is not known as the correspondent of any established humanist, or indeed of anyone at all. Apart from the dedicatory epistles of his works, not a single letter either to him or from him is known; and only one letter, written by Konrad Kluppel, makes a brief allusion to him (see p. 28). Otherwise, practically the only documents which mention him are the official university re-

---

[1] Mehl, 'Humanism in the Home Town of the "Obscure Men"', p. 38.

cords, including the few tantalizing references in their 'unofficial' stratum. By contrast with the rich networks of friendship, intellectual affiliation and patronage which can be demonstrated for many Cologne humanists, Schotten seems almost pitifully isolated, to an extent that leads one to wonder about the tenability of his position in the Laurentiana and the University as a whole.

The time is now long past when it was widely assumed that humanism was marginalized in a city and university dominated by the *viri obscuri*. More recent scholarship has recognized the considerable extent to which humanist ideas circulated in the University, and even, in the early sixteenth century, began to penetrate and change the intellectual structures of the institution.[2] In recent years an impressive amount of material has become available on the humanists of Cologne University, including Götz-Rüdiger Tewes's magisterial study of the structures and personnel of the Cologne *bursae*, which painstakingly investigates the personal and intellectual allegiances of the Arts Faculty masters. His work is frequently cited here. Tewes, like Mehl, sees 'humanism' not only as an intellectual programme, but also as a set of relationships, of networks and networking within and without the structures of the university.

Bursae

The obvious first place to search for traces of Schotten networks is in his own *bursa*, where he spent so many years as student and don.

The long story of how the *bursae*, student halls or colleges, came to dominate arts teaching at Cologne cannot

---

[2] E.g. Meuthen, 'Artesfakultät', pp. 391–92; id., *Universität*, pp. 208–09, 214–18, 287–89, etc.

be told in detail here.³ The origin of the *bursa* was the house of the individual master who took in students as lodgers and offered them extra tuition in the Arts curriculum, a must for the many students who arrived linguistically underprepared. These masters had a long tradition of taking on young boys not yet officially members of the University. Over time, and especially in the early fifteenth century, these private arrangements developed into institutions on a larger scale, a development seen all over Germany, but particularly marked in Cologne.⁴ The Cologne *bursae* were 'entrepreneurial', financed almost entirely by student fees.⁵ Their formula (board and lodging, intensive and if necessary remedial teaching, moral tutelage and a sense of community) was understandably a winning one. Whilst the *bursae* at first simply repeated the Arts classes held in the Faculty building, by the end of the fifteenth century they effectively were the Faculty: almost all Arts teaching went on there, with the Faculty responsible for little beyond examinations.⁶ This in practice opened an academic career only to someone appointed as a lecturer (*lector* or *regens*) in a *bursa*. There, as a salaried *commensalis*, he would have board, lodging and the means to study in one of the higher faculties; he was in line for one of the lucrative Faculty offices, or if a cleric, for one of the benefices at the Cologne parish churches which were in his *bursa*'s gift.⁷ Especially be-

---

3   See esp. Meuthen, 'Artesfakultät'; id., *Universität*, pp. 91–100; Tewes, 'Die Studentenburse des Magisters Nikolaus Mommer von Raemsdonck', passim; Schwinges, 'Sozialgeschichtliche Aspekte', pp. 545–64.
4   Meuthen, 'Artesfakultät', pp. 367–69.
5   'Unternehmerbursen', the term used by Schwinges, 'Sozialgeschichtliche Aspekte', p. 537; cf. Meuthen, 'Artesfakultät', p. 373: 'Major investments of late-medieval professor-entrepreneurs'.
6   Meuthen, 'Artesfakultät', esp. pp. 367–69, 379–80, 385.
7   Tewes, *Bursen*, pp. 121–219; Meuthen, 'Artesfakultät', pp. 378, 384; id., *Universität*, p. 237; Kuckhoff, *Geschichte des*

tween 1510 and 1540, as student numbers at Cologne plummeted, the material security enjoyed by the *bursa* lector was enviable.[8]

Arts teaching at Cologne was at the outset largely Nominalist in character, and in 1414–1416 a formal attempt to introduce Realism, the 'Terministenstreit', failed; but in the 1420s there arrived at the University two masters trained at Paris in the *via antiqua*: the Thomist Heinrich von Gorkum, and Heimericus de Campo, a follower of Albertus Magnus. These men not only succeeded in establishing the Realist tradition that would triumphantly prevail at Cologne; they founded the first two of the 'principal' *bursae*. Heinrich founded the Thomist Montana; Heimericus set up the Laurentiana to teach the Albertist *via*.[9] This Thomist–Albertist opposition would characterize Arts teaching in Cologne, and the ethos of the *bursae*, for centuries to come.

As well as the Montana and Laurentiana there were two other 'principal' *bursae* in the Faculty: the Thomist Bursa Corneliana, founded in the 1420s,[10] and the Albertist Bursa Kuck (Kuyck, Cucana), an overspill foundation from the Laurentiana, set up in 1450 by Johann von Kuck.[11] These four *bursae* had a monopoly, indeed a stranglehold, on Arts teaching in Cologne. They were implacably opposed to new foundations, as was demon-

---

Gymnasium Tricoronatum, p. 17; Schwinges, 'Soziale Aspekte', pp. 545, 547; Fletcher, 'Wealth and Poverty', pp. 413–18.

[8] Eulenburg, *Die Frequenz der deutschen Universitäten*, pp. 285–99; Meuthen, *Universität*, pp. 77–79; Nauert, 'Humanists, Scholastics [...]', pp. 50–51. See pp. 32–33 above.

[9] Meuthen, *Universität*, pp. 61, 172, 177–89, 228, etc.; id. 'Artesfakultät', pp. 386–87 and n. 102; Lohr, 'Medieval Latin Aristotle Commentaries', pp. 224–26; Tewes, *Bursen*, p. 47. Further literature cited in Meuthen, 'Artesfakultät', p. 374, n. 32.

[10] Tewes, *Bursen*, p. 73; HAStK, 150, 84, fol. 9ʳ.

[11] *Matrikel*, 170,27; Meuthen, 'Artesfakultät', p. 377; Kuckhoff, *Geschichte des Gymnasium Tricoronatum*, pp. 56–101.

strated in the fate of two smaller houses when they attempted to become members of the 'club' of major *bursae*. The Raemsdonck, founded by Nicolaus Raemsdonck, was absorbed by the Montana in 1477–1480;[12] the Ottonis, founded by Otto von Bleeck of Xanten, was forced to close in 1502–1503, despite healthy student numbers. This may partly have been because it was engaged in teaching a curriculum close to that of humanist *gymnasia*, which in turn may explain its popularity with the leading Cologne families.[13]

Tewes distinguishes the ways in which humanism was articulated in the Thomist *bursae* (the Montana and the Corneliana) and those which followed the Albertist way (the Laurentiana and the Kuck). In the Thomist *bursae*, humanist activity seems to have been easily integrated and encouraged; in the Albertist *bursae*, by contrast, a more rigorous morality, a more serious piety and a more inflexible religious ethos made them less open to humanism, and less likely to accept and integrate individual humanists. It is telling that in the two major controversies of the early sixteenth century, those concerning Reuchlin and Luther, the Albertists were almost invariably on the conservative side.[14]

The Bursa Laurentiana

The Laurentiana was founded by Heymericus de Campo in 1420, though its own mythology represented it as go-

---

12   Tewes, 'Die Studentenburse [...]', passim; Meuthen, 'Artesfakultät', p. 378.
13   Meuthen, *Universität*, p. 97; id., 'Artesfakultät', p. 378; Tewes, *Bursen*, esp. pp. 108–10, 112–16, 427–39.
14   Meuthen, *Universität*, p. 221; Tewes, *Bursen*, pp. 748–86.

ing back to the very beginnings of the University.[15] The house had a regional 'power base' in Heymericus's home in the Kampen–Amersfoort–Zwolle area of the Netherlands, from which the leading figures continued to hail.[16] The records amply demonstrate the nepotism endemic in late-medieval university structures: those in control of the *bursa* regularly favoured their own kith and kin (see p. 49). In Schotten's time the *bursa* was in the Schmierstraße (now Komödienstraße) where it had been placed by Laurentius Buninch of Groningen in the 1440s, and where it remained till a move in 1569 to a house near the Franciscan convent.[17] The *bursa* strictly observed the Albertist *via*.[18] The Laurentiana had once been the largest *bursa*, though in Schotten's time its numbers, like those of the university as a whole, were already declining. It was also, despite its Dutch power-base, the most cosmopolitan *bursa*, though not one where Hessians like Schotten were particularly well represented.[19]

Despite its strict Albertist orientation, the Laurentiana had by no means entirely excluded humanist scholars. A supreme example was Rudolf von Langen, who on coming to Cologne reacted against the scholastic training he had received at Erfurt (1456–1460); he was later the guiding spirit of the humanist curricular reform at the Münster Cathedral School.[20] His Cologne associates in-

---

[15] Tewes, *Bursen*, pp. 47–48; Meuthen, 'Artesfakultät', pp. 375–77; HAStK, 150, A 760, a MS history of the Laurentiana. Heymericus de Campo: *Matrikel*, 132,124. The foundation in 1388 by Theodoricus Kerckering de Monasterio (*Matrikel*, 1,16) alleged in HAStK, 150, A 760, fol. 1ʳ, is a fifteenth-sixteenth-century fiction.

[16] Meuthen, 'Artesfakultät', p. 377; see data in Tewes, *Bursen*, pp. 47–73.

[17] *Topogr.*, II, 108b, 17, 18. Tewes, *Bursen*, pp. 254–57, 273–77.

[18] Meuthen, *Universität*, pp. 93, 143, 145, 187; id. 'Artesfakultät', p. 390; cf. p. 376, n. 40.

[19] Schwinges, 'Sozialgeschichtliche Aspekte', p. 549.

[20] Langen: *Matrikel*, 382,10; *NDB*, XIII, pp. 578–80; *CoE*, II,

cluded active humanists like Johannes Kerckmeister, the author of the Latin drama *Codrus*; Anton Frey (Liber) von Soest, who edited the humanist *Familiarum epistolarum compendium* (*ca.* 1473); Arnold Bevelen von Hildesheim, rector of the Emmerich school till 1502; the Laurentiana graduate Lambert von Venroed, Arnold's successor at Emmerich till 1513 or after, and the teacher there of Jakob Siberti von Münstereifel, later a Benedictine, a friend of Johann Butzbach. Others included Johannes (de Aqua) de Bercha, and the Laurentiana masters Johannes de Mechlinia and Gerardus de Harderwijck. Langen also collaborated in producing several teaching texts used by the Laurentiana.[21] Another leading humanist who enjoyed friendly relations with the Laurentiana was Hermannus Buschius (1468–1534), who wrote a poem in praise of the *bursa* in 1498, and contributed an epigram to a 1508 edition of the life of St Suitbert edited there.[22] He lived at the Laurentiana when he returned to Cologne in 1508, and again in 1518, to see to the printing of his *Vallum humanitatis* (see p. 180). Ortwin Gratius (*ca.* 1480–1542), though mercilessly satirized in the *Epistolae obscurorum virorum*, was indeed a humanist; in a poem of 1508 he described the Laurentiana as a centre of the 'disciplinae liberales'.[23] Johannes Murmellius (1480–1517), the humanist educator, contributed a poem praising Albertus Magnus to an edition of the Lauentiana master Gerhard von Harderwijck's logic textbook in 1511.[24]

The Laurentiana personnel began to be more systematically 'humanized' in the 1490s, when two Nuremberg

---

pp. 290–91. *Rhodolphi Langii [...] Carmina* (1486), ed. by Hugenroth (Münster: Regensberg, 1991).
[21] On Langen's connections see Tewes, *Bursen*, pp. 715–26, including details of all the figures mentioned here.
[22] Tewes, *Bursen*, pp. 725, 727. Poem: Liessem, *Hermann van dem Busche*, p. 6; epigram: ibid., pp. 43–44; *Regesten*, 2524.
[23] Tewes, *Bursen*, pp. 727–29, 734–35.
[24] Tewes, *Bursen*, p. 735. Murmellius: *Matrikel*, 430,9.

humanists were brought to the *bursa*: Georg Beheim and Peter Kamerer. Beheim, though designated as the successor to the principalship, eventually went back to Nuremberg; Kamerer, the owner of a good collection of humanistic books, died very prematurely in 1503.[25] Tewes is probably right to surmise that the Laurentiana would have become a more humanistically inclined institution had these two dynamic young figures stayed at the *bursa* for longer; nonetheless, he concludes that there seems to have been more tolerance, even enthusiasm, for humanism at the Laurentiana than previously supposed. He notes discreet humanist tendencies in such Laurentiana masters as Johannes de Buscoducis (*ca.* 1482–1543), who was for example involved in the humanist-dominated Quodlibet of 1522, and Bernardus Witte de Affelen (b. *ca.* 1520).[26]

Yet, though the Laurentiana may have been an environment not entirely hostile to humanist colleagues and humanist thought, there is nowhere any documentary evidence of Schotten asserting himself as a humanist within the *bursa*, or forging any personal affiliations with other lectors. Traces of personal networks have to be sought beyond the immediate confines of the Laurentiana.

---

[25] Beheim: Tewes, *Bursen*, p. 726 (cf. pp. 585–91); HAStK, 150, A 760, fol. 11ʳ; *Regesten*, 2373. Kamerer: *Matrikel*, 428, 39; Tewes, *Bursen*, p. 726 (cf. p. 586, n. 1214); *Regesten*, 2400.

[26] Tewes, *Bursen*, pp. 726–27. J. de Buscoducis: *Matrikel*, 434,132; cf. HAStK, 150, A 481, fol. 146ᵛ; Tewes, *Bursen*, pp. 68, 727, 745. B. Witte: Tewes, *Bursen*, esp. p. 68.

Schotten's dedications

The only extant letters of Schotten are the dedicatory letters to his various works. Those most helpful in putting Schotten in some kind of context are in two works written in 1527: the *Vita honesta*, a brief treatise on the virtuous life, and the *Ludus imperatorius*, an allegorical play on the state of the Holy Roman Empire.

The *Vita honesta* is dedicated by Schotten to Johann (III) Rinck, a member of one of the leading patrician families in Cologne.[27] The dedication is dated 4 April 1527; a brief valediction is dated 26 April.[28]

Johann was the first person to whom Schotten, 'infimae fortunae literariae, inter literas discentes unus' (sig. Aii^r) thought of dedicating the work. His family is famed far beyond Cologne. The Rincks fittingly bear the name of the ring. It is round, the noblest of shapes, made of precious metal, and worn to be displayed to the inspection of all. Just so, Rincks have always lived lives of 'virtus' and 'prudentia' in the public gaze (sig. Aii^r–Aiii^r).

Schotten now reviews the Rinck clan, beginning with Johann's late father, Johann (II). A man distinguished by learning, virtue and piety, he has given the city splendid buildings and churches; like Augustus in Rome and Lorenzo de' Medici in Florence, he fitted out his house, which is rightly called the 'House of the Muses', with a fine scholarly library (sig. Aiii^{r-v}). Schotten then eulogizes Johann (II)'s three surviving brothers: Adolf, the incorruptible magistrate and staunch supporter of Catholic religion; Hermann (II), the wise counsellor of Emperor

---

[27] 'Eruditissimo ac maxime egregio viro Ioanni Rynckx patritiae familiae apud Colonienses, iuris utriusque doctori Mecænati suo', Schotten, *Vita honesta*, quoted from the edition of Antwerp: A. Goinus, 1540, sig. Aii^r–v^r (Aii^r).

[28] 'Coloniae ex aedibus meis, Pridiae [sic] Idus Aprilis. M. D. XXVII.', *Vita honesta*, sig. Av^r. 'Coloniae sexto Kalendas Mai.', ibid., sig. Eiii^v.

Charles V and the king of England; Conrad (II), in his hoary old age like a Roman senator (sig. Aiii^v–iv^r; Aiv^r; Aiv^v). He also briefly mentions Johann (III)'s brother Hermann (III), recently elected to the city council (sig. Aiv^v).

Finally Schotten addresses Johann (III) himself. Like Pythagoras, Johann left his native soil to study abroad. At Bologna, then at Cologne, he became Doctor of Canon, then of Civil Law. He is a protector of the Observant Franciscans and a patron of scholars, and his house is truly the 'House of Maecenas' (sig. Aiv^v). Schotten ends with further greetings to Johann and to his pregnant wife (Anna Bars, known as Olisleger), and best wishes for her confinement and for the children she will produce.[29]

Only six months later, on 22 October 1527, Schotten dedicated his *Ludus imperatorius* to Johann (III)'s uncle Hermann (II).[30] In the brief letter Schotten compares Charles V, whose counsellor Hermann is, with the Caesars, Alexander and Charlemagne. Clemency is the watchword of his dealings with enemies (sig. A2^v). Schotten's play is a shadowing forth, an 'umbratica imago', of the causes of the disastrous state of the present age, celebrating Charles's supreme victories (sig. A2^v). He dedicates it to Hermann as the emperor's counsellor, asking him to consider not the size or value of the gift, but the spirit in which it is given. He bids farewell to a 'uir integerrim[us], simul et prudentissim[us]' (sig. A3^r).

---

[29] 'Rursum uale cum honestissima uxore tua, nunc feliciter impregnata, felicius faxit Deus ut pariat: felicissime pulchra faciat te prole parentem', Schotten, *Vita honesta*, sig. Av^r.

[30] 'Prudentissimo et integerrimo viro Hermanno Rinco seniori, patricio Coloniensi, equiti aurato, necnon illustrissimi Regis Angliae, & inuictissimi Caroli quinti Ro. imperatoris, a consiliis, Hermannus Scottennius [sic] Hessus S. P. D.', Schotten, *Ludus imperatorius siue caesareus, continens umbraticam imaginem, horum temporum, regnante Diuo Carolo quinto [...]* (Cologne: P. Quentel, 1527), sig. A1^v.

In these dedications to the Rincks, Schotten was ingratiating himself with one of the leading dynasties of Cologne.³¹ The success of their family business in trade, property and finance had made them one of the wealthiest Cologne families.³² The Rinck 'patriarch', Johann (I), probably moved to Cologne early in the fifteenth century.³³ It was however his nephew Hermann (I) (d. *ca.* 1496) who really established the dynasty, and Hermann's sons Johann (II) (*ca.* 1457–1516), Hermann (II) (d. after 1528), Conrad (II) (d. 1531) and Adolf (1472?–1541) who consolidated its power.³⁴

Wealth bought political clout. The Rincks appear constantly as Cologne councillors and mayors.³⁵ A particularly influential time was from 1512–1539, when Johann (II) and Adolf were mayors: this coincided with Schotten's time in Cologne.³⁶ The Rincks forged marriage alliances with Cologne's other dominant families.³⁷ They also gained considerable political influence in the Empire and further afield.

---

31 Herborn, 'Zur Rekonstruktion [...] der Kölner Bürgermeisterliste [...], p. 180; *Slg. Ketten*, IV, pp. 265–79; *RHV*, 3096–105. Family tree, ibid., pp. 480–81 and Schmid, *Stifter*, p. 604.
32 Irsigler, 'Hansekaufleute', pp. 313–27, esp. 320–22; Hegel, *St. Kolumba in Köln*, p. 98.
33 Mentioned as a Cologne merchant in 1423: *Hansisches Urkundenbuch*, VI, no. 491; became a Cologne citizen in 1432: *Neubürger*, I, p. 78 (1432, no. 6, 20.2.1432); Kuske, *Quellen*, II, p. 574, no. 1143; Irsigler, 'Hansekaufleute', pp. 313–16; Schmid, *Stifter*, pp. 26–62.
34 Hermann (I): Irsigler, 'Hansekaufleute', esp. pp. 316–17, 320–22; Schmid, *Stifter*, pp. 140–58. Hermann's sons: ibid., pp. 160–90; Irsigler, 'Hansekaufleute', p. 319.
35 *RHV*, 3096–105.
36 Schmid, *Stifter*, p. 159. List in Herborn, 'Zur Rekonstruktion [...]', pp. 131–33: Johann (II) was mayor 1512–14; Adolf was mayor nine times between 1514 and 1539.
37 *RHV*, pp. 480–81. Family trees recording alliances with Hardenraths, Kannengießers, etc.: *Slg. Ketten*, IV, pp. 270–73; Schmid, *Stifter*, pp. 223–494 and Stammtafel 2–12, pp. 605–15.

Many Rincks studied at the University and maintained close connections with it. Peter (*ca.* 1429–1501) entered in 1452, and from 1459 taught in the Law Faculty.[38] Two of Hermann (I)'s sons studied at Cologne. Johann (II) matriculated in Arts in 1471.[39] Like many patrician youths he left without a degree, but he remained connected with and devoted to the University, notably as a city council *Provisor* of University affairs,[40] and it was that devotion which in May 1516 earned him a glowing obituary in the Arts *Dekanatsbuch*.[41] Adolf, who entered as a minor in 1485, succeeded Johann as University *Provisor* in 1516.[42] Johann (II)'s son Hermann (III) matriculated in Arts in 1505, and was for a while a member of the Law Faculty.[43] His brother Johann (III) began Law in 1508, taking his doctorate ten years later. He held various university positions, resigning the rectorship of 1558–1559 owing to ill health.[44] Five other Rincks are recorded as students.[45]

---

[38] *Matrikel*, 255,51; Schmid, *Stifter*, pp. 63–139.
[39] *Matrikel*, 331,9.
[40] *Regesten*, 2659; *BRStK*, II, 1514, no. 292; Schmid, *Stifter*, pp. 182–83. On the duties of the *Provisores*, see *Alte Un.*, pp. 95–101.
[41] 'Vir clarissimus [...] in ordine patriciorum vel primus vel inter primis': HAStK, 150, A 481, fol. 110ʳ; *Matrikel*, 331,9.
[42] *Matrikel*, 385,47. The birthdate of 1472 (*Slg. Ketten*, IV, p. 268, n. 4) fits this matriculation date. As *Provisor*: *Regesten*, 2742; *BRStK*, II, 1516, no. 315; Schmid, *Stifter*, p. 182.
[43] *Matrikel*, 467,55: Law Faculty member, 1513. *Ratsherr*, 1519–39; cf. *RHV*, 3100.
[44] *Matrikel*, 480,1. *CoE*, III, pp. 161–62.
[45] Heinrich (unidentified): *Matrikel*, 320,7: matriculated 1469; Rutger (unidentified): matriculated 1470: *Matrikel*, 329,63; Irsigler, 'Hansekaufleute', p. 313. Hieronymus, illegitimate son of Peter: *Matrikel*, 425,6: matriculated 1495; BA 1497; MA 1499; Tewes, *Bursen*, pp. 49, 433; Irsigler, 'Peter Rinck', pp. 65–66. Hermann and Peter, sons of Hermann (III): *Matrikel*, 631,16 and 17 (matriculated as minors, 30 September 1546). Keussen implicitly, and wrongly, identifies Peter with Peter (II) (d. 1568), who was already a merchant by 1528, and a councillor 1534–68: *RHV*, 3105; cf. Schmid, *Stifter*, p. 166

Rinck allegiances with specific *bursae* are less certain. Peter Rinck's illegitimate son Hieronymus matriculated as a minor in 1495 at the Ottonis, and in 1485 Hermann (I)'s son Adolf, also a minor, was promised for by an Ottonis master, virtually guaranteeing that he too was there.[46] Hieronymus went to the Laurentiana for his MA, incepting in 1499 under Arnold von Tongeren:[47] Ottonis bachelors frequently migrated to other *bursae* for the MA and higher degrees.[48] An unidentified Heinrich Rinck (entered 1469) determined BA under Cornelius Baes de Breda at the Bursa Kuck, which maintained close connections with the Laurentiana, its parent *bursa*.[49] Cornelius had studied at the Laurentiana, and was close to the Laurentiana Albertist circle of Johannes de Mechlinia, rector of St Kolumba: along with Peter Rinck and others he executed Johannes's will.[50] When the Ottonis closed the Rincks may have transferred allegiance to the Montana.[51] This suggests that the antagonisms between the Albertist and Thomist *bursae* which Tewes sketches so

---

and n. 54. Hermann (LicLeg 1558, d. before 1591) may be identical with the Hermann Rinck who started Law in 1554: *Matrikel*, 663,15; LicLeg under Conrad Betzdorf: HAStK, 150, A 11, 204ʳ; Keussen does not make this identification.

[46] Hieronymus: *Matrikel*, 425,6; Tewes, *Bursen*, pp. 49, 433; Irsigler, 'Peter Rinck', pp. 65–66. Adolf: *Matrikel*, 385,47: 'n[on] i[uravit], sed m. Nic. Lynnich promisit in forma.'; cf. Tewes, *Bursen*, pp. 432–33. Nicolaus Heerl de Linnich (*Matrikel*, 283,31) was co-principal of the Ottonis from 1473 at latest: Tewes, *Bursen*, p. 109.

[47] *Matrikel*, 425,6: inception 11 April 1499; Tewes, *Bursen*, p. 433. Arnold von Tongeren: *Matrikel*, 392,67.

[48] Tewes, *Bursen*, pp. 425–27.

[49] *Matrikel*, 320,7: determined BA 20 June 1470 under Cornelius de Breda; MA 1472.

[50] Baes: *Matrikel*, 217,28; Tewes, *Bursen*, pp. 95, 443–44.

[51] Johann (III) Rinck, matriculated 1508 (*Matrikel*, 480,1) was promoted DLeg by P. de Clapis, who also promoted Conrad Betzdorf (Montana): *Matrikel*, 579,29.

emphatically may at times have been bridged by close personal relationships.

In the narrowest institutional terms, then, the Rincks and the Laurentiana seem not closely connected. But this impression is misleading: other networks associated the Rincks with the *bursa* in very powerful ways.

The parish of St Kolumba

The Rincks, the most important artistic patrons and donors in late-medieval Cologne, focused their generosity on religious institutions, and particularly on one which brought them into contact with the Bursa Laurentiana. The main Rinck family home, Königstein, being on the north side of the Schildergasse, was in the parish of St Kolumba, the largest and most socially prestigious in the city.[52] The Rincks were intensely involved with the life of the important parish church. Four generations were churchwardens; Peter, Johann (II) and other Rincks were generous patrons.[53] The family played a major role in planning and financing extensive works at St Kolumba.[54]

---

[52] Königstein: *Topogr.*, I, p. 369a, 16–23; mentioned in HAStK, 241, U 1/7 of 1511, 2ᵛ. St Kolumba: Schmid, *Stifter*, pp. 31–32, citing further literature; *KD*, VI,4, pp. 194–230. On the social cachet see Greving, *Steuerlisten des Kirchspiels St. Kolumba in Köln*, and Herborn, 'Sozialtopographie des Kölner Kirchspiels St. Kolumba', quoted in Hegel, *St. Kolumba in Köln*, pp. 92–100; Tewes, *Bursen*, p. 439.

[53] Churchwardens: e.g. Peter, Hermann (I), Johann (II), Peter (II): Schmid, *Stifter*, p. 166. Patronage: e.g. Peter (will of 1500); Hermann (I); Johann (II) (will of 1512): Schmid, *Stifter*, pp. 68, 78; 144; 160.

[54] E.g. 1456 rebuilding: Tewes, *Bursen*, pp. 443–44. Choir-stalls donated by the Rincks, early sixteenth century: *KD*, VI,4, p. 214; Schmid, *Stifter*, p. 44, Ill. 7; Hegel, *St. Kolumba in Köln*, p. 140.

Much of their interest was devoted to the magnificent Marienkapelle, virtually a family chapel, where numerous Rincks were buried.[55] To it they contributed lavishly.[56]

St Kolumba was a point of contact with other influential families, such as the von Wasservas, who were also benefactors.[57] But most crucially it was an extremely important centre for the Albertists of the University, and particularly of the Laurentiana, even though the *bursa* was not physically in the parish till it moved in 1569.[58] It is above all Tewes's systematic studies which have revealed the parish as an Albertist intellectual and spiritual focus.[59] The parish had the right to appoint its own rector, and for over a century, from 1442 to 1554 – with the Rincks always conspicuously involved – it appointed seven Laurentiana academics in a sequence interrupted only by a single Montana graduate.[60] For nearly forty years (1503–1542), covering practically the whole of Schotten's time in Cologne, the incumbent was Arnoldus de Dammone; he was followed (1542–1554) by Hermann Blankenfort de Monasterio, who had been appointed Lector in the Laurentiana in 1528, perhaps in preference to Schotten (see pp. 50–51), and was by now an eminent

---

[55] Schmid, *Stifter*, esp. pp. 41–48; cf. plan, p. 617; Hegel, *St. Kolumba in Köln*, pp. 117–48; Tewes, *Bursen*, pp. 441–42. Burials: Schmid, *Stifter*, pp. 146, 162, 203–05, ill. 46.

[56] E.g. Master of the Lyversberg Passion, *Coronation of the Virgin* (now Munich, Alte Pinakothek, Inv. no. WAF 615): Schmid, *Stifter*, pp. 44–48. Johann (II)'s memorial window to his wife: Schmid, *Kölner Renaissance-Kultur*, p. 113, n. 285.

[57] Schmid, *Stifter*, pp. 144–45; Tewes, *Bursen*, p. 446, ns 307–09.

[58] Hegel, *St. Kolumba in Köln*, p. 86.

[59] 'Geistig-geistlicher Fokus': Tewes, *Bursen*, p. 447.

[60] 1442: Johannes Hulshout de Mechlinia; 1475: Heinrich Boese de Horst; 1496: Gerhard de Harderwijck; 1503: Arnold de Dammone; 1542–54: Hermann von Blankenfort; 1558–64: Sebastian Niermoell or de Novimola (Montana); 1564–1605: Johann Nopel von Lippstadt; 1605–17: Caspar Ulenberg. Cf. Tewes, *Bursen*, pp. 440–52; Hegel, *St. Kolumba in Köln*, pp. 88–89, 299–301.

theologian. Other jobs, too – as curates, sacristans, schoolmasters – went to Laurentiana men.[61]

St Kolumba facilitated close links between the Rincks and the Laurentiana. The Laurentian Johannes de Mechlinia, rector 1442–1475, was a good friend and executor of Johann (I) Rinck, whilst Peter Rinck's executors included Gerhard de Harderwijck, principal of the Laurentiana and rector of St Kolumba 1496–1503: Peter and Johann (II) had been churchwardens when he was presented to the cure.[62] In 1512 another Laurentiana principal, Arnold Luyde von Tongeren, executed Johann (II)'s will.[63]

Kloster Lämmchen: Conventus Rinckiorum

Another important point of contact between the Rincks and the Laurentiana was the Lämmchen, a convent of Augustinian nuns on the Burgmauer.[64] Johann (II) made major donations in 1502 and 1511, and the family was still supporting the house in the 1580s.[65] So generous was

---

[61] Arnoldus: *Matrikel*, 384,47: important in the Theological Faculty. Blankenfort: see pp. 50–51. Others: Tewes, *Bursen*, pp. 440–41, 444, 445, 448, 451.

[62] Johannes de Mechlinia: Tewes, *Bursen*, pp. 440–41. Gerhard de Harderwijck: *Matrikel*, 317,89; cf. HAStK, 150, A 760, 11ʳ; Schmid, *Stifter*, pp. 68–70; Tewes, *Bursen*, pp. 448 and n. 320, 469–70, 723.

[63] HAStK, 110 (Test.), 1/R 264, partially printed in Kuske, *Quellen*, no. 198, pp. 301–04; Schmid, *Stifter*, pp. 160–61. Arnoldus: *Matrikel*, 392,67; Schmid, *Stifter*, p. 167; cf. Tewes, *Bursen*, pp. 469–70.

[64] Gelenius, p. 585; von Mering and Reischert, *Die Bischöfe und Erzbischöfe von Köln*, II, p. 95; *Slg. Ketten*, IV, p. 278; Schmid, *Stifter*, pp. 167–72.

[65] 1502: Rinck 'ad perfectam monasterii formam auxit', Gelenius, p. 585. 1511: HAStK, 241, U 1/7; cf. HAStK, 295, 151; *KD*, VII,3,2, pp. 224–27. 1584: HAStK, 241, U 3/28: bequest of

the Rincks' patronage that the house was popularly known as 'Conventus Rinckiorum'.[66]

The Lämmchen, just within the parish of St Kolumba, was a mere stone's throw from the Laurentiana,[67] and a number of Laurentiana personalities were connected with it. The Tongeren regional/kinship group, the ruling circle of the *bursa*, was particularly closely involved: Arnold Luyde von Tongeren, the then principal (and Johann (II) Rinck's executor), was a Visitor in 1511; Heinrich Buschers von Tongeren, principal from 1530, left a bequest to the house in 1563 to fund his anniversary memorial.[68] The convent's confessor in 1565 was Johann Walsgartz von Tongeren, another eminent Laurentiana academic.[69] The Lämmchen, a focus for Albertist *bursa* loyalties and personal friendships, demonstrates no less clearly than St Kolumba the close connections between members of the Rinck family and the Laurentiana.

In other ways, too, the Lämmchen and the Laurentiana seem to be linked. We know little of the nuns, since the Lämmchen was founded only in the late fifteenth century, and its inmates are not systematically recorded.[70] But one document, relating to a donation of Johann (II)

Adelheit Rinck to the Lämmchen.
[66] *Slg. Ketten*, IV, p. 278: 'vulgo conventus Rinckiorum nuncupatur'.
[67] *Topogr.*, I, p. 303b, 8–12 and pl. VIII (Lämmchen); II, p. 108a, 17, 18 and pl. XI (Laurentiana).
[68] Arnoldus: *Matrikel*, 392,67; Schmid, *Stifter*, p. 167; cf. Tewes, *Bursen*, pp. 469–70. Heinrich: *Matrikel*, 488,59; his bequest: HAStK, 241, U 2/22, 31.10.1563.
[69] Walsgartz: *Matrikel*, 659,90: matriculated 27 March 1554, his fee paid by rector Hermann Blankenfort de Monasterio, Bursa Laurentiana. Taught in Arts Faculty, 1559–65; numerous offices, including dean of Arts and rector; refused principalship of the Laurentiana in 1564; Cathedral canonry. See Keussen's note to *Matrikel*, 659,90; Schmid, *Stifter*, p. 167, n. 62.
[70] No Lämmchen nuns are listed in Militzer, *Kölner Geistliche*, II. *Frauen*.

Rinck, lists the twenty sisters there in 1511.⁷¹ Their surnames are not those of the Cologne elite: the Lämmchen was clearly not in the same social league as the Benedictine Machabäer convent (Maviren), or St Mauritius, where the Rincks placed their own daughters.⁷² But the names are not completely obscure either. Ten of the sixteen match those of respectable Cologne burgher families: Bruwer, van Clarenbach, Eschwiler, Kleffer (probably van Kleve), Koch, van Lunschet (Lüdenscheidt), van Sent Truden, van deme Sterne, Steynmetzer, van Tzons (Zons), names frequent in the standard literature on the Cologne burgher class in the Middle Ages,⁷³ on the city council,⁷⁴ and in wills.⁷⁵

---

71   HAStK, 295, 151, fol. 2ʳ: In alphabetical order: Joanna van Arbelen; Elsgin Bartscherer; Styngin Bruwer; Yrmgin van Clarenbach; Gertgin van Coln; Bela and Ffigin Eschwiler; Agnese and Tringyn Kleffer; Meysgin Koch; Druitgin Koster; Tringin van Lunschet; Druitgyn van Sent Truden; Leyngin and Tringin van deme Sterne(n); Druitgyn and Tzeychin Steynmetzer; Luckart van Tzons; Engin Vorloin; Eltzgin van Wertzborch.

72   Hermann (I)'s daughters Klara (Klairgin) and Benigna (Gutgin) were at the Machabäer in the period 1492–1494: Militzer, *Kölner Geistliche*, II, pp. 504–05. Klara was still there in 1527: HAStK, 295 (GA), 160, 28ᵛ, and 161, 2ʳ. In 1521 Gutgin was prioress: Kloft, *Inventar [...]*, II, no. 911. Anna and Katharina Rinck, nuns at St Mauritius, may have been daughters or nieces of Hermann (III): Militzer, *Kölner Geistliche*, II, pp. 655–58; Schmid, *Stifter*, pp. 211–13 and ills 51 and 52.

73   *Slg. Ketten*; *RHV*; *Neubürger*; Herborn, *Die politische Führungsschicht*; Irsigler, *Die wirtschaftliche Stellung der Stadt Köln [...]*; Kellenbenz, 'Die wohlhabendsten Kölner Bürger um 1515'; Knipping, *Die Kölner Stadtrechnungen des Mittelalters*; von Loesch, *Die Kölner Zunfturkunden*; Militzer, *Die vermögenden Kölner 1417–1418*. None, however, occurs in Militzer, *Kölner Geistliche*, II.

74   Councillors: Bruwer (*RHV*, 529, 595–99); Eschwiler (*RHV*, 1086–88; *BRStK*, VI, p. 56); Koch (*RHV*, 2175, 2177; *BRStK*, VI, pp. 106–07); van sent Truden (*RHV*, 858–60; *BRStK*, VI, pp. 177–78); Steynmetzer (*RHV*, 3394); van Zons (*RHV*, 4005, 4007, 4010–14; *BRStK*, VI, pp. 209–10) (and possibly Kleffer, if

Might these families have been connected with the Laurentiana? This is harder to say. Whilst most of the nuns had probably lived in or near Cologne, names of boys matriculating may be simple toponymics. Conservative university usage often preferred geographical over family names, and did not always clearly record its students' home dioceses;[76] and the *bursa* of many entrants who never took a degree is unknown. But when the focus is restricted to entrants from the Cologne area, then, allowing for the inevitably approximate nature of the data, it does seem possible that boys from Cologne with these surnames who matriculated from the 1490s on had a preference for the Laurentiana. Amongst those who definitely or probably entered the *bursa* the names Bruwer, Clarenbach, Eschwiler, Koch, van Lunschet, van St Truden, and Zons are well represented.[77] Of only three Clarenbachs

---

identical to van Kleve: *RHV*, 2143, 2144). Mayors: Bruwer (*RHV*, 529); van Kleve (*RHV*, 2144).

[75] All references to HAStK, 110 (Test.): Bruwer: 2/B 891 (1494); 1/B 901 (1550); Eschwiler: 3/E 276 (1481); 3/S 278 (1566); van Kleve: 3/C 447 (1518); 3/C 446 (1521); 3/L 216 (1539); Koch: 3/K 509–510, 519, 521–523, S/K 528, 3/K 529–531, 534, 2/K 535, 536, 3/K 538 (1484–1595); van Lunschet: 3/L 433 (1544); 3/L 434 (1571); 3/L 435 (1566); van Sent Truden: 3/T 148 (1508); 3/T 149 (1542); 3/T 150 (1518); van deme Sterne: 3/S 1084 (1400); 3/S 1087 (1509); Steynmetzer: 3/S 1074 (1564); 3/S 1075 (1579); van Zons: 3/Z 42–47, 3/Z 51–52, 3/Z 54 (1485–1598).

[76] Cf. Schwinges, *Deutsche Universitätsbesucher*, pp. 435–41 and fig. 42, pp. 436–38, on the difficulty of reliably attributing Cologne students to Cologne families.

[77] Bruwer: *Matrikel*, 448,56 (1500); 464,33 (1504); 505,11 (1515); probably also 573,13 (1532): he matriculated with a van St Truden (573,12), a definite Laurentiana entrant. Clarenbach: *Matrikel*, 478,3 (1508); 503,19 (1514). Eschwiler: *Matrikel*, 463,24 (1504), 478,23 (1508). Koch: *Matrikel*, 422,109 (1494). Van Ludenscheid: *Matrikel*, 494,111 (1512), 514,64 (1517); possibly 508,33 (1515; determined BA under Johannes de Busco, Laurentiana). De St Truden: *Matrikel*, Nachtrag, 1599 (1514), 508,46 (1515), 573,12, 16 (1532). Zons: *Matrikel*,

who matriculated at Cologne, two were at the Laurentiana.[78] Another good example are the Eschwilers, the family of Bela (Belchin), superior in 1511, and succeeded by her sister Sophie (Ffigin).[79] The surname is uncommon at the University: before 1559 there were only nine entrants with that name, one probably unconnected with Cologne.[80] Six (only two definitely from Cologne diocese) cannot be ascribed to any *bursa*;[81] but two were definitely at the Laurentiana,[82] making it the only *bursa* which Eschwilers are positively known to have attended. Focusing on boys matriculated from the 1490s on, when the Lämmchen had been founded and the connection with the Rincks and the Laurentiana was established, shows that two out of four Eschwilers were at the *bursa*.[83]

---

[78] 380,97 (1483): *bursa* not recorded, but he matriculated in a large block of Laurentiana entrants (*Matrikel*, 330,97–109: 98, 100, 102, 103, 105, 108, 109 are all definitely Laurentiana). Laurentiana: Gottschalk, 4.4.1508 (*Matrikel*, 478,3); Adolf, August 1514 (*Matrikel*, 503,19). Bursa unknown: Johann, 18.10.1486 (*Matrikel*, 392,13).

[79] Bela: HAStK, 241, U 3/5, 14.7.1508; HAStK, 295, 151, 2ʳ. Sophie: as superior in HAStK, 241, U 2/9 (1517).

[80] *Matrikel*, III, 'Alphabetisches Hauptregister', p. 355. Non-Cologne: *Matrikel*, 311,3, Nicholas de Wilss, a tutor accompanying Johann de Wilss (311,2), a canon of Trier, in 1466.

[81] Definitely from Cologne diocese: Gerhard, 1463, (*Matrikel*, 297,42); Peter, 1473 (*Matrikel*, 340,14). Diocese not given: Matthias, 1457 (*Matrikel*, 275,19); Servatius, 1482 (*Matrikel*, 375,53); Werner, 1492 (*Matrikel*, 414,135); Flammingus, 1500 (*Matrikel*, 447,16).

[82] *Matrikel*, 463, 24: Johannes Eschwijlre, matriculated 17.8.1504, determined BA under Johannes de Noerdingen, Laurentiana, 17 June 1505. *Matrikel*, 478, 23: Johannes Esswyler, Cologne diocese, matriculated 8 August 1508, determined BA under Johannes de Venlo, Laurentiana, 23 November 1508.

[83] Bursa unknown: *Matrikel*, 414,135, Werner (1492); 447,16, Flammingus (1500). Laurentiana: 463, 24, Johannes (1504); 478, 23, Johannes (1508).

These data must not be forced, but they certainly suggest that the Lämmchen was another institution which brought the Rincks and members of the Laurentiana together.

To be at the Laurentiana, then, was to be connected, at least to some extent, with the Rincks. And to be connected with the Rincks was to know a family whose links with humanist figures are amply documented. Johann (II), a friend and correspondent of Rudolph Agricola, also had links with such figures as Raimundus Mithridates, Johann Potken, Wimpheling, Brant, Glarean, Buschius and Petrus Ravennas.[84] Peter, a friend of Langen, Buschius and Petrus Ravennas, may have been instrumental in bringing Raimundus Mithridates to Cologne University; Johann (II)'s son Hermann (III) had been at several Italian universities.[85] Rincks were dedicatees of various humanist works.[86] Johann (III), with whom Schotten had the most immediate contact, corresponded with Erasmus in tones that suggest genuine warmth and mutual respect.[87] The

---

[84] Agricola, *Letters*, ed. by van der Laan and Akkermann, pp. 173, 203, 219, 341–42; Schmid, *Stifter*, p. 183; Meuthen, *Universität*, p. 209.

[85] Peter: Hegel, *St. Kolumba in Köln*, pp. 151–52; Irsigler, 'Peter Rinck', passim. Hermann: *Matrikel*, 467,55.

[86] E.g. Buschius, works dedicated to Johann (II) and Hermann (II): Schmid, *Stifter*, p. 183; Tewes, *Bursen*, p. 724. Langen, *Horae de Sancta Cruce* (1496) dedicated to Johann (II): Tewes, *Bursen*, p. 722; Agricola, *Letters*, ed. by van der Laan and Akkermann, pp. 341–42. Langen, *Rosarium uirginis beatissime [...] ad uirum egregium M. Petrum Rincum* (1493): Tewes, *Bursen*, p. 722; Schmid, *Stifter*, p. 64 and n. 13. *Dicta septem sapientium Greciae*, transl. by Mithridates, dedicated to Peter: Schmid, *Stifter*, p. 64 and n. 12; Mehl, 'Humanism in the Home Town of the "Obscure Men"', p. 9.

[87] Letters survive from 1530–1535: Erasmus, *Epistolae*, 2285, 2355, 2534, 2618 (Erasmus to Rinck), 3004 (Rinck to Erasmus); cf. 2277. 'Amice incomparabilis' (2285, l. 138); 'vir amicorum candidissime' (2618, l. 9); 'Erasme multis nominibus charissime' (3004, ll. 1–2). Cf. *CoE*, III, pp. 161–62.

Rincks were collectors of antiquities.[88] At least two had sizeable personal libraries: Peter's will left a 'remarkable number of books'; Schotten himself praised the library of Johann (II).[89]
No doubt it was Schotten's Laurentiana background that had brought him into contact with that powerful clan, since it is hard to see any other way in which Schotten, in 1527 the obscure young schoolmaster, a Hessian 'foreigner' in Cologne, without a secure university position, and perhaps even in the eyes of some senior dons something of a humanist maverick, could have managed to have the Rincks as 'patrons' in any sense of the word. The question, of course, is precisely what sense of the word did apply; and here again we come up against the dearth of detail in so many of the documents relating to Schotten. His dedication of the *Vita honesta* to Johann (III) Rinck, though fulsome, is sparse in terms of information. How intimate was his connection with the Rincks, or at least with Johann? Was he addressing a man whom he already knew well, and of whose patronage and benevolence he could be sure? Or was he making a much more tentative approach to a family to which his Laurentiana affiliation gave him a certain right of access, but with no certainty that the approach would work? In the midst of all this slightly hazy information, however, comes a brief shaft of light. As Schotten bids Johann farewell, he quite directly asks him for a job: 'If you have any position which needs to be filled, continue to regard me as one of

---

[88] Keussen, 'Die drei Reisen', I, pp. 65–66; II, p. 55.
[89] Peter: 'Ein mirckliche gezall van bücheren': HAStK, 110, 3/R 270 (5.5.1500); Kuske, *Quellen*, III, pp. 304–05 (no. 200); Irsigler, 'Peter Rinck', pp. 62–63; Werhahn, 'Die Bücher des Dr. Peter Rinck', passim; Schmid, *Stifter*, pp. 85–89; Quarg, '*Ganz Köln steckt voller Bücherschätze*' [...]', pp. 105–08. Johann (II): 'Bibliotheca literaria [...] ex omni sententiarum genere, libris collectis & coemptis', Schotten, *Vita honesta*, sig. Aiii^v–Aiv^r); Schmid, *Stifter*, p. 183 and n. 171.

your friends, as you have begun to do'.⁹⁰ This request echoes, and corroborates, the other evidence that Schotten was moving back from school to university at exactly this time, 1527 (see pp. 46–47). Either he had never thought of schoolteaching as a permanent career, or else no longer found it satisfactory. The appeal also raises the possibility that Schotten might actually have preferred employment with Johann Rinck to a return to the University; but in the event no offer seems to have been forthcoming.

In the same dedication, Schotten mentions that Johann's late father Johann (II) had been planning the rebuilding of a Latin school, 'gymnasium quoddam literarium' (sig. Aiii^v); he had collected books from family members, and would have completed the project at his own expense had not death intervened (in May 1516).⁹¹ Where was this school? Did it have any connection with Schotten's schoolteaching activity? None of these questions is answered, either by the dedication or by anything else we know of Schotten or the Rincks.

The short dedication of the *Ludus imperatorius* to Hermann (II) Rinck is even sparser than that to Johann, and even less specific about Hermann. The second dedication to a Rinck in six months suggests that the family were not unhappy to have Schotten dedicate his work to them, and in some sense to be his 'patrons' – but it is unclear exactly what that meant.

---

90   'Vale uir humanissime, et apud te si quis locus uacat in album tuorum amicorum ut coepisti, me numera', Schotten, *Vita honesta*, sig. Av^r.
91   'Literarum amator fuit, ideo gimnasio construendo insumere argentum uoluit, ideo supellectilem librorum intra penates colligit'; 'Deinde ad [...] reficiendum aere suo subuenisset, nisi auster floribus inmissus fuisset', ibid., sig. Aiii^v.

The Antonite monastery

Only a step away from the Rinck family home, Königstein on the Schildergasse, was another religious institution which proves to play an important part in Schotten's networks of friendship and possibly patronage; the house of the Antonite order.

In colloquy 58, 'De suprema cena Christi cum discipulis et die Parasceves', Matthias plans to go to the Maundy Thursday *mandatum* at a church called 'St Anthony's' (l. 25). This demonstrably refers to the Cologne Antonite house. The superior is called the preceptor: 'uulgus Praeceptorem appellat' (l. 40) which was the usual style in the Antonites, as in other hospitaller orders.[92]

The Antonites originated in the eleventh century as a lay brotherhood caring for sick pilgrims to the reputed relics of St Anthony, the third-to-fourth-century Egyptian hermit, in a village now called Saint-Antoine-l'Abbaye near Romans in France. Its renown spread rapidly, and it had soon extended to other countries: by the end of the twelfth century there were houses in Germany. In 1232 the loosely organized brotherhood accepted stricter statutes, becoming in 1247 an independent monastic, not lay, order under the Augustinian rule.[93]

---

[92] E.g. the Teutonic Knights and the Knights Hospitallers of St John of Jerusalem: Mischlewski, 'Antoniter', pp. 832–33; id., 'Expansion', p. 206.

[93] Michlewski, 'Antoniter'; see also id., 'Der Antoniterorden in Deutschland'; id., 'Die Antoniter und ihr Haus in Köln'; id., 'Expansion et structures de l'ordre hospitalier de Saint-Antoine-en-Viennois'; id., 'Das Antoniusfeuer in Mittelalter und früher Neuzeit'; id., 'Beobachtungen zur Erwerbspolitik ...'; id., *Grundzüge der Geschichte des Antoniterordens*; id., 'Soziale Aspekte der spätmittelalterlichen Antoniusverehrung'. K. Frank, 'Antonianer. VII. Hospitäler', *LThK³*, I, col. 783.

The Antonites specialized in the treatment of 'St Anthony's fire', properly ergotism, a tissue-wasting disease caused by a fungal infection of rye, but also applied to other diseases with similar effects, such as erysipelas and gangrene.[94] Much of the order's income came from the yearly collections which it had papal authorization to make over wide geographical areas, the 'viagia' or 'Quest'.[95] Another distinctive source of revenue were the 'St Anthony's pigs' which were donated to the order: wearing a bell and marked with a tau cross, they had the right to roam in the cities, were fed on scraps by all and sundry, and their meat, or its price, went to the Antonites.[96] St Anthony is nearly always depicted with a pig in attendance.[97]

Anthony was one of the most popular saints of the later Middle Ages: of the many visual depictions, perhaps a devotional woodcut by Hans Weiditz (*ca.* 1522) most effectively communicates the fatherly care which the age associated with the saint;[98] though Anthony was sometimes imagined as vindictively sending 'St Anthony's fire' as a punishment.[99] The Cologne house was founded in 1298 from Rossdorf near Hanau, in the convent of the

---

[94] Mischlewski, 'Antoniter', p. 830; id., 'Die Antoniter und ihr Haus in Köln', pp. 25–26; id., 'Antoniusfeuer', esp. pp. 260–62; id., *Grundzüge*, pp. 349–51; Bauer, *Das Antoniusfeuer in Kunst und Medizin*, passim.
[95] Mischlewski, *Grundzüge*, pp. 35–36; id., 'Antoniter', p. 832; id., 'Erwerbspolitik', p. 189.
[96] Michlewski, 'Antoniter', p. 832; id., 'Soziale Aspekte', pp. 144–45; id., *Grundzüge*, pp. 36–38, citing further literature.
[97] Chaumartin, 'Le compagnon de Saint-Antoine', passim; *LCI*, V, col. 207.
[98] Geisberg, G. 1504; see illustration on p. 150. Other woodcuts include Geisberg, G. 593, *Temptation of St Anthony*; Geisberg, G. 702, Dürer, *Sts Anthony and Paul, ca.* 1504.
[99] E.g. Mischlewski, 'Soziale Aspekte', pp. 31–32 and ns 79 and 80, citing examples and literature. Cf. W. Kuhn, 'Gestalt und antike Vorbilder des Antonius Eremita', *Psyche*, 2 (1948), 71–96.

dissolved 'Sackbrüder' on the present-day Antoniterstraße. In a few decades it had expanded northwards onto the Schildergasse, where its late-fourteenth-century Gothic church still stands.[100] Though never very numerous in Cologne, the order prospered there, as elsewhere in Germany.[101] The 'Quest' was lucrative. Important bequests came from laypeople: many became pensioners of the Antonites, making over their houses in return for board and lodging for life.[102] At its height the Cologne house was one of the richest in Germany.[103] Apart from the Antonite church itself, the main focus of the cult of St Anthony in Cologne was St Kunibert, which since 1222 had owned a relic of the saint's beard.[104] The other Cologne churches also housed many paintings and sculptures of the saint.[105]

The colloquy is significant as a topical reference, and as the sole surviving description of the form of the *Man-*

---

[100] R. Janin, 'Antoniusorden (6)', *LThK²*, I, cols 676–77; *GEK*, II/1, pp. 577–78; *Topogr*, I, pp. 230b–31a and Tafel VII; *KiM*, p. 149; Winheim, *Sacrarium Agrippinae*, pp. 123–27; Crusenius, *Monasticon Augustinianum*, pp. 90, 142; von Mering and Reischert, *Die Bischöfe und Erzbischöfe von Köln*, I, pp. 317–27; Stohlmann, 'Zum Lobe Kölns', p. 52.

[101] *GEK*, II/1, pp. 577–78 suggests that there were never more than about fifteen. Of 3435 male religious documented by Militzer, *Kölner Geistliche*, I, esp. p. 11, Tabelle 1, only twenty-two are Antonites.

[102] 'Kostgenger, provener oder porcionarien [...] zu sant Anthonio': *BW*, V, pp. 221–22. Half the inmates of the Antonite hospital in Rossdorf may have been pensioners: Mischlewski, 'Antoniter', p. 835.

[103] Mischlewski, 'Die Antoniter und ihr Haus in Köln', p. 26: the house had forty-two farms, some as far away as Brabant.

[104] Büttner, 'Antonius in Köln', pp. 272–74: the magnificent bust reliquary, ibid., ill. 2, p. 273. Other St Anthony relics in St Kunibert: ibid., pp. 274–79.

[105] Büttner, 'Antonius in Köln', passim. Particularly important is Meister der Heiligen Sippe, *Legend of St Anthony*, originally Cologne, Antonite church, now Munich, Alte Pinakothek, Inv. No. WAF 452 (Büttner, p. 269 and ill. 1, p. 270 ; *LCI*, V, cols 213–14).

datum in this house. But the most interesting detail is Matthias's description of the superior of the house as 'uere litteratorum Maecenas' (l. 41). Such enthusiastic approval of a monk is quite untypical even of the generally orthodox *Confabulationes*.

The eulogized superior can be identified. Documents relating to the Cologne Antonite house show that the preceptor in 1525 was one Matthias Wagener (also spelt Wagner, Wegener, Wener, Wehener, etc.): his period of office dates from August 1519 to at least March, and at latest September 1526.[106] Though almost nothing is known of Wagener, one fact corroborates the colloquy's verdict on him as a literary patron: it was to him that Johannes Phrissemius, one of the leading and most militant humanists then at Cologne University, dedicated his pioneering commented 1523 edition of Rodolphus Agricola's *De inventione dialectica*.[107] The dedication, reprinted in over thirty subsequent editions, is a conventional humanist *laudatio* which tells us nothing concrete about Wagener's character or achievements. However, the very fact that Phrissemius, who might have offered his influential edition of this seminal dialectic work to any one of his many humanist colleagues, chose a monk is remarkable; doubly so because he had suffered attacks on his religious orthodoxy from the monastic-scholastic faction in Co-

---

[106] HAStK, 295, 11e, fol. 1r: a list of preceptors. HAStK, 202 (Antoniter) contains several documents signed by or for Wagener: U 2/346 (11 August 1519) to U 1/356 (5 March 1526) inclusive. U 3/358 (3 October 1526) is the first signed by Gerhard Kerckerinck, Wagener's successor. See details in the bibliography.

[107] *Rodolphi Agricolae Phrisii de Inventione dialectica libri tres, cum scholiis Ioannis Matthaei Phrissemii* (Cologne: Hero Alopecius, 1523), sig. *1ᵛ–*2ᵛ; Krafft, 'Mittheilungen aus der niederrheinischen Reformationsgeschichte', p. 218; Macardle, 'Matthias Wagener and Traces of Antonite Humanism in Cologne'.

logne.[108] Wagener must have been at the very least favourably disposed to humanism, possibly even an active humanist himself. Yet Agricola scholars have failed to recognize that Wagener was a monk, some assuming that 'praeceptor' meant 'schoolmaster'.[109]

Nor was Wagener uncharacteristic of the Antonite order as a whole. Forty Antonites matriculated at Cologne University between 1422 and 1548, and nine of the preceptor's *familia* who for the most part were not monks.[110] This remarkably high number of matriculations for such a small house also reveals a very distinctive orientation of studies. Whilst other orders in Cologne organized their own Arts teaching, and matriculated predominantly in the Theological Faculty, only four Antonites matriculated in Theology, against twenty-three in Civil or Canon Law and seventeen in Arts (in five cases the faculty is unknown). This is an academic profile quite different from that of other monastic orders. Schwinges wrongly includes the Antonites amongst the monks and friars, whereas their distinctly uncloistered pattern of studies is in fact closer to that of secular clerics and canons regular.[111] The bias towards Law is typical of an order which supplied the Paris Canon Law Faculty with several emi-

---

[108] *CoE*, III, p. 79; Meuthen, *Universität*, pp. 245–46.
[109] Erasmus, *Epistolae*, 1978, n. 9: 'Matthias Wagener, schoolmaster of St Antony's church'; Ong, *Ramus and Talon Inventory*, p. 539: 'the Cologne teacher, Matthias Wagener'; no comment on Wagener in Huisman, *Rudolph Agricola*, no. 14, or in Agricola, *De inventione dialectica*, ed. by Mundt.
[110] Keussen's indexes to the *Matrikel* ('Register der Orden: Antoniter', *Matrikel*, III, p. 1094, and 'Alphabetisches Hauptregister: Köln, S. Antonius', III, p. 624, are incomplete. These figures are derived from an independent reading of the *Matrikel*.
[111] Schwinges, *Deutsche Universitätsbesucher*, pp. 482–83. Antonites are such a small group that Schwinges's sampling methods have misrepresented them.

nent teachers and numerous students during the first half of the fifteenth century.[112]

The Antonites' relationship with the University seems to have been particularly cordial. Their matriculation fee was waived or reduced much more frequently than in the case of other monastic or hospitaller orders. Nineteen such remissions – almost 40% of all matriculations – are recorded in the Matricula, usually in favour of preceptors, or of their relatives or protégés, most of whom were not monks.[113] A few, however, were conceded to ordinary monks of the order.[114]

Two other facts about the Cologne Antonites emerge from the University records and other documents: that the order apparently had a history of humanist interests; and that it had an association with the Bursa Laurentiana. A testimony to early humanist taste in Cologne is a MS codex of 1444 containing Petrarch's *Bucolicum carmen* and *Epistola ad Italiam* and Lactantius's *De ave phoenice*, copied in Cologne for Aymo de Poypone, whose relative Antonius de Poypone was Antonite preceptor in the city at the time (1439–1458).[115] Aymo entered the Cologne Arts Faculty in June 1439 together with his brother Johannes, who definitely studied at the Bursa Laurentiana,

---

[112] Mischlewski, *Grundzüge*, pp. 365–76: Beilage IX. 'Die Antoniter an der Pariser Dekretisten-Fakultät'.
[113] Preceptors: *Matrikel*, 298,30, Johannes Alhardi, 1463; 333,35, Heinrich Stauffenbergh, 1472; 404,58, Wilhelm Ingynberti, 1489; 437,27, Wenzeslaus Ulner, 1498. Preceptor's *familia*: *Matrikel*, 135,29, Mathias Wambier, 1422; 201,41, Johannes de Poypone, 1439; 302,34, Wilhelm de Wadenhau, 1464; 404,88, Colinus Parvi, 1489; 445,30, Jaspar Rosbach, 1500; 455,3, Gerhard Kerckerinck, 1502; 457,44, Petrus Maisseck, 1503; 478,95, Nicholas Airheyen, 1508; 638,12, Rutger Stoirbrinck, 1548.
[114] Monks: *Matrikel*, 201,40 (1439); 230,22, 23 (1446); 404,11 (1489); 437,28 (1498).
[115] HAStK, W. Kf. 348; Sottili, 'Codici del Petrarca nella Germania occidentale', pp. 409–10; cf. Meuthen, *Universität*, p. 205.

and taught there from 1451.¹¹⁶ Aymo, who succeeded Antonius as preceptor in 1459, will have studied at the same *bursa*.¹¹⁷

Goswin de Orsoy, who matriculated in Arts in September 1467, became Antonite preceptor in Lichtenberg and in 1502 the first Chancellor of the new University of Wittenberg. At this university, where humanist methods were welcomed early and enthusiastically by German standards, Goswin was in the company of humanists such as Martin Polich von Mellerstadt, Petrus Ravennas, Georgius Sibutus, and pre-eminently Hermann Buschius.¹¹⁸ Several had connections with Cologne, and Buschius is linked specifically with the Cologne Antonites. When staying in Cologne in early 1518 to see his *Vallum humanitatis* through the press he dined almost daily with Wenzeslaus Ulner de Arhelgin, who preceded Wagener as preceptor from 1497 to 1519.¹¹⁹ Some Antonites at least were evidently very different from the monks and scholastics whom Buschius's associates had satirized in the *Epistolae obscurorum virorum*.

Since only a few Antonites matriculated in Arts, and even fewer took degrees, it is not possible to link the order firmly with a *bursa*. It is interesting, however, that all five men connected with the house who can be assigned

---

[116] Aymo: *Matrikel*, 201,40; Johannes: *Matrikel*, 201,41 (incepted MA 1442, LicTh 1451; other University offices).

[117] *Regesten*, 1181.3; cf. Hayn, 'Aus den Annaten-Registern der Päpste Eugen IV., Pius II., Paul II. und Sixtus IV', p. 142, no. 366; p. 144, no. 381.

[118] *Matrikel*, 314,32. Meuthen, *Universität*, p. 204; Bauch, *Geschichte des Leipziger Frühhumanismus*, pp. 162, 166; *Album Academiae Vitebergensis*, ed. by Foerstemann, pp. 1–2; Friedensburg, *Geschichte der Universität Wittenberg*, p. 20 (Orsoy); p. 10 (Mellerstadt); pp. 70–71 (Sibutus); pp. 69–70 (Buschius); Meuthen, *Universität*, p. 215.

[119] *Matrikel*, 437,27. Ulner is shown as donor in the painting formerly in the Antonite church, now Munich, Alte Pinakothek, Inv. no. WAF 452: see n. 105.

to a *bursa* were at the Laurentiana.[120] In some cases this may be more of a family connection: it is not surprising that Gerhard Kerckerinck of Münster, a relative of Ulner's, matriculated at the Laurentiana in 1502, since his ancestor Theodoricus Kerckering was the (legendary) founder of that *bursa*, and three other family members went there too.[121] Gerhard succeeded Wagener as preceptor (1526–1557) and in turn sent two of his own *familia*, neither of them monks, to the Laurentiana.[122] Whether Kerckerinck was following a family tradition or an Antonite one (or both) is impossible to say: though in either case it does mean that in the first half of the sixteenth century there were very concrete personal cordial relations between the Antonite house and the Laurentiana. Given that Aymo and Johannes de Poypone were at the Laurentiana early in the fifteenth century, and that there is no positive evidence of a link with any other *bursa*, it certainly looks as though the Laurentiana was that of the Antonite house as a whole.

Other data suggest close Antonite–Laurentiana relations. In February 1510 Wenzeslaus Ulner entertained Wilhelm, son of Count Philipp of Waldeck, who was studying at the Laurentiana for a year, to dinner. There was no obvious connection between the two men. Admittedly, the generally rich Antonite houses did enjoy cordial relations with the nobility,[123] but in this case the

---

[120] *Matrikel*, 201,40 and 41; 455,3; 552,12; 638,12.
[121] Gerhard: *Matrikel*, 455,3 (matriculated 27 June 1502); Theodoricus: *Matrikel*, I, 16. Johann: *Matrikel*, 497,14 (1512); Christoph: 650,172 (1551); Johann: 654,5 (1552).
[122] *Matrikel*, 552,12 : Kerckerinck's nephew Johannes Schulen, November 1526; DDecr; 1548 University Rector; 1533–60 Cathedral canon and Cantor; d. 1560; *Alte Un.*, p. 399. *Matrikel*, 638,12: Kerckerinck's relative Rutger Stoirbrinck, May 1548.
[123] Michlewski, 'Antoniter', pp. 836–37, records numerous aristocratic guests entertained in the Antonite houses at Alzey and Frankfurt. Id., 'Soziale Aspekte', pp. 145–49, notes keen aristocratic involvement with the cult of St Anthony in the late

link could very well have been personal. It is likely that the Laurentiana was the *bursa* favoured by the ruling house of Waldeck (see pp. 199–201). Ulner's nephew Nicholas de Airheyen entered the Arts Faculty in 1508; and though his *bursa* is not recorded his fee was remitted by the rector, Arnold Luyde von Tongeren, the eminent Laurentiana don.[124] This probably means that Nicholas was at the Laurentiana, and that Ulner invited the young nobleman as a near-contemporary *bursa* mate of his nephew.

All the evidence, then, suggests particularly cordial relations between the Antonites and the Laurentiana: the complimentary reference to Ulner's successor Wagener, made by Schotten the Laurentiana graduate, may well be another testimony to these relations. In addition, it must stand beside Phrissemius's dedication of *De inventione dialectica* to Wagener and the other more indirect evidence as an indication that the Cologne Antonites were sympathetic to, perhaps even actively engaged in, humanism.

Information on the religious orders' involvement in humanism is still scanty, particularly in Cologne, where nothing beyond the Carthusians' limited contributions has been recorded, and the Antonites effectively go unmentioned.[125] Even these few details on the Cologne Antonites, therefore, are a helpful pointer to the order's intellectual history. But just as importantly, the colloquy

---

Middle Ages, including the formation of exclusively aristocratic guilds.

[124] *Matrikel*, 478,95: 'Nyc. Airheyen, d. Mog., nepos d. preceptoris s. Anthonii ex sorore; [...] n[on] recepi.' (24 June 1508).

[125] Kristeller, 'The Contribution of Religious Orders to Renaissance Thought and Learning'; Meuthen, *Universität*, pp. 216–17; Chaix, *Réforme et contre-réforme catholiques*. Mischlewski, 'Die Antoniter und ihr Haus in Köln', p. 26, merely cites Buschius's frequenting of the Cologne house as an indication that 'zu Anfang des 16. Jahrhunderts dringen humanistische Gedanken ein'.

helps to situate Schotten. The boy Matthias's judgement on Wagener is also Schotten's tribute to a man who seems to have been a personal acquaintance and may have been a fellow humanist. The fact that Wagener's first name is given to the boy who praises him is part of the literary gesture: the semi-fictive world of the *Confabulationes* connects with the real world as Schotten writes himself into the humanist milieu of 1520s Cologne.

The Antonite church was home to a number of *Bruderschaften*, lay guilds or confraternities joined by bonds of prayer and mutual charity, which usually supported some specific aspect of the church's worship. Militzer's systematic study of the *Bruderschaften* of Cologne reveals the names of many citizens associated with the guilds at St Anthony's.[126] The guild records confirm the connection between the Antonite house and the Bursa Laurentiana. In the guild of Our Lady and St Anthony, re-founded in 1539,[127] are listed ten identifiable university men. Four are linked with the Laurentiana.[128]

And as always where there is a Laurentiana connection, one finds the Rincks. They appear time and again as members, often as office-holders. Johann (II), Hermann (II) and Conrad (II) were all masters of the 'Bruderschaft von den drei Kertzen' ('Guild of the three candles'), and Hermann (II) was an official of the original guild of Our

---

[126] Militzer, *Laienbruderschaften*, I, pp. 51–109 (five different guilds).

[127] Ibid., I, pp. 94–102; Mischlewski, 'Die Antoniter und ihr Haus in Köln', p. 30: 'Bruderschaft Beatae Virginis Mariae et S. Anthonii' united in 1539 from three former guilds.

[128] Peter Steinwich: *Matrikel*, 626,109 (matriculated 1546; LicLeg 1558; later DLeg; 1558–85 Prof. of Law; 1571 Dean of Law; d. 1585): Militzer, *Laienbruderschaften*, I, p. 102. Paulus Wylich: *Matrikel*, 470,133 (matriculated 1506; LicA 1509); Militzer, *Laienbruderschaften*, I, p. 95. Johann Schulen: Militzer, *Laienbruderschaften*, I, p. 95; a relative of Gerhard Kerckerinck: see n. 122. Bernhard Kerckering: *Matrikel*, 494,44 (matriculated 1512); Militzer, *Laienbruderschaften*, I, p. 100.

Lady and St Anthony.[129] In 1539, when it was reconstituted as one united guild, Adolf Rinck was one of the few remaining original members; the new body included Hermann (II), Peter and his wife, and Hermann (III).[130] The intensive engagement of the Rincks in the Antonite guilds suggests a connection with that house which should be added to the better-documented links with St Kolumba and the Lämmchen: for all the family's involvement with St Kolumba, there is no evidence of Rinck membership in any of the five guilds there, of which extensive records survive.[131]

Once again, it is important not to try to extract from such data as these more than they can deliver. But the evidence certainly suggests two things about the Antonite house. Firstly, that it was an as yet unrecognized niche of humanist activity in Cologne. Second, that it was another, also unrecognized, part of the Laurentiana Albertist – St Kolumba – Rinck network which was clearly so significant for Schotten; though as with the Rincks, the precise kind of support which Wagener and the Antonites offered Schotten remains uncertain.

---

[129] Drei Kertzen: Johann (1499, 1511): Militzer, *Laienbruderschaften*, I, pp. 52, 53, 54. Hermann (1503), Conrad (1504): ibid., p. 53. Our Lady and St Anthony: Hermann (1499, 1501): ibid., pp. 72, 76, 77.

[130] Adolf: Militzer, *Laienbruderschaften*, I, p. 90. Hermann (II), etc.: ibid., pp. 95, 96. (From HAStK, 295 (GA), 11a, a nineteenth-century copy of the lost HAStK, 295 (GA), 11, the 'Bruderschaftsbuch' of the new guild).

[131] Records from the later fifteenth and earlier sixteenth century: Militzer, *Laienbruderschaften*, II, pp. 785–96, nos 56–60.

The Starckenberg family

The Antonite guild provides an interesting connection with another of Schotten's patrons. Among the members in 1539 was one Johann Starckenberg.[132] It was to his son Gisbert that Schotten dedicated the *Confabulationes*.[133] In the dedication, much of Schotten's attention focuses on Johann, 'patris tui, uiri prudentissimi, mihique amicissimi' [...] 'uirtutum uerum domicilium' (ll. 13–14, 20). He is a Cologne councillor 'prudentia nulli secundus' (l. 21) who has made every effort and sacrifice, even to the extent of living as a widower without taking another wife, in order to set his children up in life.[134]

Amongst Johann's children Schotten mentions Gisbert's two brothers, Johannes and Matthias, and unidentified sisters (ll. 14–15, 23–24). Schotten's connection with the Starckenbergs continued at least for a few years, for in August 1527 he dedicated his *Instructio prima puerorum* to Gisbert's youngest brother Matthias, who at that time was also his pupil.[135]

Von der Ketten's genealogical survey does not treat the Starckenbergs in their own right, but does record their fifteenth- and sixteenth-century marriage alliances with the important Cologne families of Gropper, Imhoff, and Lublar (or Liblar).[136] The Starckenbergs, long settled

---

[132] Militzer, *Laienbruderschaften*, I, p. 94 ('Johan Starckenburch').

[133] Schotten, *Confabulationes* (Cologne: Quentel, 1526), sig. A2^r; Schotten, *Confabulationes*, ed. by Macardle, 'Et genere et moribus adolescenti ingenuo Gisberto Sterckenberg [...]'.

[134] '[...] omni conatu, omne mouendo saxum, etiam et caelibem ducendo uitam, id unicum agit, quo te tuosque fratres et sorores ditet, locuplet, uobis ut congerat reliquae uitae commeatum', Ibid., ll. 21–24. No Starckenberg wills mention Johann (II) living unmarried.

[135] Schotten, *Instructio prima puerorum [...] per colloquia mutua* (Cologne: P. Quentel, 1527), sig. A3^v. See below.

[136] *Slg. Ketten*, II, p. 331 (Gropper); III, p. 24 (Imhoff); III, p. 409

in Cologne, had been affluent and influential since the late fourteenth century.[137] A Johann Starckenberg wealthy enough to lend the city sixty Gulden in 1513 must either have been Gisbert's father Johann (II) or his grandfather Johann the Elder (d. 1515).[138] Starckenbergs were prominent on the city council in the later fourteenth century, and again from the middle of the fifteenth.[139] By far the most active was Gisbert's father Johann (II), who served from 1515 till 1540 and figures over 300 times in the council records.[140] Four wills of 1483, 1514, 1515 and 1553 give glimpses of the Starckenbergs' fortunes and connections in Schotten's time.[141] Johann Starckenberg

---

(Liblar).

[137] Knipping, *Die Kölner Stadtrechnungen des Mittelalters*: Johannes, canon of St Mariengraden, and Hadewigis, pensioners of the city of Cologne, 1371–1381: I, p. 226; Heinrich, 1376, 1392: II, p. 238, I, p. 62; Johannes, *Ratsherr*, 1370-1390s: I, p. 15– II, p. 21, and frequently; son of Johannes, 1374: II, pp. 128, 158. Militzer, *Die vermögenden Kölner 1417–1418*, p. 189: Herbord, Schöffe of the Niederich district, 1417; ibid., p. 231: Johann, member of the Gaffel Gürtelmacher, early fifteenth century.

[138] Kellenbenz, 'Die wohlhabenden Kölner Bürger um 1515', p. 278 (original: HAStK, 30 (V+V), 74, fols 127ʳ–33ᵛ).

[139] *RHV*, 3374; Herborn, *Die politische Führungsschicht*, pp. 493, 597; Knipping, *Die Kölner Stadtrechnungen des Mittelalters*, I, p. 15 (1370). *BRStK*, I, p. 625 (1382) mentions Johann (deceased) and his son Heinrich. Heinrich (1455–1458): *RHV*, 3373; *BRStK*, I, p. 265 (1455, 31). Johann (I) (1474–1511): *RHV*, 3375; *BRStK*, I, p. 718 (1488, 5); I, p. 752 (1491, 2); I, p. 837 (1503, 23); I, p. 862 (1506, 11). Von Loesch, *Die Kölner Zunfturkunden*, II, pp. 381–82; cf. *BRStK*, I, p. 748 (1490, 34; Johann Starckenberg not named).

[140] *RHV*, 3376; *Matrikel*, 528,69. *BRStK*, VI, p. 185, index: mentioned approximately 330 times between 3.10.1515 (*BRStK*, II, p. 266: 1515, 428) and 17.11.1540 (ibid., IV, p. 706: 1540, 424). The *BRStK* index (VI, p. 185), lists four references which are probably to Johann Starckenberg (I) under Johann Starckenberg (II): 1513, 26, 523 and 1042; 1514, 163.

[141] HAStK, 110 (Test.), 3/S 1014 (Johann the Elder, 1483); 3/S 1015 (Johann the Elder, 1514), summary in Kuske, *Quellen*,

the Elder (d. 1515) and his wife Gertrud (Druitgin) had at least four children: Johann, Jaspar, Heinrich and Gertraud.[142] The eldest, Johann (II), had reached majority by the time of the 1483 will; Jaspar and Heinrich were still minors.[143] Johann (II) fathered at least three children: yet another Johann, and Gisbert and Matthias, later Schotten's pupils, who, then probably less than seven years old, were each left six silver spoons by their uncle Heinrich in 1515.[144]

In the late fifteenth century the family lived in the parish of St Alban.[145] By 1515, their estate was already considerable.[146] By the time Schotten's pupil Gisbert (d. 1583) made his own will in 1553, they had moved to the Glockengasse in the parish of St Kolumba, and so probably up the social scale;[147] they had left the parish, however, before 1589.[148] The Starckenberg wills also reveal the kinship networks the family had developed. Heinrich's sister Gertraud had married the widowed Johann von Lublar, from one of the most important families in Cologne civic

---

III, pp. 333–34; 3/S 1013 (Heinrich, 1515), summary in Kuske, *Quellen*, III, pp. 332–33; 3/S 1012 (Gisbert, 12.7.1553).

[142] HAStK, 110, 3/S 1014 and 3/S 1015.
[143] HAStK, 110, 3/S 1014.
[144] HAStK, 110, 3/S 1013: 'Seess silueren leffele mit kurtzen steelen'.
[145] At the Haus zum (Großen) Schauenberg, Martinsstraße: HAStK, 110, 3/S 1013, 3/S 1014, 3/S 1015. Schauenberg: *Topogr.*, I, p. 166b, 2, 3.
[146] Heinrich owned six houses in Cologne and a farm near Hülchrath (HAStK, 110, 3/S 1013).
[147] HAStK, 110, 3/S 1012 (also stipulating burial in St Kolumba). Glockengasse: *Topogr.*, I, p. 317a, 1–8, esp. 2. On the social cachet of St Kolumba, see Greving, *Steuerlisten des Kirchspiels St. Kolumba in Köln*, and Herborn, 'Sozialtopographie des Kölner Kirchspiels St. Kolumba', cited in Hegel, *St. Kolumba in Köln*, pp. 92–100; Tewes, *Bursen*, p. 439.
[148] Not included in the 1589 tax census: Greving, *Steuerlisten des Kirchspiels St. Kolumba in Köln*, pp. 19–21, 27–31.

life.¹⁴⁹ Heinrich left legacies to two of his Lublar nephews Heinrich and Johann.¹⁵⁰

The Starckenbergs were pillars of civic life, but not of learning or the University: of the Cologne family only Gisbert and Johann, and a Gottfried who matriculated in 1550 studied there.¹⁵¹ Gottfried's relationship to the family is unknown. His likely birthdate of 1536 or earlier would put him in the generation below Gisbert; he could perhaps be a nephew of Gisbert's.

There are definite signs of a Starckenberg affinity with the Bursa Laurentiana. The *bursa* of the brothers Johann and Gisbert, minors on matriculation in December 1520, is not recorded; but the matriculating rector, who described them as 'sons of the provident Johann Starckenberg', was Johannes Schudherinck de Nussia, a jurist and ecclesiastic who later endowed a free place at the Laurentiana; so that *bursa* is a very likely choice.¹⁵²

---

149 Between 1483 and 1617, there were only fourteen years (1501–1509 and 1511–1515) without a Lublar on the council (*RHV*, 2430–38).
150 HAStK, 110, 3/S 1013. Lublar family (also Liblaer, Lubeer): *Slg. Ketten*, III, pp. 408–09; p. 409 records the marriage of Johann von Lublar to an unnamed female Starckenberg. The name Gertraud, and the complex history of the Lublar progeny, emerges in a court case of 1624: HAStK, 310 (Reichskammergericht Köln), H 41. Note also a lengthy lawsuit of some kind between Johann (II) Starckenberg and Melchior and Jaspar Lublar in 1524: *BRStK*, III, p. 145 (1524, 694, 19.8.1524); appeal by Gisbert: *BRStK*, V, p. 460 (1546, 819).
151 *Matrikel*, 528,69 (Johann); 528,70 (Gisbert); 645,54 (Gottfried). Three others are probably not from the Cologne family: *Matrikel*, 402,2: Johann Starckenberg, Trier diocese (matriculated 1489); 517,18: 'Johannes Lybbelener iunior, alias Sterckenberch' (1518); 601,5: 'Antonius Raesselt alias Starckenberch' (1539).
152 *Matrikel*, 528,69, 70: 'Joh. et Gisb. Starckenberch de Colonia, fratres, minorennes, filii providi Johannis Starckenberch, civis Col.'. Schudherinck: *Matrikel*, 445,4 (matriculated 1500). Will of 1535: *Regesten*, 3053; Bianco, I,2, pp. 870–74; Tewes, *Bursen*, pp. 274–75.

Later events point in the same direction: one of the witnesses of Gisbert's will, Gerhard van Arwiler, was a Laurentiana graduate, and Gottfried Starckenberg studied there too.[153] The Laurentiana connection would have been of a piece with the Starckenbergs' residence in the parish of St Kolumba. Their move there cannot be dated more precisely than between 1515 and 1553, but if Johann and Gisbert matriculated at the Laurentiana in 1520 it is possible that the family had moved to St Kolumba not long after Heinrich's death in 1515, though their connection with the *bursa* could of course have predated their coming to the parish.

In this, the dedication in his first major work, Schotten was cultivating a burgher family, admittedly a step or two down the hierarchy from the Rincks, but nonetheless one with wealth and influence, and almost certainly involved with the same networks as the Rincks. He was not addressing humanist colleagues or equals, or a family known for its intellectual interests, but people who would be in a position to help him financially. We know nothing of the success of this strategy; but it was an entirely understandable one for a presumably impecunious young scholar, and in the same mould as the approach two years later to Johann Rinck.

The dedications to the Starckenbergs tell us something about Schotten's tactics, and a little about the chronology of his career. Gisbert and his older brother Johann matriculated in Arts on 10 December 1520, as minors.[154] Even if Gisbert was not far short of the minimum age of fourteen, he cannot have been born before 1507. Since he

---

[153] Arwiler: *Matrikel*, 617,40: matriculated 2 August 1543; LicA 1545. Starckenberg: *Matrikel*, 645,54 (listed as Gottfried Linner: see p. 198-99).

[154] *Matrikel*, 528,69, 70: 'Joh. et Gisb. Starckenberch de Colonia, fratres, minorennes, [...] pro quibus ipse pater i[uravit] et promisit, ut dum ad etatem legitimam pervenerint, per se ipsos iurabunt.'

died in 1583, he may well have been born some years later, and have been considerably underage at matriculation, which would certainly have been in the Cologne tradition. In December 1520, Schotten, perhaps not so many years older than Gisbert, was still at the Laurentiana. With his MA behind him, he was working towards membership of the Arts Faculty *consilium*, which involved teaching in Arts, and he may already have begun his studies in Theology (see pp. 22, 47). Since Gisbert and Johann were probably at the Laurentiana, Schotten may even have taught them there for a while. But the dedication to Gisbert in February 1525 is over four years after Gisbert's matriculation, and almost certainly after Schotten left the Laurentiana, probably in 1522 or 1523 (see p. 47). Not even dim students took that long to reach the BA; yet in 1525 Gisbert was still working at a 'trivial', pre-university level in Latin. Schotten describes the *Confabulationes* as a systematic collection of colloquies which he had authored for the use of his pupils, including Gisbert:

> Latinas locutiones, quas hactenus satis abunde tibi tuisque commilitonibus litterariis dictaui, in unum hunc confabulationum libellum congessi.[155]

The sequence of events which these details suggest is this: Gisbert's time at the Laurentiana was unsuccessful, either because he was too young or too incompetent, or because the Laurentiana teaching was unsatisfactory; the boy left after an unknown period and transferred to Schotten's school; in early 1525, aged at most eighteen, though possibly one or two years younger, he was still there. He never took a university degree.

The situation implied by Schotten's dedication of the *Instructio prima puerorum* to Gisbert's younger brother

---

[155] Schotten, *Confabulationes*, ed. by Macardle, 'Et genere et moribus adolescenti ingenuo Gisberto Sterckenberg', ll. 9–11.

Matthias in August 1527 is strikingly similar. In this book, Schotten assures Matthias, he will not find boring and pedestrian elementaries, 'casus et tempora, quae nuper didicisti (scis ubi) nescio quanta cum fruge, certe magna dispendio temporis, et laboris sudore' (sig. A3ᵛ). This is a standard humanist gibe at old-fashioned schools, where boys put in immense amounts of effort, yet gained little competence in Latin. The sentence suggests that Matthias had recently transferred from such a school to Schotten's own, superior establishment, in exactly the same way as Gisbert seems to have done.

In August 1527, when he penned this, Schotten was almost certainly still at his trivial school (see pp. 46–47). The fact that Gisbert had begun at the Laurentiana but had left and gone to wherever Schotten was teaching in 1524–1525 virtually guarantees that that school was somewhere entirely separate from the Laurentiana, and not a semi-clandestine remedial or pre-university stream at the *bursa* itself. Indeed the gibe about Matthias's previous place of education might actually refer to the Laurentiana. Matthias does not appear in the Cologne matricula, but his entry could easily have gone unrecorded (see p. 198, and n.180). If he was at a *bursa*, it would presumably have been the Laurentiana, where both his brothers had probably been sent.

Unfortunately, as with most material concerning Schotten, all this provides a tantalizing amount of highly suggestive detail, but not quite enough to give definitive answers to the questions about Schotten's career that one would really like to have answered.

Georg Lauer

The *Ludus martius* of 1526 is dedicated to the cleric Georg Lauer or Lauwer:

> Egregio ac literato uiro Georgio Lauwer Herbipolensi, artium ingenuarum magistro, aedis sanctorum Apostolorum in Agrippina Colonia canonico et ecclesiae in Moxstat praeposito, domino et Maecoenati suo Her. Scottenius Hessus S.P.D.[156]

Lauer matriculated in the Cologne Arts Faculty in 1496, incepting MA in 1499. He had a University prebend at St Aposteln by 1509 and was a canon by 1510. By 1526, the date of Schotten's dedication, he was provost of St Martin in Mockstadt in the Mainz diocese; in 1534 he was rector of St Peter in Cologne.[157] A picture of him, painted in 1553, the year he died, hangs in St Aposteln.[158]

Schotten's dedication is brief. After lamenting the devastation caused by the Peasants' War, he concludes with an allusion to Lauer's generosity, not least to Schotten himself. He promises to celebrate Lauer in his future writings, and to be attentive to his patron's wishes:

> Elegantius quandoque mittam, in quo tuam [dicam] humanitatem erga literatos omnes, liberalitatem in egentes pueros literarios et me, cui Maecoenas esse soles non minus quam ille Horatio et Virgilio quondam fuit. Par pari referre cum nequeam opibus, omni pede in te honestando consistam. Chartis meis te non silebo.[159]

The promise did not materialize: not another word of Schotten's mentioning Lauer survives.

As with all Schotten's dedications, this delivers little concrete information on Schotten's relationship to the dedicatee. Lauer, Schotten says, was as much of a patron to him as the original Maecenas was to Horace and Vergil:

---

[156] Schotten, *Ludus martius siue bellicus* (Cologne: Quentel, 1526), sig. A1^v.
[157] *Matrikel*, 430,42 (Bursa Montana). *Regesten*, 2386 lists Lauer as prebendary in 1509; Ennen, *Geschichte*, IV, pp. 195, 355.
[158] H. Schaefer, 'Ein Verzeichniss von Kölner Prälaten- und Stiftsherrenbildern aus dem Jahre 1635', p. 103.
[159] Schotten, *Ludus martius siue bellicus*, sig. A2^v.

in what did this generosity consist? Might Lauer have used his connections with St Aposteln to secure Schotten a teaching post there? This is by no means impossible. The schoolmaster there at the time is not clearly identified.[160] Several topographical allusions in the *Confabulationes* are suggestive. The alehouse in the Schaafenstraße is mentioned twice (colloquies 26, 97); other locations, like the vineyards (colloquy 69), would fit the outlying, semi-rural St Aposteln better than an inner-city parish. But Schotten makes no clear reference to working there, which is interesting given that he mentions having performed the *Ludus martius* with his schoolboys that Shrovetide, which had ended only a month before he wrote the letter (in mid-Lent).[161] Had the play been staged at St Aposteln, Schotten would almost certainly have made some reference to the fact.

It is uncertain what Schotten's connection with Lauer was. It was not *bursa*-based, for Lauer was at the Montana; this is another friendship across the Thomist/Albertist divide. It was not regional, for Schotten was born about 100 km from Lauer's *Heimat* of Würzburg. Might it have involved affinities of thought? Nothing is known directly of Lauer's sympathies in theology or any other area. He was however a friend of Johannes Cochlaeus, a fellow Franconian from near Nuremberg, and certainly a humanist, but also a virulent anti-Lutheran. It was with Lauer that Cochlaeus stayed when forced by a popular Lutheran uprising to leave Frankfurt in 1525,[162] and during this stay he was instrumental in

---

[160] Thomas Leusman de Fredeborch was schoolmaster in 1503, but it is not clear whether he continued till 1532, when Tilman Kalthuys von Breckerfeld is mentioned: Oediger, 'Die niederrheinischen Schulen', p. 389.

[161] '[Pueri mei], quos hoc exhibendo ludo exercui, his Bacchanalibus die[bus]', *Ludus martius*, sig. A2ᵛ. 1526: Ash Wednesday 14 February, Easter 1 April.

[162] Krafft, 'Mittheilungen aus der Matrikel', p. 471; Ennen, *Geschichte*, IV, p. 195; *CoE*, I, p. 322; *NDB*, III, p. 305.

frustrating the attempt by William Tyndale and William Roye to have Tyndale's controversial English New Testament translation printed in Cologne by Peter Quentel.[163]

Did Lauer approve of his guest Cochlaeus's attitude and actions? And might Schotten's friendship with Lauer have meant that he did as well? Some facts do point in that direction. Cochlaeus was assisted by another of Schotten's patrons, Hermann (II) Rinck; and Hermann had a track record of rather aggressive Catholic conservatism. He had earlier lived in England, and as a *confidant* of Henry VIII had helped to negotiate trading privileges between England and the Empire.[164] In 1528 he wrote to Cardinal Wolsey, offering to ask Emperor Charles V to renew these privileges, which now included an extradition clause on all English subjects who were traitors to Henry VIII, or Lutherans: under this arrangement a number of Protestants would later be extradited.[165] In this exchange of correspondence the Observant Franciscans, to whom the Rincks were so devoted, had acted as couriers.[166]

Johann (III) Rinck, with whom Schotten had the most immediate contact, seems to have had a similar religious vision. Johann was a correspondent of Erasmus (see p. 172), but in his only surviving letter to Erasmus, he includes the most virulent invective against Luther as a monster from hell, who has spawned all the current Prot-

---

[163] Giesen, 'Ein Brief des Kölner Ratsherrn Hermann Rinck [...]', p. 371.

[164] Irsigler, 'Hansekaufleute', p. 322.

[165] Hermann Rinck's letter, 4 October 1528: British Library, Vitellius B. XXI, 43; printed in William Arber, *The First Printed English New Testament Translated by William Tyndale* (London: Bloomsbury, 1871), p. 32. See Giesen, 'Ein Brief des Kölner Ratsherrn Hermann Rinck [...]', pp. 372–76.

[166] A letter from Henry VIII of 5 August 1526 was passed to Hermann Rinck by Johann West, an Observant Franciscan priest: Giesen, 'Ein Brief des Kölner Ratsherrn Hermann Rinck [...]', p. 372.

estant heresies.[167] He approvingly mentions Cochlaeus, the humanist who did so much to establish this image of Luther as diabolically deranged heresiarch.[168] Whilst the *Confabulationes* do not go this far, they certainly present an extremely negative image of Lutheranism, and of its dire effects on the Catholic status quo, particularly on attitudes towards the clergy. Priests everywhere are 'the object of hate on the part of those who support Luther'; in some places they are 'ostracized and treated as if they were Jews' (colloquy 88, ll. 26–27, 30–31); almost no one pays clerics for the traditional funeral rites because 'people are siding with Luther' (colloquy 107, ll. 30–32); monks are deserting their orders because of the hostility of 'worthless people' (colloquy 117, ll. 40–41). These are of course sentiments utterly foreign to Erasmus's colloquies.

The Linner family

Schotten dedicated his *Colloquia moralia* of October 1535 to one Heinrich Linner, whom he addresses as a BA and an intending medical student.[169] This identifies him as the Heinrich Linner who matriculated in Arts in 1534 (giving him a birthdate of *ca.* 1520 at latest), and who, after rapid progression to MA, had his BMed by 1538; von der Ketten later records him as a DMed and mayor of Wesel.[170]

---

[167] 'Nae monstrum horrendum Lutherus ab infernalibus Furiis missum in orbem turbandis omnibus', Erasmus, *Epistolae*, 3004, ll. 31–33; and cf. ll. 26–48.

[168] Erasmus, *Epistolae*, 3004, ll. 26–31. See Herte, *Das katholische Lutherbild*, passim.

[169] Schotten, *Colloquia moralia* (Cologne: P. Quentel, 1535), sigs a1^v, q7^r.

[170] *Matrikel*, 583,15 (listed as 'Henonus Linner' in *Matrikel*, index, III, p. 694). Matriculated 1 October 1534; BA 16 October

The Linners were another eminently respectable Cologne burgher family, though one whose history is less well recorded than is the Starckenbergs', or the Rincks'. Wills and various University and municipal documents do however give some idea of the family's status in Schotten's time.

The origin of the name Linner or Lynner is probably toponymic, from Linn near Krefeld.[171] The 'patriarch' of the Cologne family was Heinrich (I) von Linner (d. 1529), who became a Cologne citizen in 1517, and was an active councillor and municipal officer; he lived in the parish of St Laurenz.[172] He married twice, first Hilwich (Heilwigis), surname unknown, then Ursula von Breinich.[173] The widowed Ursula married Heinrich van Broich,[174] creating a close enough link with that considerable Cologne family for one of Heinrich (I) von Linner's sons, Andreas, to remember the Mayor Heinrich van Broich in his will of 1548.[175] The same will reveals that Andreas's sister Sevis was married to the jurist Conrad von Betzdorf, also from an important Cologne family.[176]

By comparison with the Starckenbergs however, the Linners were not particularly well connected. They were oriented less towards the city, more towards the Uni-

---

       1534; MA May 1536; BMed 25 April 1538: HAStK, 150, A 516, 76ᵛ, 80ᵛ; *Slg. Ketten*, III, p. 413.
[171] *Neubürger*, index, IV, p. 412. Some fourteenth- and fifteenth-century 'von Lynne's may not be directly related to the sixteenth-century Cologne Linners.
[172] In the Budengasse: *Topogr.*, I, pp. 187a–93b; Glasner, II, pp. 95–96. Heinrich: *Neubürger*, I, p. 113: 1517, no. 7, 1.7.1517. HAStK, 30 (V+V), C 656, fol. 9ᵛ. *RHV*, 2463: councillor 1518–1527.
[173] Hilwich: HAStK, 110, 3/ L 255, will of Heinrich and Hilwich, 17.3.1515. Ursula, and von Breinich family: *Slg. Ketten*, III, p. 413.
[174] *Slg. Ketten*, III, p. 413. Van Broich family: ibid., I, p. 433; Heinrich van Broich (d. 1553): *RHV*, 549.
[175] HAStK, 110, 2/ L 253, Andreas's will of 20.7.1548.
[176] HAStK, 110, 2/ L 253.

versity. Only Heinrich (I) is recorded on the city council (1518–1527); but an impressive seven Linners, most of them definitely from Cologne, studied at the University in under fifty years. Some cannot be identified.[177] Presumably not all branches of the family are recorded; and the Cologne burgher class enthusiastically fathered illegitimate children.[178] One of these unidentifiable Linners is a Heinrich who matriculated in Law in 1540, and whom Keussen identifies as Schotten's dedicatee.[179] This however is clearly a mistake. The man whom Schotten addresses, must have been Heinrich (II) Linner, another son of Heinrich (I), and the brother of Andreas.

Another son of Heinrich (I) is Conrad Linner who took his BA in 1543, but whose matriculation, probably in 1541 or 1542, has not been recorded.[180] Since he incepted MA under the Montana master Jacob van Hoogstraten, he will have been at the Montana.[181] He must have been born about 1527, shortly before Heinrich (I)'s death; Heinrich's son Andreas mentions him in his will.[182]

---

[177] Nicolaus Linner, matriculated in Law 14.8.1509 (thus born by ca. 1492): *Matrikel*, 483,20. Heinrich Linner, matriculated in Arts, 1517 (hence born by ca. 1503): *Matrikel*, 516,38.

[178] E.g. Peter Rinck's illegitimate son Hieronymus: *Matrikel*, 425,6; Heinrich Starckenberg's natural daughter Magdalena: HAStK, 110 (Test.), 3/S 1015; Weinsberg's brother Christian's illegitimate daughter: *BW*, V, p. 461.

[179] *Matrikel*, 605,4: matriculated 2 January 1540; BLeg in absentia (ill with plague): HAStK, 150, A 516, fols 91^v, 94^r. LicLeg 18 March 1542; DMed 29 May 1556. Keussen's note wrongly identifies him as Schotten's pupil.

[180] *Matrikel*, III, Nachtrag 1939 (= III, p. 115). BA 14 November 1543: HAStK, 150, A 481, fol. 228^v; LicA 1545: ibid., fol. 233^r; MA 1545: ibid., fol. 233^v. On the reasons why students are missing from the Matricula, see *Matrikel*, I, pp. 16*–17*, and III, p. 1.

[181] HAStK, 150, A 481, fol. 233^v (19 March 1545). Hoogstraten: *Matrikel*, 555,6.

[182] HAStK, 110, 2/ L 253.

A Gottfried Linner of Cologne, who matriculated in Arts in 1550 at the Laurentiana, became the subject of an interesting confusion with a Gottfried Starckenberg which led Keussen to suggest that the two men were identical.[183] On close inspection this proves to be a clerical muddle, stemming from incomplete or incorrect entries in the Receptor's book, too complex to be summarized here.[184] It may also have reflected the fact that there were close connections between the Linner and Starckenberg families. For Gisbert's will shows that a sister of his wife Elß Gummeradt had married into the Linner family, and Gisbert left a bequest to their son Peter.[185] This must be the Peter Linner who matriculated at the University in 1551, and so must have been born by 1537 at the latest.[186] Gisbert also mentions a Truigen van Linner, an aunt of Peter's.[187] Catharina von Linner made her brother-in-law Johann Starckenberg an executor of her will of 1540.[188]

It is interesting that the *Colloquia moralia* dedication, written by a Schotten now firmly established in the

---

[183] In *Matrikel*, 'Alphabetisches Hauptregister', III, pp. 694, 956, Keussen lists G. Linner and G. Starckenberg under the same matriculation number (645,54). In *Matrikel*, 645,44, G. Linner, his note attributes the name 'Stairckeberch'.

[184] E.g. 1553: G. Starckenberg was examined (HAStK, 150, 481, fol. 253^v) but omitted from the list of fee-payers (HAStK, 150, A 516, fol. 125^{r-v}).

[185] HAStK, 110, 3/S 1012. On the von Gummeraide family (Gummeradt, Gumroide, etc.) see *RHV*, 1516. Elß's own will (1583): HAStK, 110, 3/G 506.

[186] *Matrikel*, 650,6. Matriculated 19 April 1551, Laurentiana. BA 1551; MA 1553; *Receptus ad consilium* of the Arts Faculty 1558. 1559 Dean, 1561 Quodlibetarius and Receptor. 1559 BTh designate; 1563 BLeg, 1568 LicLeg. He edited or commented on Pierre Loriot, *In usus feudorum commentarius* (Cologne: A. Birckmann, 1566 and 1567) (*VD 16*, L 2600, 2601).

[187] HAStK, 110, 3/S 1012.

[188] HAStK, 110, 3/L 254. Hermann Linner and Johann Starckenberg worked together as city councillors on a criminal case in August 1524: *BRStK*, III, p. 148 (1524, 722).

Laurentiana and in the University in general, addresses a member of a family distinguished less by wealth and civic influence than by intellectual interests and competence. Schotten, now a salaried academic with an assured future, probably did not need to cultivate material patronage as much as he had in the more precarious days of his relative youth, and could afford the cultural gesture of affinity with a man who, even if he did not develop into a 'humanist', went on to gain learning and to exercise a learned profession.

The House of Waldeck

Material concerns may not, however, have been completely foreign to Schotten: this at least is suggested by his dedication of the *Colloquia philosophica* (23 August 1535) to Philipp and Johann, counts of Waldeck.[189]

The small principality of Waldeck, already economically weak, weakened itself further internally by its tendency to split the ruling line: for much of the sixteenth century three lines (Wildungen, Eisenberg and Landau) existed simultaneously.[190] Cologne had originally pursued a policy of containment towards Waldeck; but by the later fifteenth century relationships had become more cordial, and from the late 1460s on, it became customary for boys from the house of Waldeck to study at Cologne: between 1468 and 1548 eight are recorded, most, like

---

[189] 'Generosis ac illustribus adolescentibus et dominis, Philippo, Moguntinensis et Iohanni, Coloniensis ecclesiarum Cathedralium Canonicis, fratribus Germanis Comitibus Vvaldeccensibus, dominis suis perpetuo obseruandis. Hermannus Schottennius Hessus salutis exoptat plurimum': Schotten, *Colloquia philosophica*, sig. A1ᵛ.

[190] Demandt, *Geschichte des Landes Hessen*, pp. 521-33, 'Das Fürstentum Waldeck'; cf. genealogical table facing p. 528.

Schotten's pupils Philipp and Johann, from the Eisenberg line. The first, in 1468, was the grandfather of Schotten's pupils, Junggraf Philipp (1452 or 1453–1524), later Count Philipp II.[191] In 1495 came Philipp's sons Georg (1483–1504) and Philipp (1486–1539), later Count Philipp III.[192] Schotten's pupils Philipp and Johann, Philipp III's sons, matriculated in 1534.[193] Philipp (b. 1519 or 1520) was later Philipp V 'the Deaf'. Johann (1521 or 1522–1567), later Johann I 'the Pious', was the first of the junior Landau line. Like others of the House of Waldeck, Johann was a canon of Cologne Cathedral (from 1535). Philipp, in 1535 a canon of Mainz, became one of Cologne as well, in 1550.[194]

The other branch of the Waldeck house represented at Cologne was the senior Wildungen line. In 1509 Junggraf Wilhelm matriculated for a stay of a year.[195] In 1548 it was the turn of Daniel (1530–1577) and Heinrich (d. 1577), the sons of Philipp IV of the same line.[196] They are the last of the House of Waldeck recorded in the Cologne *matricula*.

Since none of the Waldeck boys took a degree, their *bursae* are not recorded in the University books. But Junggraf Wilhelm is known to have been at the Laurentiana from a record of his expenses there for 1509–1510;[197] and Philipp and Johann must have been there too if Schotten was their master. If fathers in both lines were

---

[191] *Matrikel*, 317,112 (2 June 1468).
[192] *Matrikel*, 425,18 (Georg), 425,19 (Philipp) (22 February 1495).
[193] *Matrikel*, 583,23: 'Phil. ex comitibus de Waldeck'; 583,24: 'Joh. com. de Waldeck' (13 October 1534).
[194] Note to *Matrikel*, 583,23, 24. Cf. Schotten's greeting (see n. 189).
[195] *Matrikel*, 484,24 (21 October 1509).
[196] *Matrikel*, 638,19 (Daniel), 638,20 (Heinrich) (9 July 1548).
[197] Huyskens, 'Junggraf Wilhelm von Waldeck', passim. 'In achademia necnon burse [sic] Laurentii Coloniensis': ibid., p. 92.

sending their sons to the Laurentiana, it was very likely the Waldeck *bursa*.

Schotten's conventionally formulated dedication praises the Waldeck boys as modest and unassuming;[198] he celebrates the good judgement of their father and their uncle Franz, bishop of Münster (sig. A2^{r-v}). Further addresses to the counts precede the second and third sections of the *Colloquia*. In the first, Schotten exhorts them to fortitude, clemency, moderation and *humanitas* (sig. P1^r–2^r); in the second, he cautions them against pride and self-exaltation (sig. Y4^r). Schotten begs the boys to accept his poor literary gift in the spirit of the Persian king Artaxerxes accepting a handful of water offered him by the poor Plutarch (sig. A3^r). He must have forgotten that Plutarch (who lived half a millennium after Artaxerxes) merely recorded this anecdote, and that the water was offered by a poor labourer; but perhaps he remembered that Artaxerxes's reward was a golden goblet and a thousand gold pieces, and was angling for a similar recognition of his own poor 'chartaceum munusculum'.[199] Beyond this, however, the dedication reveals nothing about his relationship to the boys or their dynasty.

Conclusion

Yet despite this wealth of evidence of Schotten's 'networking', Schotten's career as a whole can still only be glimpsed in outline. What emerges most clearly are the traces of his typically Albertist connections in Cologne: whether or not he had been marginalized at the Lauren-

---

[198] 'Ingenua vestra et laudata morum modestia, ac digna verecundia', *Colloquia philosophica*, sig. A3^r.

[199] Plutarch, *Artaxerxes*, 5. Artaxerxes died 425 BC; Plutarch died AD 140.

tiana, or perhaps even ejected at the time of the 1523 Quodlibet, he had access of some sort to the Rincks and the Starckenbergs, in both cases almost certainly via the Albertist network of St Kolumba and the Laurentiana. Yet Schotten's relationship with these families seems essentially that of client to patron. The Starckenbergs were not a learned family, and most definitely not humanists, even if Schotten seems to have been doing his best to mould Gisbert and Matthias into humanist schoolboys. The Rincks were scholarly, and had humanist connections, but in his dedications to them Schotten seems not so much to be cultivating humanist acquaintances as seeking material patronage, as is borne out in his candid appeal for employment to Johann Rinck. As noted above, this comes at precisely the time, around 1527, when there are other signs that Schotten was quitting the classroom and making a return to the university (see pp. 172–173). It seems unlikely that Johann Rinck gave Schotten a job as such; but perhaps some Rinck influence or Rinck subsidy helped Schotten make the transition. This career change suggests that Schotten, whatever his pedagogical gifts (and the *Confabulationes* suggest they were considerable) was typical of his age in seeing schoolteaching as a temporary career rather than a lifetime vocation.

The other patrons whom Schotten addresses are almost certainly connected in some way with this basic Laurentiana Albertist network. The Linners were related to the Starckenbergs; the Antonites were in a friendly relationship with the Laurentiana; the Waldeck boys were students there. Schotten's relationship with Georg Lauer might have been based on teaching at St Aposteln, but perhaps more plausibly reflects connections of Lauer (via Cochlaeus) with the Rincks: connections which suggest that Schotten was content, for the sake of material support, to be allied with men whose Catholicism was not merely conservative but sternly repressive; or even that his own religion was more conservatively orthodox than a reading of the *Confabulationes* might suggest. This would add force to the argument that Schotten reworked Erasmus largely to avoid or counter Erasmus's 'progressive' theology (see Chapter 3).

But the one thing which all these data fail to produce is evidence of Schotten affiliated as an equal (or indeed in any capacity) with other humanists. The closest Schotten ever comes to this scenario is in the dedication to Heinrich Linner, a young man rather than a boy, not from a conspicuously wealthy family, and clearly of scholarly inclinations. Even Matthias Wagener is eulogized as a patron, 'litteratorum Maecenas', rather than a scholar in his own right. Nowhere does Schotten speak, as humanist dedications regularly do, of humanist third parties known to him and the dedicatee, recording, celebrating and cementing intellectual networks and affinities. There is still the sense that Schotten was ploughing a rather lonely humanist furrow in a *bursa* and a university that were, if not actively hostile to him, more than a little indifferent.

Cologne, St Maria im Kapitol, from Anton Woensam, *Große Ansicht von Köln* (1531).

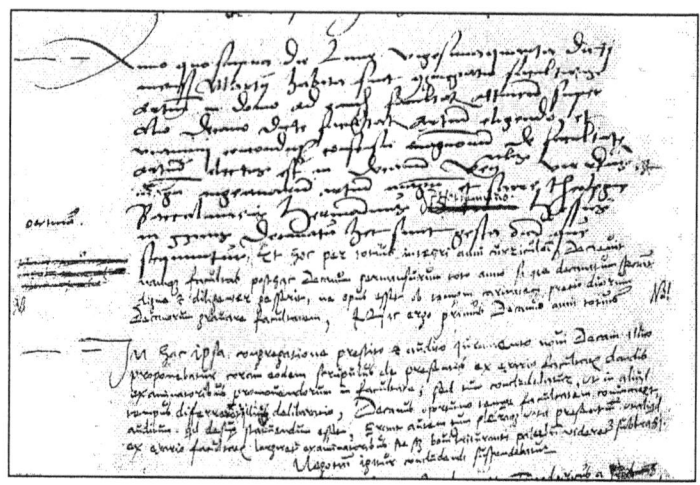

Hermann Schotten's handwriting, at the start of the record of his deanship of the Cologne Arts Faculty, HAStK, 150, A 481, fol. 187ᵛ (lower half).

Conclusions

After pursuing Schotten and his work along some fairly intricate trails, it is worthwhile standing back and briefly taking stock of the man and his achievement.

The *Confabulationes* emerge as not only one of the most substantial colloquy collections of the sixteenth century, but as amongst the most interesting. Schotten's use of model humanist texts, in this case Erasmus's *Colloquia*, Mosellanus's *Paedologia* and Hegendorff's *Dialogi*, is an almost schoolbook example of emulation; indeed the detailed comparison of the *Confabulationes* with these previous collections shows just how deeply Erasmus and Mosellanus in particular had impressed themselves on Schotten. Yet this does not make him a merely derivative writer: the *Confabulationes* have their own distinctive voice. This is not merely a question of Schotten's particular diction and his own, to some extent idiolectal, version of humanist Classical Latin, as explored in Chapter 4, though this is certainly part of it. More important is Schotten's supreme ability, and complete willingness, to immerse himself in the physical and mental world of real schoolboys, something virtually unparalleled in the age. Reading the *Confabulationes* as a whole will confirm that their vivid, small-scale, at times almost photographic recording of everyday reality makes them an important document of literary realism. This aesthetic aspect really needs a more detailed examination than can be pursued in the confines of this study, and I hope to be able to return to it at a later opportunity.

It is clear that Schotten's voice was one which the educational world at large greatly appreciated. That the *Confabulationes* were printed nearly sixty times in the teeth of competition from Erasmus, Mosellanus and

Vives, as well as from lesser lights, shows that they could hold their own even in an extremely competitive market. It is frustrating that no recorded statements exist which might give a precise idea of what contemporary readers thought about the *Confabulationes*. It would be particularly interesting to know how masters and pupils in the Protestant regions served by south and east German printing centres like Augsburg, Nuremberg and Leipzig made of a text produced by a Catholic in Cologne, and depicting so many distinctive features of the Catholic life, culture and attitudes of that Rhineland city. Yet make something of it they must have, or the work would not have sold so well. Though I have not yet examined all the sixteenth-century printings in detail, there is no indication that later editions altered Schotten's text other than in minor ways. There are occasional changes to the names of the speakers in a few colloquies, but nothing along the lines of elision or rewriting to adapt the content to another German regional or confessional culture. Perhaps the *Confabulationes* covered so much larger a range of situations than any other colloquies that their pedagogical usefulness outweighed their regional and confessional bias.

Setting Schotten in his professional contexts has not been easy. The goings-on in the Cologne Arts Faculty need careful interpretation. It is all too simple and gratifying to read the sparse facts concerning Schotten's debarment from the Quodlibet and his eventual return to the Laurentiana as a kind of fairy-tale of the hero's exile and his triumphant return after the death of the wicked witch. The skeletal framework of documentary traces of events may mask a slightly different story, which possibly amounts to little more than that Schotten had the misfortune to be at the University at a time when the disastrous drop in student numbers had reduced the need for permanent teaching staff (and the good fortune to be available when at last there was a position he could fill). If there is one major regret, it is that the garrulous Hermann von Weinsberg, who studied at the Laurentiana when Schotten was there, who was examined by him, and who may even have been taught by him, did not include any reference to Schotten in his memoirs. Nonetheless, Schotten's modest career shows that a humanist could fill a position in the Cologne Arts Faculty to the satisfaction of the authorities, and also presumably to some extent to his own satisfaction.

Schotten's personal networks have not proved easy to reconstruct; but there is certainly evidence of his Laurentiana Albertist affiliations as well as of other, more personal connections which suggest material support from eminent Cologne families. Perhaps Schotten's data can be combined with results from future studies of Cologne figures. Tewes's tracing of the complex trail of persons in the Arts Faculty has considerably advanced our understanding of the affiliations of the masters, both as individuals and in groups, and there seems little doubt that future detailed studies of individuals and groups will flesh out the picture considerably, and perhaps even generate more data relevant to Schotten. This kind of study, however, is still in its infancy. The information-gathering requires computerized processing of very large amounts of data on persons and organizations. Only thus will as yet unsuspected networks and affiliations begin to emerge, as will ways in which these intersected with one another. The immense amount of archival material in Cologne would provide an excellent basis. The work of Schwinges has shown something of what could be achieved, and the work on the Weinsberg project should also produce relevant results, since one of its aims is to look systematically at the numerous individuals and groups of people recorded by Weinsberg.

This study contends that Schotten is a fascinating figure, not that he was a particularly original humanist. He can perhaps best be seen as epitomizing the Cologne humanists as Erich Meuthen describes them: characterized less by originality than by intelligent receptivity, an ability to absorb the impulses of humanism and hand them on to future generations: representatives of a 'solider Schulhumanismus'.[1] This is a kind of mediocrity, but precisely the kind which is absolutely necessary for any intellectual movement to take root in a culture. Only a few genial figures are needed to lead such movements, but many lesser lights are indispensable to pass on the ideas, inculcate them successfully in later generations, and generally turn them from elite, avant-garde positions into mainstream culture. At the most obvious level, Schotten and those like him did this simply by being competent, if not always brilliant, classroom teachers, who also had enough sympathy with the humanist programme, and enough understanding of its classical linguistic and literary basis, to hand on a changing Latinity and a changing intellectual and aesthetic vision. But of course the vast majority of this mostly forgotten army did not author anything themselves, or at least nothing that has survived: no doubt some, like Schotten, wrote texts for their own classroom use. Schotten, by publishing his material, reached the next level, that of author, in principle able to put his own spin on humanist pedagogy and give it lasting form. Yet the essentially 'occasional' nature of his material makes it unlikely that he designed the *Confabulationes* as a consistent, programmatic 'authorial' statement. Not all the effects the collection makes were necessarily ones he intended.

Schotten's rewriting of Erasmus in a more orthodox Catholic vein (see Chapter 3) was probably intentional. Yet even this had effects which go beyond what Schotten's immediate aim may have been. Erasmus simplified matters somewhat. The critique of medieval Catholic praxis which he put into his boys' mouths was contextualized in, and supported by, the vision of religious reform expounded in the *Colloquia* as a whole, and in his other

---

[1] Meuthen, *Universität*, p. 262.

writings. But this was a vision unrealised anywhere other than in small and isolated circles. Everywhere in Europe, people had to live out their own religious visions and aspirations against the background of church life as it actually was: in Cologne, a Catholicism deeply entrenched in every aspect of the city's culture and structures of power, and on the whole unsympathetic to humanism. Schotten was too much of a realist simply to reiterate Erasmus's religious views in a book which reflected life in Cologne; and probably too conventional a Catholic to ascribe to them unreservedly. So what he presents is a broadly Erasmian piety, but expressed within a much more orthodox Catholic framework. Whether it was his conscious intention or not, the effect must have been one of mediation between the 'Erasmian' and the 'orthodox' positions, at a time when that perceived opposition was becoming ever sharper. The result was perhaps to ensure some Erasmian ideas an easier passage into the consciousness of Cologne boys than the original *Colloquia* would have done.

The question of how the very many schoolboys from quite different cities who read the *Confabulationes* saw all this is of course a separate one, and probably now unanswerable. But for the real Cologne schoolboys – Schotten's own pupils – for whom he had expressly designed the text, the effect is fairly evident, though again it may not have been one consciously designed by Schotten. The *Confabulationes* implicitly communicate the message that learning and using humanist Classical Latin was not an activity divorced from their real lives as citizens of a late-medieval or early modern city. The sheer bulk of detail on the life and culture of that city implicitly suggests that that life and culture were worthy of record, and deserving of discussion by learned people. Linguistically the *Confabulationes* demonstrate that the Latin of classical times and classical authors was a medium perfectly suited to that recording and discussion. The precise contours of that Latin were still under negotiation. Schotten implicitly demonstrates that a Terentian Latin can be expanded judiciously by using elements of the post-classical and medieval language necessary to comprehend the realities of the early modern world. He demonstrates that that expansion does not represent 'impurity', barbarism, or deformation of the classical language, but a necessary enrichment of its means.

All in all, the boys who used the *Confabulationes* must have had an impression of continuity: continuity of what they were learning both with the values of Classical Antiquity and with the realities of their own time and their own city; the sense of being citizens simultaneously of Cologne and of the *respublica litterarum*. It was noted in Chapter 2 that Schotten nowhere alludes to the (bogus) legends of the origins of the Cologne patricians in a number of Roman families, or to the (perfectly genuine) Roman origins of the city. It is perhaps because the *Confabulationes* implicitly set up such strong linguistic, textual and cultural continuities between classical times and values and those of his readers' world that Schotten had no need of these fictive or archaeological continuities.

Schotten's career and work, most especially the *Confabulationes*, show him to have been an obscure humanist, but by no means an insignificant one. They make an important contribution to the gradually emerging picture of how humanism was lived out in the earlier part of the sixteenth century in the City and University of Cologne.

Boats designed for the central Rhine (left) and the lower Rhine (right), from Anton Woensam, *Große Ansicht von Köln* (1531).

Select Bibliography

Items are listed either under abbreviated titles, or in the main list of secondary literature.

Abbreviations:

Periodicals, series, and frequently cited works referred to by abbreviated titles.

ADB:	*Allgemeine Deutsche Biographie*, ed. by Historische Commission bei der königlichen Akademie der Wissenschaften (Bayern), 66 vols (Leipzig: Duncker und Humblot, 1875–1912).
AfK:	*Archiv für Kulturgeschichte.*
AHVN:	*Annalen des Historischen Vereins für den Niederrhein, insbesondere die alte Diözese Köln.*
AK:	*Alt-Köln, Zeitschrift herausgegeben vom Verein Alt-Köln.*
Alte Un.:	Keussen, Hermann, *Die alte Universität Köln: Grundzüge ihrer Verfassung und Geschichte*, VKGV, 10 (Cologne: Creutzer, 1934).
AMKG:	*Archiv für mittelrheinische Kirchengeschichte.*
ANRhKG:	*Annalen für niederrheinische Kirchengeschichte.*
ARG:	*Archiv für Reformationsgeschichte.*

ASD:	Erasmus, Desiderius, of Rotterdam, *Opera omnia Desiderii Erasmi Roterodami*, ed. by Jan Hendrik Waszink and others (Amsterdam: North Holland, 1969–).
Bianco, I:	Bianco, Franz Joseph von, *Die alte Universität Köln und die späteren Gelehrten-Schulen dieser Stadt, nach archivarischen und anderen zuverlässigen Quellen*. I. Theil. Erste Abtheilung: *Die alte Universität Köln* (Cologne: Gehly, 1855).
Bianco, I,2:	Bianco, Franz Joseph von, *Die ehemalige Universität und die Gymnasien zu Köln, so wie die an diese Lehr-Anstalten geknüpften Studien-Stiftungen von ihrem Ursprunge bis auf unsere Zeiten*. II. Theil, 2nd edn (Cologne: Gehly, 1850).
BRStK:	*Beschlüsse des Rates der Stadt Köln 1320–1550*, ed. by Manfred Huiskes and Manfred Groten, PGRG, 65, 5 vols (Düsseldorf: Droste, 1988–1990).
BW:	*Das Buch Weinsberg. Kölner Denkwürdigkeiten aus dem 16. Jahrhundert*, ed. by Konstantin Höhlbaum and others, PGRG, 3, 4, 16, 5 vols (Leipzig: Dürr, and Bonn: Hanstein, 1886–1926; repr. Düsseldorf: Droste, 2000).
CCFr:	*Catalogue Collectif de France* (Paris, Bibliothèque Nationale de France), online at: <http://ccfr.bnf.fr/portailccfr/servlet/LoginServlet>
CIC:	*Corpus Iuris Canonici In Tres Partes Distinctum; Glossis Diversorum illustratum [...]*, 3 vols (Lyon: J.A. Huguetan and G. Barbier, 1671).
CIC, ed. by Friedberg:	*Corpus Iuris Canonici*, ed. by Emil Friedberg, 2 vols (Leipzig: Tauchnitz, 1879, 1881).

Bibliography

CoE: Contemporaries of Erasmus. A Biographical Register of the Renaissance and Reformation, ed. by Peter G. Bietenholz and Thomas B. Deutscher, 3 vols (Toronto: University of Toronto Press, 1985–1987).

CWE: Collected Works of Erasmus, ed. by Alexander Dalzell and others (Toronto, University of Toronto Press, 1974–).

DBE: Deutsche Biographische Enzyklopädie, ed. by Walter Killy and others, 13 vols in 15 (Munich: Saur, 1995–2000).

DBI: Deutscher Biographischer Index, ed. by Willi Gorzny and others, 4 vols (Munich–London–New York–Oxford–Paris: Saur, 1986).

DMLBS: Dictionary of Medieval Latin from British Sources, ed. by R.E. Latham and D.R. Howlett (Oxford: Oxford University Press for the British Academy, 1975–).

DuC: Du Cange, Charles, Glossarium mediae et infimae Latinitatis, rev. edn, ed. by Léopold Favre, 10 vols (Niort: Favre, 1883–1887).

EETS: Early English Text Society, Publications.

Erasmus, Epistolae: Opus Epistolarum Desiderii Erasmi Roterodami, ed. by P.S. Allen and others, 11 vols (Oxford: Clarendon, 1907–1945).

Festschr. Ennen: Die Stadt in der europäischen Geschichte. Festschrift für Edith Ennen, ed. by Werner Besch and others (Bonn: Röhrscheid, 1972).

Festschr. Köln: Festschrift zur Erinnerung an die Gründung der alten Universität Köln im Jahre 1388, ed. by Hubert Graven (Cologne: Schroeder, 1938).

Geisberg :	Geisberg, Max, *The German Single-Leaf Woodcut. 1500–1550*, rev. and ed. by Walter L. Strauss, 4 vols (New York: Hacker Art Books, 1974).
GEK:	*Geschichte des Erzbistums Köln*, ed. by Norbert Trippen and others (Cologne: Bachem, 1972–).
Gelenius:	Gelenius, Aegidius, *De admiranda, sacra et civili magnitudine Coloniae Claudiae Agrippinensis Augustae Ubiorum urbis libri IV* (Cologne: J. Kalkhoff, 1645).
GiK:	*Geschichte in Köln*.
Glasner:	Glasner, Peter, *Die Lesbarkeit der Stadt*, 2 vols. [I]. *Kulturgeschichte der mittelalterlichen Straßennamen Kölns*. [II]. *Lexikon der mittelalterlichen Straßennamen Kölns* (Cologne: DuMont, 2002).
Grimm:	Grimm, Jakob and Wilhelm Grimm, *Deutsches Wörterbuch*, 16 vols and index (Leipzig: Hirzel, 1854–1971).
GW:	*Gesamtkatalog der Wiegendrucke*, ed. by Kommission für den Gesamtkatalog der Wiegendrucke (Leipzig: Hiersemann, then Stuttgart: Hiersemann and Berlin: Akademie, then Stuttgart: Hiersemann, 1925–).
HAStK:	Cologne, Historisches Archiv der Stadt Köln.
HbKJL:	*Handbuch zur Kinder- und Jugendliteratur 1570 bis 1750*, ed. by Theodor Brüggemann and Otto Brunken, 2 vols (Stuttgart: Metzler, 1987–1991).
HL:	*Humanistica Lovaniensia*.
HU:	*History of Universities*.

HUE:	A History of the University in Europe, ed. by Walter Rüegg, 4 vols (Cambridge: Cambridge University Press). I. *Universities in the Middle Ages*, ed. by Hilde de Ridder-Symoens (1992). II. *Universities in Early Modern Europe (1500–1800)*, ed. by Hilde de Ridder-Symoens (1996).
Isenmann:	Isenmann, Eberhard, *Die deutsche Stadt im Spätmittelalter 1250–1500. Stadtgestalt, Recht, Stadtregiment, Kirche, Gesellschaft, Wirtschaft*, UTB Große Reihe (Stuttgart: Ulmer, 1988).
JKGV:	*Jahrbuch des Kölnischen Geschichtsvereins*.
JMRS:	*The Journal of Medieval and Renaissance Studies*.
JWCI:	*Journal of the Warburg and Courtauld Institutes*.
KD:	*Die Kunstdenkmäler der Stadt Köln*, ed. by Paul Clemen, 2 vols. (=*Die Kunstdenkmäler der Rheinprovinz*, VI, VII) (Düsseldorf: Schwann, 1905–1938; repr. Düsseldorf: Schwann, 1980).
KiM:	Keussen, Hermann, *Köln im Mittelalter: Topographie und Verfassung* (Bonn: Hanstein, 1918).
KL:	*Kirchenlexikon oder Encyclopädie der katholischen Theologie und ihrer Hilfswissenschaften*, ed. by Heinrich Joseph Wetzer and Benedikt Welte, 2nd edn, rev. by Joseph Cardinal Hergenröther and Franz Kaulen, 12 vols (Freiburg im Breisgau: Herder, 1886–1901).
Klersch:	Klersch, Joseph, *Volkstum und Volksleben in Köln. Ein Beitrag zur historischen Soziologie der Stadt*, 3 vols (Cologne: Bachem, 1965–1969).
Kuske, Quellen:	*Quellen zur Geschichte des Kölner Handels und Verkehrs im Mittelalter*, ed. by Bruno Kuske, PGRG, 33, 4 vols (Bonn: Hanstein, 1917–1934; repr. Düsseldorf: Droste, 1978).

KVK: Karlsruher Virtueller Katalog (Universität Karlsruhe, Universitätsbibliothek), online at: <http://www.ubka.uni-karlsruhe.de/kvk.html>.

LB: Erasmus, Desiderius, of Rotterdam, *Opera omnia emendatiora et auctiora [...]*, ed. By Jean Le Clerc, 10 vols (Leiden: P. Vander Aa, 1703–1706).

LCI: *Lexikon der christlichen Ikonographie*, ed. by Engelbert Kirschbaum, SJ and Wolfgang Braunfels, 8 vols (Rome–Freiburg–Basel–Vienna: Herder, 1968–1976).

Legenda aurea: Voragine, Jacobus de, *Legenda aurea: vulgo Historia Lombardica dicta*, ed. by Theodor Graesse (Dresden–Leipzig, Arnold, 1846).

LLMA: Blaise, Albert, *Lexicon Latinitatis Medii Aevi praesertim ad res ecclesiasticas investigandas pertinens. Dictionnaire latin-français des auteurs du Moyen-Age*, Corpus Christianorum Continuatio Medievalis (Turnhout: Brepols, 1975).

LThK: *Lexikon für Theologie und Kirche*, 2nd edition, ed. by Josef Höfer and Karl Rahner, 10 vols and index (Freiburg: Herder, 1957–1967).

LThK³: *Lexikon für Theologie und Kirche*, 3rd edition, ed. by Walter Kasper and others (Freiburg: Herder, 1993–).

Matrikel: *Die Matrikel der Universität Köln*, ed. by Hermann Keussen and others, 7 vols, PGRG, 8 (Bonn: Hanstein). I. *1389–1475* (²1928); II. *1476–1559* (1919); III. *Nachträge 1389–1559 und Register zu Bd. I und II* (1931); IV. 1559–1675, bearb. Ulrike Nyassi and Mechthild Wilkes (1981); V. 1675–1797, bearb. Ulrike Nyassi and Mechthild Wilkes (1981); VI. Register, 1559–1797, A–H, bearb. Manfred Groten and Manfred Huiskes (1981); VII. Register,

	1559–1797, I–Z, bearb. Manfred Groten and Manfred Huiskes (1981).
Meuthen, Universität:	Kölner Universitätsgeschichte. Herausgegeben von der Senatskommission für die Geschichte der Universität zu Köln, 3 vols (Cologne–Vienna: Böhlau, 1988), I: Meuthen, Erich, Die alte Universität.
Militzer, Laienbruderschaften:	Quellen zur Geschichte der Kölner Laienbruderschaften vom 12. Jahrhundert bis 1562/63, ed. by Klaus Militzer, PGRG, 71, 4 vols (1997–2000).
MStAK:	Mitteilungen aus dem Stadtarchiv von Köln.
NCE:	The New Catholic Encyclopedia, 2nd edn, ed. by Bernard L. Marthaler, OFMConv and others, 15 vols (Detroit: Thomson Gale, 2003).
NDB:	Neue Deutsche Biographie, ed. by Historische Kommission bei der Bayerischen Akademie der Wissenschaften (Berlin: Duncker & Humblot, 1952–).
Neubürger:	Stehkämper, Hugo, Gerd Müller and others, Kölner Neubürger 1356–1798, 4 vols, MStAK, 61–64 (Cologne: Böhlau, 1975–1983).
N&K:	Nijhoff, Wouter, and M.E. Kronenberg, Nederlandsche Bibliographie van 1500 tot 1540, 3 vols (The Hague: Martinus Nijhoff, 1923–1971).
NUC:	The National Union Catalog. Pre-1956 Imprints, ed. by the American Library Association, 754 vols (London–Chicago: Mansell, 1968–1981).
ÖH:	Ökumenisches Heiligenlexikon, online at <http://www.heiligenlexikon.de>.
OLD:	Oxford Latin Dictionary, ed. by P.J.W. Glare, corrected edn (Oxford: Clarendon Press, 1996).

Otto:	Otto, August, *Die Sprichwörter und sprichwörtlichen Redensarten der Römer* (Leipzig: Teubner, 1890).
PGRG:	Publikationen der Gesellschaft für Rheinische Geschichtskunde.
PL:	*Patrologiae cursus completus [...] Series Latina*, ed. by Jacques-Paul Migne, 221 vols (Paris: Migne; last vol. Garnier, 1844–1890).
QGSK	*Quellen zur Geschichte der Stadt Köln*, ed. by Joachim Deeters and others, 2 vols (Cologne: Bachem, 1996).
Regesten:	Keussen, Hermann, *Regesten und Auszüge zur Geschichte der Universität Köln 1388–1559*, MStAK, 36, 37 (Cologne: DuMont-Schauberg, 1918).
RHV:	*Ratsherrenverzeichnis von Köln zu reichsstädtischer Zeit von 1396 bis 1796*, ed. by Herbert M. Schleicher, Veröffentlichungen der Westdeutschen Gesellschaft für Familienkunde, N.F. 19 (Cologne: Westdeutsche Gesellschaft für Familienkunde, 1982).
RL:	*Rheinische Lebensbilder* (Gesellschaft für Rheinische Geschichtskunde).
RQ:	*Renaissance Quarterly.*
RST:	*Reformationsgeschichtliche Studien und Texte* (Münster: Aschendorff).
RVB:	*Rheinische Vierteljahrsblätter.*
SCJ:	*The Sixteenth Century Journal.*

Slg. Ketten:	*Die genealogisch-heraldische Sammlung des Kanonikus Joh. Gabriel von der Ketten in Köln*, ed. by Herbert M. Schleicher, Veröffentlichungen der Westdeutschen Gesellschaft für Familienkunde, N.F. 22, 24, 27, 32, 33, 5 vols (Cologne: Westdeutsche Gesellschaft für Familienkunde, 1983–1986).
Stein:	*Akten zur Geschichte der Verfassung und Verwaltung der Stadt Köln im 14. und 15. Jahrhundert*, ed. by Walther Stein, 2 vols, PGRG, 10 and 10.2 (Bonn: Behrendt, 1893–1895; repr. Düsseldorf: Droste, 1993).
Stotz:	Stotz, Peter, *Handbuch zur lateinischen Sprache des Mittelalters*, 5 vols (Munich: Beck, 1996–2004). (Citations refer not to the volumes but to the seven books into which the work is divided.)
TLL:	*Thesaurus Linguae Latinae*, ed. auctoritate et consilio academiarum quinque Germanicarum: Berolinensis, Gottingensis, Lipsiensis, Monacensis, Vindobonensis (Leipzig, then Stuttgart: Teubner, 1900–).
Topogr.:	Keussen, Hermann, *Topographie der Stadt Köln im Mittelalter*, 2 vols (Bonn: Hanstein, 1910; repr. Düsseldorf: Droste, 1986).
VD 16:	*Verzeichnis der im deutschen Sprachbereich erschienenen Drucke des XVI. Jahrhunderts*, hrsg. von der Bayerischen Staatsbibliothek in München in Verbindung mit der Herzog August Bibliothek in Wolfenbüttel (Stuttgart: Hiersemann, 1983–).
VD 16 online	<http://bvba2.bib-bvb.de/V/8UNFJN7GXVRLP1K8C4Q1UIA2FYRJX7Y25FCKMFNHJ9DQD6VH52-67766?func=file&file_name=search_vd16>

VKGV:	Veröffentlichungen des Kölnischen Geschichtsvereins, e.V.
VL:	*Die deutsche Literatur des Mittelalters. Verfasserlexikon.* 2nd edn, ed. by Kurt Ruh and others (Berlin–New York: de Gruyter, 1978–).
WA:	Luther, Martin, *Werke. Kritische Gesamtausgabe (Weimarer Ausgabe)* (Weimar: Böhlau, 1883–).
WABr:	Luther, Martin, *Werke. Kritische Gesamtausgabe (Weimarer Ausgabe), Briefe*, 18 vols (Weimar: Böhlau, 1930–1985).
Walther:	*Proverbia sententiaeque Latinitatis medii aevi. Lateinische Sprichwörter und Sentenzen des Mittelalters in alphabetischer Anordnung*, gesammelt und hrsg. von Hans Walther, 6 vols, Carmina Medii Aevi Posterioris Latina, II/1–6 (Göttingen: Vandenhoeck & Ruprecht, 1963–1967). and *Proverbia sententiaeque Latinitatis medii ac recentioris aevi. Nova series. Lateinische Sprichwörter und Sentenzen des Mittelalters und der frühen Neuzeit in alphabetischer Anordnung, aus dem Nachlaß von Hans Walther* hrsg. von Paul Gerhard Schmidt, 3 vols, Carmina Medii Aevi Posterioris Latina, II/7–9 (Göttingen: Vandenhoeck & Ruprecht, 1982–1986). The numbering of the items in the two series is continuous.
Wander:	Wander, Karl Friedrich Wilhelm, *Deutsches Sprichwörter-Lexikon. Ein Hausschatz für das deutsche Volk*, 5 vols (Leipzig: Brockhaus, 1867–1880; repr. Darmstadt, Wissenschaftliche Buchgesellschaft, 1964).
ZdPh:	*Zeitschrift für deutsche Philologie.*

ZfdA:	*Zeitschrift für deutsches Altertum und deutsche Literatur.*
ZhTh:	*Zeitschrift für die historische Theologie.*
ZkTh:	*Zeitschrift für katholische Theologie.*
ZVV:	*Zeitschrift des Vereins für Volkskunde.*
Zwei Jahr-tausende:	*Zwei Jahrtausende Kölner Wirtschaft.* Herausgegeben im Auftrag des Rheinisch-Westfälischen Wirtschaftsarchivs zu Köln von Hermann Kellenbenz, unter Mitarbeit von Klara von Eyll, 2 vols (Cologne: Greven, 1975).

Archival Sources:

Cologne, Historisches Archiv der Stadt Köln (HAStK). (See Kuphal, 'Die Archive der Universität Köln', and Deeters, *Die Bestände des Stadtarchivs Köln bis 1814*.)

Bestand 30 (Verfassung und Verwaltung) (V+V):

G 204: 'Liber malefactorum': alphabetical list of criminals and their crimes, 1510–1522.

N 230: Collection of printed broadsheet funeral regulations from the years 1578–1795. Relevant items are listed separately in the bibliography below.

N 807: Two funeral regulations, 1578, 1592.

V 108: (fols 17^r–19^r): Reply of the City Council to the 1525 citizens' articles (see Bestand 56, 385).

Bestand 56 (Köln contra Köln) (KcK):

385: (fols 76^r–88^v): The articles presented by the leaders of the 1525 citizens' uprising.

Bestand 110 (Testamente):

Full details of all wills cited are given in the footnotes.

Bestand 150 (Universität) (Un):

A 11: *Liber Rectorum matricule quarte vniversitatis studii Coloniensis [...]* Acta rectoralia, Liber rectoralis relating to the fourth *Matricula*, 1502–1558.

A 36–42: University of Cologne, Matricula, 7 vols. 36: I (1389–1425). 37: II (1425–1466). 38: III (1466–1502). 39: IV (1502–1559). 40: V (1559–1627). 41: VI (1627–1709). 42: VII (1754–1788) and University chronicle.

A 74: 'Conceptus dati per singulas facultates super reformatione universitatis' (1525).

A 84: MS history of the *Bursa Corneliana*, 16th c.

A 229: Extracts from the *Dekanatsbuch* of the Theological Faculty, made by Hermann Crombach, SJ and Joseph Hartzheim, SJ.

A 230 (previously 114a): 19th–20th-c. copy of extracts made by Nikolaus Brewer from the *Dekanatsbuch* of the Theology Faculty. I: 1398–1658. (Not Brewer, *Collectio statutorum, decretorum et responsorum facultatis theologicae* as stated in *Matrikel*, II, p. 793)).

A 236: Nikolaus Brewer, index of the statutes, decisions and notable proceedings of the Theological Faculty *Dekanatsbücher*, 1795.

A 317: 87^r–92^v: copy of 150, A 74 by Stephan Broelmann.

A 478–482: University of Cologne, *Dekanatsbuch* of the Arts Faculty, 5 vols. 478: I (1406–1440). 479: II (1440–1457). 480: III (1458–1499). 481: IV (1500–1565). 482: V (1565–1612).

A 516: Receptor's (Treasurer's) Book of the Arts Faculty, 1518–1564.

A 759 (previously 390): MS list of principals of the Bursa Laurentiana, 1440–1772. Till 1530 follows 760; after 1530 gives a detailed account by the principal Paul Kuckhovius (d. 1585).

A 760 (previously 390a): *Historia ACADEMIAE ARTIVM AGRIPPINENSIS. praecipuè Gymnasii Laurentiani, et Artium aliorum omnium*, a short history of the *Bursa Laurentiana*, to 1530, with continuations up to 1788. Paper MS, 14 fols.

Bestand 202 (Antoniter):

U 2/345: Mass foundation by Wenzeslaus Ulner as preceptor of the Cologne Antonite monastery, 28 July 1519.

U 2/346: Document confirming W. Ulner's Mass foundation signed by Matthias Wagener as preceptor of the Cologne Antonite monastery, 11 August 1519.

U 1/349: Rent contract signed by M. Wagener as preceptor, 20 February 1520.

U 2/351 and 2/352: Rent contract signed by M. Wagener as preceptor, 16 June 1520 (2 copies).

U 2/354: Rent contract signed by M. Wagener as preceptor, 12 January 1523 (2 copies).

U 1/356: Assignment of altar benefice, signed by M. Wagener as preceptor, 5 March 1526.

U 3/358: Rent contract signed by G. Kerckerinck as preceptor of the Cologne Antonite monastery, 3 October 1526.

Bestand 241 (Lämmchen auf der Burgmauer) (LBur):

U 3/5: Document naming Bela von Eschwiler as superior of the Lämmchen, 14 July 1508.

U 2/9: Document naming Sophie von Eschwiler as superior of the Lämmchen, 1517.

U 1/7: Donation of Johann (II) Rinck to the Lämmchen, 1511.

U 2/22: Bequest of Heinrich Buschers von Tongeren to the Lämmchen, 31 October 1563.

U 3/28: Bequest of Adelheit Rinck to the Lämmchen, 1584.

Bestand 290 (Clerus secundarius intraneus Coloniensis) (CSIC):

A. 2: *Conceptum Prouincialis Concilij Archiep[iscopatus] Coloniensis de anno 1536.* A MS draft of the 1538 *Canones concilii prouincialis Coloniensis*, largely identical with the printed version.

Bestand 295 (Geistliche Abteilung) (GA):

11a: 19th-c. copy by J.J. Merlo of the lost GA 11, the 'Bruderschaftsbuch' of the combined guild of St Anthony, Antonite monastery.

11e: MS list of the preceptors and monks of the Cologne Antonite house, 1358–1775.

150: Augustinian convent of the Lämmchen. Rules (16th c.) and historical details (1645–1805).
151: Mass and memorial foundations (1511) of Johann Rinck (d. 1516). Includes list of Lämmchen nuns.
209: 'Pfarrerbruderschaft': kalendar; order of burial of priests; lists of members, deceased and entitled to the brotherhood's prayers. 14th–15th c.
209a: 'Pfarrerbruderschaft': statutes, as revised in 1668. Vellum MS, 41 fols.
209b: 'Pfarrerbruderschaft': statutes, as revised in 1668. Paper MS, same text as 209a. Possibly a working copy, with notes and emendations, no signatures.

Bestand 310 (Reichskammergericht Köln):
H 41: Documents of a court case of 1624.

Bestand 7004:
27: Cookbook, Rheinfranken or Mainfranken, 15th c., second half. Paper, 66 fols (Previously Hs. G.B. 4º 27).

Bestand 7030 (Chroniken und Darstellungen) (C+D):
8: *Cronica presulum et Archiepiscoporum Coloniensis ecclesiae*, till 1508. MS, paper, 74 fols: text on fols 1–45.
19: Heinrich von Beeck, *Agrippina*, MS A (15th c.).
20: Heinrich von Beeck, *Agrippina*, MS B (15th c.).
29: *Koelhoffsche Chronik*, with MS additions, 1499. Paper MS.
49–52: *Das Buch Weinsberg*, the chronicle of Hermann von Weinsberg. 49: 'Liber iuventutis', 1518–1577; 50: 'Liber senectutis', 1578–1587; 51: 'Liber decrepitudinis', 1588–1597; 52: 'Claickboich'.
53–60: Various documents, accounts, wills and codicils pertaining to Hermann von Weinsberg's chronicle.
128: Interleaved copy of Hartzheim, *Bibliotheca Coloniensis* (q.v.), with numerous annotations and additions.
129: MS volume of additions to Hartzheim, *Bibliotheca Coloniensis* (q.v.).

Bestand 7657 (Genealogische Abteilung):
67: Family chronicle of Werner Overstolz, 1446.

Bestand 8830:

12. *Kleine Kölnische Chronik*, 1528: 19th-c. copy of the end of Darmstadt, Hessische Landesbibliothek, Hs. 131, an extract from the *Koelhoffsche Chronik*, with additions up to 1528. Previously Bestand 7030 (C+D), 30.

Manuscripts:

W. Kf. 348: MS codex of 1444, containing works by Petrarch and Lactantius, written for Aymo de Poypone.

Schotten's Works:

Ludus grammaticus latinae Linguae tramitem ostendens (Cologne: S. Kruffter, 1525). Sole known copy: Augsburg, Staats- und Stadtbibliothek, shelfmark Phil. 1226.

Meta Studii literarii [e]t quomodo in eam sint ducenda omnium scientiarum genera, necnon cur sit inuentus labor literarius: Et quantum toto coelo, nunc aberrent hij, qui a literis se abdicant/ Autore Hermanno Scottennio Heßo (Cologne: S. Kruffter, [1525]). *VD 16*, S 4029.

Confabulationes tyronum literariorum, ad amussim Colloquiorum Erasmi Roterodami, authore Hermanno Schotten. Heso [sic] (Augsburg: S. Ruff, July 1525). *VD 16*, S 4005.

Confabulationes tironum litterariorum, ed. by Peter Macardle, Durham Modern Languages Series, GT02 (Durham: DMLS, 2007).

Ludus martius sive bellicus, co[n]tinens simulachrum, originem, fabulam, & finem dissidij, habiti inter Rusticos & Principes Germaniae Orie[n]talis. Anno. 1525 Autore Hermanno Schotte[n]nio Hesso. [...] (Cologne: P. Quentel, 1526). *VD 16 online*, ZV 24274.

Ludus Martius sive bellicus: Mars- oder Kriegsspiel, ed. and trans. by H.-G. Roloff, Bibliotheca Neolatina, 1 (Bern–Frankfurt–New York–Paris: Lang, 1990).

Ludus imperatorius sive caesareus, continens umbraticam imaginem, horum temporum, regnante Diuo Carolo quinto, illiusque Caesaris diuinas uictorias, imperij felicem exitum, &

laudem, autore Hermanno Schottennio Hesso. Cui accedit, & Ludus Martius, de discordia principum & rusticorum Germaniae, anni M. D. XXV (Cologne: P. Quentel, 1527). VD 16, S 4027.

Instructio prima puerorum [...] per colloquia mutua (Cologne: [P. Quentel], 1527). VD 16, S 4026.

Vita honesta sive virtutis [...] (Cologne: P. Quentel, 1527). VD 16, S 4030 (much reprinted). Quoted from the edition of Antwerp: A. Goinus, 1540.

Elementale Dialectices Eivsdem quoq[ue] artis origo, utilitas & fructus pingui minerua a Grammatica ad Dialecticam progressuris prelibandum & frugiferum, Autore Hermanno Schottennio Hesso (Cologne: [P. Quentel], 1528). VD 16 online, ZV 25766.

Centuria epistolarum proverbialium quibus in providentia humanarum rerum. instructio. eruditio. & calliditas per adagia docentur & traduntur (Cologne: [P. Quentel], 1529). VD 16, S 4002.

Colloquia philosophica, & consolatoria, ac exhortatoria, vtriusque fortunæ ferendæ modum docentia, iuxta Senecæ & Francisci Petrarche consilia, ne inexperta rerum adolescentia temere sapiat, neve in prosperis plus æquo gestiat, atque in aduersis animam non despondeat. Authore Hermanno Schottennio Hesso (Cologne: P. Quentel, 1535). VD 16, S 4004.

Colloquia moralia ex variis philosophorum dictis condita [...] (Cologne: P. Quentel, 1535). VD 16, S 4003.

Other Sources:

References to classical literature, unless otherwise stated, are not to specific editions; any convenient edition may be used.

Agricola, Rodolphus, *Rodolphi Agricolae Phrisii de Inventione dialectica libri tres, cum scholiis Ioannis Matthaei Phrissemii* (Cologne: Hero Alopecius, 1523). VD 16, A 1098.

——, *De inventione dialectica libri tres. Drei Bücher über die Inventio Dialectica. Auf der Grundlage der Edition von Alardus von Amsterdam (1539) kritisch herausgegeben von Lothar Mundt* (Tübingen: Niemeyer, 1992).

——, *Letters*, ed. and trans. by Adrie van der Laan and Fokke Akkerman, Medieval and Renaissance Texts and Studies, 216 (Assen: van Gorcum, 2002).

Albala, Ken, *Eating Right in the Renaissance*, California Studies in Food and Culture, 2 (Berkeley: University of California Press, 2002).

Album Academiae Vitebergensis ab anno Christi MDII usque ad annum MDLX, ed. by Carolus Eduardus Foerstemann (Leipzig: Tauchnitz, 1841).

Anthologia Latina, sive Poesis latinae supplementum, ed. by Franz Buecheler and Alexander Riese, 5 vols (Leipzig: Teubner, 1894–1926; repr. Amsterdam: Hakkert, 1964).

Apostolios, Michael, of Byzantium, *Proverbia*, quoted from *Michaelis Apostolii Paroemiae [...]* (Leiden: Elzevier, 1619).

Bahlmann, P., 'Die Lambertus-Feier zu Münster i.W.', *ZVV*, 5 (1895), 174–80.

Barlandus, Hadrianus, *Dialogi XLII ad profligandam e scholis barbariem utilissimi* (Louvain: P. Martin Alost, 1524); cited from the edition of Antwerp: J. van der Loe, 1550.

Barth, Susanne, 'Manuale scolarium', in *HbKJL*, I, cols 321–31.

——, 'Johannes Murmellius: *Pappa*. Köln 1513', in *HbKJL*, I, cols 371–77.

——, 'Desiderius Erasmus: *Colloquia familiaria*', in *HbKJL*, I, cols 377–413.

——, 'Petrus Mosellanus: *Paedologia*', in *HbKJL*, I, cols 414–29.

Bauch, Gustav, *Geschichte des Leipziger Frühhumanismus*, Centralblatt für Bibliothekswesen, Beiheft 22 (Leipzig: Harrassowitz, 1899).

Bauer, Veit Harold, *Das Antoniusfeuer in Kunst und Medizin*, Supplement zu den Sitzungsberichten der Heidelberger Akademie der Wissenschaften, Mathematisch-Naturwissenschaftliche Klasse (Berlin: Springer, 1973).

Bayle, Edith, and others, *Répertoire automatisé des livres du seizième siècle à la bibliothèque municipale de Rouen* (Paris: Saur, 1983).

Bebel, Heinrich, *Facetien: drei Bücher. Historisch-kritische Ausgabe*, ed. by Gustav Bebermeyer, Bibliothek des Literarischen Vereins in Stuttgart, 276 (Leipzig: Hiersemann, 1931; repr. Hildesheim: Olms, 1967).

———, *Facetiarum [...] libri tres, a mendis repurgati [...]* (Tübingen: [Widow of U. Morhard], 1570).

Beemelmans, Wilhelm, 'Bilder aus dem Kölner Volksleben im XVI. Jahrhundert', *JKGV*, 15 (1933), 135–52.

Behr, Hans-Joachim, 'Franz von Waldeck (um 1491–1553)', *Westfälische Lebensbilder*, 14 (1987), 38–62.

Berry, Lilian Gay, 'A Fifteenth-Century Guide to Latin Conversation for University Students', *The Classical Journal*, 23 (1928), 520–30.

Bierlaire, Franz, 'Le *Libellus Colloquiorum* de mars 1522 et Nicolas Baechem, dit *Egmondanus*', in *Scrinium Erasmianum*, ed. by J. Coppens, 2 vols (Leiden: Brill, 1969), I, pp. 55–81.

———, 'Un livre du maître au XVIᵉ siècle: Erasme expliqué par Hegendorf', *Quaerendo*, 2 (1972), 200–20.

———, *Les Colloques d'Erasme: réforme des études, réforme des mœurs et réforme de L'Eglise au XVIᵉ siècle* (Paris: Les Belles Lettres, 1978).

———, 'Les "Dialogi pueriles" de Christophe Hegendorff', in *Acta Conventus Neo-Latini Turonensis. 3ᵉ Congrès International d'Etudes Néo-Latines, Tours 1976*, ed. by J.-C. Margolin (Paris: Vrin, 1980), pp. 389–401.

Bömer, Alois, *Die lateinischen Schülergespräche der Humanisten. Auszüge mit Einleitungen, Anmerkungen und Namen- und Sachregister. Quellen für die Schul- und Universitätsgeschichte des 15. und 16. Jahrhunderts*, Texte und Forschungen zur Geschichte der Erziehung und des Unterrichts in den Ländern deutscher Zunge, 1 (Berlin: Harrwitz, 1897; repr. Amsterdam: Schippers, 1966).

———, 'Hermannus Buschius', *Westfälische Lebensbilder*, 1 (1930), 50–67.

Breuer, Wimmar, *Burgbann und Burgmeile von Köln* (Cologne: Jacobi, 1921).

Breviarium Romanum ex decreto Sacrosancti Concilii Tridentini restitutum [...] (Florence: Birindelli, 1857).

Brincken, Anna-Dorothee von den, 'Johann Potken aus Schwerte, Propst von St. Georg in Köln, der erste Äthiopologe des Abendlandes', in *Aus kölnischer und rheinischer Geschichte. Festgabe Arnold Güttsches zum 65. Geburtstag*, VKGV, 29 (Cologne: Wamper, 1969), pp. 81–114.

——, 'Die Stadt Köln und ihre hohen Schulen', in *Stadt und Universität im Mittelalter und in der früheren Neuzeit*, ed. by Erich Maschke and Jürgen Sydow, Stadt in der Geschichte. Veröffentlichungen des Südwestdeutschen Arbeitskreises für Stadtgeschichtsforschung, 3 (Sigmaringen: Thorbecke, 1977), pp. 27–52.

Brunken, Otto, 'Desiderius Erasmus: *De civilitate morum puerilium*', in *HbKJL*, I, cols 632–56.

Büttner, Andreas, 'Antonius in Köln. Auf den Spuren eines Heiligen im Mittelalter', in *Thesaurus Coloniensis. Beiträge zur mittelalterlichen Kunstgeschichte Kölns. Festschrift für Anton von Euw*, ed. by Ulrich Krings, Wolfgang Schmitz, and Hiltrud Westermann-Angerhausen, VKGV, 41 (1999), pp. 265–96.

Buschius, Hermannus, *Hermanni Buschii Monasteriense Epigrammaton sententiis utilibus [...]* ([Cologne]: J. Landen, [1498]). *GW*, 5798.

——, *De saluberrimo fructuosissimoq[ue] diue virgi[ni]s Marie psalterio triplex Hecatostichon cum alijs ad eandem quibusdam carminibus elegantissimis* (Leipzig: M. Landsberg, *ca.* 1500). *VD 16*, B 9939.

Canones concilii prouincialis Coloniensis [...] celebrati. Anno 1536 [...] (Cologne: P. Quentel, 1538).

Carmina Burana, ed. by Alfons Hilka and Otto Schumann, 2 vols (Heidelberg: Winter, 1930–1970).

Chaix, Gérald, *Réforme et contre-réforme catholiques. Recherches sur la Chartreuse de Cologne au XVIe siècle*, Analecta Cartusiana, 80, 3 vols (Salzburg: Universität Salzburg, Institut für Anglistik und Amerikanistik, 1981).

——, 'Humanisme et élites urbaines à Cologne au XVIe siècle', in *Humanismus und höfisch-städtische Eliten im 16. Jahrhundert*, ed. by Klaus Malettke and Jürgen Voss (Bonn: Bouvier, 1989), pp. 195–210.

——, 'De la cité chrétienne à la métropole catholique. Vie religieuse et conscience civique à Cologne au XVIᵉ siècle' (unpubl. doctoral thesis, University of Strasbourg, 1994).

Chaumartin, H., 'Le compagnon de Saint-Antoine', *Aesculape*, 20 (1930), 233–56.

Claes, 'De lexicografie in de zestiende eeuw', in *Geschiedenis van de Nederlandse taalkunde*, ed. by Dirk M. Bakker and G.R.W. Dibbets (Den Bosch: Malmberg, 1977), pp. 206–17.

Clemen, Carl, 'Der Ursprung des Martinsfestes', *ZVV*, 28 (1918), 1–14.

Cobban, Alan B., 'Medieval Student Power', *Past and Present*, 53 (1971), 28–66.

Coellen eyn Croyn. Renaissance und Barock in Köln, ed. by Werner Schäfke, Der Riss im Himmel, 1 (Cologne: DuMont, 1999).

Cordier, Mathurin, *Colloquiorum scholasticorum libri IIII, ad pueros in sermone latino paulatim exercendos, Mathurini Corderii* (Lyon: T. Straton, 1564).

Cornelius, Antonius, de Linnich, *Oratio habita Coloniae coram frequenti clero, ab Antonio Cornelio Lynnichano, qua ecclesiae proceres sui officij admonet, & cuiusmodi Euangelici gregis pastores esse debeant, ostendit [...]* ([Cologne: E. Cervicornus, 1527]). *VD16*, C 5155.

Corsten, Severin, 'Universität und Buchdruck in Köln. Versuch eines Überblicks für das 15. Jahrhundert', in Severin Corsten, *Studien zum Kölner Frühdruck. Gesammelte Beiträge 1955–1985*, Kölner Arbeiten zum Bibliotheks- und Dokumentationswesen, 7 (Cologne: Greven, 1985), pp. 123–37.

Crahay, R., 'Les censeurs louvanistes d'Erasme', in *Scrinium Erasmianum*, ed. by J. Coppens, 2 vols (Leiden: Brill, 1969), I, pp. 221–49.

Cratepoleus, Petrus Merssaeus, *De electorum ecclesiasticorum archi-episcoporum ac episcoporum Coloniensium Origine et Successione à Primo Christianae Religionis exordio usque ad praesens saeculum Historica Tractatio [...]* (Cologne 1580); cited from the edition of Cologne: O. Steinhauss, 1736).

Creutz, Rudolf, 'Pest und Pestabwehr im alten Köln', *JKGV*, 15 (1933), 79–119.

Cronica van der hilliger stat van Coellen (also known as *Koelhoffsche Chronik*), ed. by Hermann Cardauns, *Die Chroniken der deutschen Städte vom 14. bis ins 16. Jahrhundert*, ed. by Historische Commission bei der Königlichen Akademie der Wissenschaften (of Bavaria) (Leipzig: Hirzel, 1875–1877; repr. Göttingen: Vandenhoeck & Ruprecht, 1968), XIII and XIV.

Crusenius, Nicolaus, *Monasticon Augustinianum in quo omnium ordinum sub regula S. Augustini militantium [...] origines, atque incrementa [...] explicantur* (Munich: J. Hertsroy, 1623).

Decreta et Statuta dioecesanae synodi Coloniensis ([Cologne: J. Busaeus, 1661?]).

Decreta et Statuta dioecesanae synodi Coloniensis (Cologne: J. Busaeus, 1667).

Deeters, Joachim, *Die Bestände des Stadtarchivs Köln bis 1814. Eine Übersicht*, MStAK, 76 (Cologne–Weimar–Vienna: Böhlau, 1994).

Dekker, A.M.M., 'Three Unknown "Cantilenae martinianae" by Georgius Macropedius: A Contribution to the Study of the Utrecht *Carmina Scholastica*', *HL*, 23 (1974), 188–227.

Demandt, Karl E., *Geschichte des Landes Hessen*, rev. repr. of 2nd edn (Kassel: Stauda, 1980).

Didier, Nikolaus, *Nikolaus Mameranus. Ein Luxemburger Humanist des XVI. Jahrhunderts am Hofe der Habsburger. Sein Leben und seine Werke* (Freiburg: Herder, 1915).

Dohrn-van Rossum, Gerhard, *The History of the Hour. Clocks and Modern Temporal Orders*, trans. by Thomas Dunlap (Chicago–London: University of Chicago Press, 1996).

Dorn, Johannes, 'Der Ursprung der Pfarreien und die Anfänge des Pfarrwahlrechts im mittelalterlichen Köln', *Zeitschrift der Savigny-Stiftung für Rechtsgeschichte, Kanonistische Abteilung*, 5 (1915), 122–64.

Dürr, Franciscus Antonius, *Commentatio historica de episcopo puerorum, vulgo vom Schul-Bischoff*, in *Thesaurus iuris ecclesiastici potissimum Germanici sive dissertationes selectae in ius ecclesiasticum*, ed. by Antonius Schmidt, 7 vols (Heidelberg: Göbhardt, 1772–1778), III, pp. 58–83.

Durandus, Gulielmus, *Rationale divinorum officiorum*, ed. by Anselme Davril, OSB and Timothy M. Thibodeau, 3 vols, Corpus Christianorum Continuatio Mediaevalis, 140–40B (Turnhout: Brepols, 1995–2000).

Ebeling, Dietrich and Irsigler, Franz, *Getreideumsatz, Getreide- und Brotpreise in Köln 1368–1797*, MStAK, 65–67, (Cologne: Böhlau, 1976–). I. *Getreideumsatz und Getreidepreise: Wochen-, Monats- und Jahrestabelle* (1976). II. *Brotgewichte und Brotpreise: Wochen-, Monats- und Jahrestabelle. Graphiken* (1977).

Engammare, Max, *L'Ordre du temps. L'invention de la ponctualité au XVIe siècle*, Les seuils de la modernité, 8 (Geneva: Droz, 2004).

Ennen, Leonard, *Quellen zur Geschichte der Stadt Köln*, 6 vols (Cologne: DuMont-Schauberg, 1860–1879; repr. Aalen: Scientia, 1970).

——, *Geschichte der Stadt Köln, meist aus den Quellen des Kölner Stadt-Archivs*, 5 vols (Cologne–Düsseldorf: Schwann, 1863–1879).

——, 'Kölner Holzfahrttag', *Zeitschrift für Kulturgeschichte*, N.F. 1 (1872), 641–42.

Erasmus, Desiderius, of Rotterdam, *Adagia*, ed. by M.L. van Poll-van de Lisdonk and others, *ASD*, II-1 (1993); II-4 (1987); II-5 (1981); II-6 (1981).

——, *Colloquia*, ed. by L.-E. Halkin and others, *ASD*, I-3 (1972).

——, *The Colloquies*, trans. by Craig R. Thompson (Chicago–London: Chicago University Press, 1965).

Erneuerte Funeral oder Begräbnüß Ordnung/ wornach alle und jede des Heil. Röm. Reichs freyer Statt Cölln Bürger und Einwohnere unter deren darbey vermelten Straffen sich zu richten und zu verhalten (Cologne: J.B. Pfeiffer von Bacharach, [1688]).

Eulenburg, Franz, *Die Frequenz der deutschen Universitäten von ihrer Gründung bis zur Gegenwart*, Abhandlungen der sächsischen Gesellschaft der Wissenschaften, philologisch-historische Klasse, 24,2 (Leipzig: Teubner, 1904; repr. Berlin: Akademie, 1994).

Feste und Feiern im Mittelalter. Paderborner Symposion des Mediävistenverbandes, ed. by Detlef Altenburg, Jörg Jarnut and Hans-Hugo Steinhoff (Sigmaringen: Thorbecke, 1991).

Fetkenheuer, Klaus, *Die Rezeption der Persius-Satiren in der lateinischen Literatur. Untersuchungen zu ihrer Wirkungsgeschichte von Lucan bis Boccaccio* (Bern: Lang, 2001).

Fletcher, John M., 'Wealth and Poverty in the Medieval German Universities with Particular Reference to the University of Heidelberg', in *Europe in the Late Middle Ages*, ed. by J.R. Hale and others (London: Faber and Faber, 1965), pp. 410–36.

——, 'Commentary' (on Gingerich, 'Matriculation Ages in Sixteenth-Century Wittenberg'), *History of Universities*, 6 (1986–87), 139–41.

[*Flores poetarum de virtutibus et viciis ac donis sancti spiritus*] (from sig. n vii^r) (Cologne: B. de Unckel, 1480). Cf. GW, 10070 (possibly not identical).

[*Funeral directive, Cologne, 1578*] Printed single sheet. No title. Begins: 'VNsere HErn vom Radte kommen in gewiße erfarung [...]' Ends: 'Sic actum et conclusum VIII. Augusti Anno LXXVIII.' (n.p., n.pr., 1578).

[*Funeral directive, Cologne, 1592*] Printed single sheet. No title. Begins: 'WJr Bürgermeister vnd Rathe des heiligen Reichs Freyer Statt Cölln/ [...]' Ends: 'Geben Mitwoch am 9. tag Septembris. Anno M.D.LXXXXJJ*. (n.p., n.pr., 1592).

[*Funeral directive, Cologne, 1597*] Booklet. No title. Begins: 'WJr Bürgermeistere vnd Rhat des Heyligen Reichs freyer Statt Cölln/ [...]' Ends: '[...] am *11. Junij. Anno M.D.XCVII*' (n.p., n.pr., 1597). Large 4°, A1–4.

Gescher, Franz, *Der Kölner Stadtdechant und die Vereinigung der stadtkölnischen Pfarrer: Urkunden und Akten bis zum Ausgang des 14. Jahrhunderts*, MStAK, 40 (Cologne: Böhlau, 1929), pp. 164–243.

——, 'Die Statuten der theologischen Fakultät an der alten Universität Köln', in *Festschr. Köln*, pp. 43–108.

Giesen, Josef, 'Ein Brief des Kölner Ratsherrn Hermann Rinck an Kardinal Wolsey', *JKGV*, 19 (1937), 370–76.

Gilmore, Myron P., 'Erasmus and Alberto Pio, Prince of Carpi', in *Action and Conviction in Early Modern Europe. Essays in Memory of E.H. Harbison*, ed. by Theodore K. Rabb and Jerrold E. Seigel (Princeton: Princeton University Press, 1969), pp. 299–318.

——, 'Italian Reactions to Erasmian Humanism', in *Iter Italicum. The Profile of the Italian Renaissance in the Mirror of its European Transformations. Dedicated to Paul Oskar Kristeller on the Occasion of his 70th Birthday*, ed. by Heiko H. Oberman and Thomas A. Brady, Jr, Studies in Medieval and Renaissance Theology, 14 (Leiden: Brill, 1975), pp. 61–115.

Gingerich, Miriam and Owen Gingerich, 'Matriculation Ages in Sixteenth-Century Wittenberg', *History of Universities*, 6 (1986–1987), 135–37.

Götze, Alfred, *Die hochdeutschen Drucker der Reformationszeit* (Berlin: de Gruyter, 1963).

Gotzen, Joseph, 'Ein kirchliches Bittlied aus der Zeit der Fieberepidemie in Köln 1529', *JKGV*, 1 (1912), 79–88.

Greving, Joseph, *Steuerlisten des Kirchspiels St. Kolumba in Köln vom 13.–16. Jahrhundert*, MStAK, 30 (Cologne: DuMont-Schauberg, 1900).

Grotefend, Hermann, *Taschenbuch der Zeitrechnung des deutschen Mittelalters und der Neuzeit*, 12th edn, rev. by Jürgen Asch (Hanover: Hahnsche Buchhandlung, 1982).

Grotefend online, ed. by H. Ruth: <http://www.manuscripta-mediaevalia.de/gaeste/grotefend/ grotefend.htm>.

Günther, Otto, *Plautuserneuerungen in der deutschen Literatur des 15.–17. Jahrhunderts und ihre Verfasser* (Leipzig: Marquart, 1886).

Gutmann, Elsbeth, *Die Colloquia familiaria des Erasmus von Rotterdam*, Basler Beiträge zur Geschichtswissenschaft, 111 (Basel–Stuttgart: Helbing und Lichtenhahn, 1967).

Halkin, Léon-Ernest, *Erasmus: A Critical Biography*, trans. by John Tonkin (Oxford: Blackwell, 1993).

Hansisches Urkundenbuch, ed. by Verein für Hansische Geschichte (Halle: Waisenhaus, then Leipzig: Duncker & Humblot, then Weimar: Böhlau, 1876–).

Hartzheim, Joseph, SJ, *Bibliotheca Coloniensis [...] omnium Archi-dioeceseos Coloniensis [...] indigenarum et incolarum scriptorum [...]* (Cologne: T. Odenall, 1747; repr. Farnborough: Gregg, 1967).

Hayn, Kasimir, 'Aus den Annaten-Registern der Päpste Eugen IV., Pius II., Paul II. und Sixtus IV. (1431–1447; 1458–1494)', *AHVN*, 61 (1895), 129–86.

Hegel, Eduard, *St. Kolumba in Köln. Eine mittelalterliche Großstadtpfarrei in ihrem Werden und Vergehen*, Studien zur Kölner Kirchengeschichte, 30 (Siegburg: Schmitt, 1996).

Hegendorff, Christoph, *Dialogi pueriles,* in Mosellanus, P., *Paedologia Petri Mosellani Protegensis in puerorum usum conscripta & aucta. Dialogi XXXVII. Dialogi pueriles Christophori Hegendorphini XII. lepidi æque, ac docti* (Strasbourg: J. Knobloch, 1 July 1523), sig. C5^v–D7^v.

Helmstaedter, Gerhard, 'Pestprävention im Kölner Raum um 1500 – Aus dem Rezeptbuch eines Brauweiler Mönches', *AHVN*, 205 (2002), 87–101.

Helvicus, Christophorus, *Familiaria colloquia, Autoritate Superiorum selecta et adornata à Christophoro Helvico [...] Jam [...] Germanice reddita [...]*, 6th edn (Gießen: C. Chemlin, 1655); many later editions. First edition not found.

Herborn, Wolfgang, 'Zur Rekonstruktion und Edition der Kölner Bürgermeisterliste bis zum Ende des Ancien Régime', *RVB*, 36 (1972), 89–183.

——, 'Bürgerliches Selbstverständnis im spätmittelalterlichen Köln. Bemerkungen zu zwei Hausbüchern aus der ersten Hälfte des 15. Jahrhunderts', in *Festschr. Ennen*, pp. 490–520.

——, 'Sozialtopographie des Kölner Kirchspiels St. Kolumba', in *Zwei Jahrtausende*, I, pp. 205–215.

——, *Die politische Führungsschicht der Stadt Köln im Spätmittelalter*, Rheinisches Archiv, 100 (Bonn: Röhrscheid, 1977).

——, 'Fast-, Fest- und Feiertage im Köln des 16. Jahrhunderts', *Rheinisches Jahrbuch für Volkskunde*, 25 (1983/1984), 27–61.

——, '"Straßen wie diese". Zum Alltagsleben einer Kölner Straße im 16. Jahrhundert', *GiK*, 15 (1984), 6–36.

——, 'Hermann von Weinsberg', *Rheinische Lebensbilder*, 11 (1988), 59–76.

Herte, Adolf, *Das katholische Lutherbild im Bann der Lutherkommentare des Cochläus*, 3 vols (Münster: Aschendorff, 1943).

Heyden, Sebaldus, *Nomenclatura rerum domesticarum* (Mainz: I. Schöffer, 1534; repr., ed. by Peter O. Müller and Gaston van der Elst, Documenta linguistica, Reihe I, Hildesheim: Olms, 1998).

——, *Formulae puerilium colloquiorum*, in id., *Nomenclatura rerum domesticarum*, ed. by Müller and van der Elst, sig. G4^v–I2^r.

Hiestand, Rudolf, 'Civis Romanus sum. Zum Selbstverständnis bürgerlicher Führungsschichten in den spätmittelalterlichen Städten', in *Herkunft und Ursprung. Historische und mythische Formen der Legitimation*, ed. by Peter Wunderli (Sigmaringen: Thorbecke, 1994), pp. 91–109.

Höhlbaum, Konstantin, 'Zur Geschichte der sogenannten Koelhoffschen Chronik', MStAK, 19 (1890), 103–12.

Hoffmann, Detlef, *The Playing Card. An Illustrated History*, 3rd edition (Leipzig: Edition Leipzig, 1973).

Hofmann, J.B., *Lateinische Syntax und Stilistik*, rev. by Anton Szantyr, *Handbuch der Altertumswissenschaft*, 2. Abteilung, 2. Teil, 2. Band (Munich: Beck, 1965).

Hofmann, Winfried, 'Hermann von Weinsberg und die kölnische Fastnacht im 16. Jahrhundert', *Rheinisch-westfälische Zeitschrift für Volkskunde*, 10 (1963), 82–98.

Hospinianus, Rodolphus, *De festis Iudaeorum et ethnicorum: Hoc est, de origine, progressu, ceremoniis et ritibus festorum dierum Iudaeorum, Graecorum, Romanorum, Turcarum et Indianorum, libri III [...]*, 2nd edn (Zürich: R. Wolf, 1611).

——, *Festa Christianorum. Hoc est, de origine, progressu, ceremoniis et ritibus festorum dierum Christianorum liber unus [...]*, 2nd edn (Zürich: R. Wolf, 1612).

Huisman, Gerda, *Rudolph Agricola: A Bibliography of Printed Works and Translations*, Bibliotheca bibliographica neerlandica, 20 (Nieuwkoop: de Graaf, 1985).

Humanismus in Köln / Humanism in Cologne, ed. by James V. Mehl, Studien zur Geschichte der Universität zu Köln, 10 (Cologne–Weimar–Vienna: Böhlau, 1992).

Huyskens, Albert, 'Junggraf Wilhelm von Waldeck an der Universität Köln 1509/10', *AHVN*, 97 (1915), 78–110.

Ijsewijn, Josef, 'Mittelalterliches Latein und Humanistenlatein', in *Die Rezeption der Antike: Zum Problem der Kontinuität zwischen Mittelalter und der Renaissance*, ed. by August Buck (Hamburg: Hauswedell, 1981), pp. 71–83.

Index des livres interdits, ed. by J.M. de Bujanda and others (Sherbrooke, Quebec: Université de Sherbrooke, 1984–).

Irsigler, Franz, 'Köln, die Frankfurter Messen und die Handelsbeziehungen mit Oberdeutschland im 15. Jahrhundert', in *Köln, das Reich und Europa. Abhandlungen über weiträumige Verflechtungen der Stadt Köln in Politik, Recht und Wirtschaft im Mittelalter*, ed. by Hugo Stehkämper, MStAK, 60 (Cologne: Neubner, 1971), pp. 341–429.

——, 'Hansekaufleute. Die Lübecker Veckinchusen und die Kölner Rinck', in *Hanse in Europa. Brücke zwischen den Märkten, 12.–17. Jahrhundert. Ausstellung des Kölnischen Stadtmuseums 9. Juni–9. September 1973* (Cologne: Kölnisches Stadtmuseum, 1973), pp. 301–27.

——, 'Getreidepreise, Getreidehandel und städtische Versorgungspolitik in Köln, vornehmlich im 15. und 16. Jahrhundert', in *Festschr. Ennen*, pp. 571–610.

——, 'Kölner Wirtschaft im Spätmittelalter', in *Zwei Jahrtausende*, I, pp. 217–319.

——, 'Getreide- und Brotpreise, Brotgewicht und Getreideverbrauch in Köln vom Spätmittelalter bis zum Ende des Ancien Régime', in *Zwei Jahrtausende*, I, pp. 519–39.

——, 'Peter Rinck († 8. Febr. 1501)', *Rheinische Lebensbilder*, 6 (1975), 55–69.

——, *Die wirtschaftliche Stellung der Stadt Köln im 14. und 15. Jahrhundert*, Vierteljahrsschrift für Sozial- und Wirtschaftsgeschichte, Beiheft 65 (Wiesbaden: Steiner, 1979).

——, and Arnold Lassotta, *Bettler und Gaukler, Dirnen und Henker. Außenseiter in einer mittelalterlichen Stadt: Köln 1300–1600*, dtv 30075 (Munich: Deutscher Taschenbuch Verlag, 1989).

Janin, R., 'Antoniusorden (6)', *LThK²*, I, cols 676–77.

Kaemmel, Heinrich Julius, *Geschichte des deutschen Schulwesens im Übergange vom Mittelalter zur Neuzeit. Aus seinem Nachlasse hrsg. von O. Kaemmel* (Leipzig: Duncker & Humblot, 1882; repr. Hildesheim: Olms, 1986).

Kahl, Willi, 'Die Musik an der alten Kölner Universität um 1500', in *Festschr. Köln*, pp. 473–501.

Kellenbenz, Hermann, 'Die wohlhabendsten Kölner Bürger um 1515', in *Geschichte in der Gesellschaft. Festschrift für Karl Bosl zum 65. Geburtstag 11.XI.1973*, ed. by Friedrich Prinz, Franz-Josef Schmale, and Ferdinand Seibt (Stuttgart: Hiersemann, 1974), pp. 264–91.

——, 'Wirtschaftsgeschichte Kölns im 16. und beginnenden 17. Jahrhundert', in *Zwei Jahrtausende*, I, pp. 321–427.

Kemp, Jacob, 'Die Wohlfahrtspflege des Kölner Rates in dem Jahrhundert nach der großen Zunftrevolution' (unpubl. doctoral thesis, University of Bonn, 1904).

Keussen, Hermann, 'Die drei Reisen des Utrechters Arnoldus Buchelius nach Deutschland, insbesondere sein Kölner Aufenthalt', I, *AHVN*, 84 (1907), 1–102; II, *AHVN*, 85 (1908), 43–114.

Klersch, Joseph, *Die Kölnische Fastnacht von ihren Anfängen bis zur Gegenwart*, Schriften des Bundes Deutscher Karveval, 1 (Cologne: Bachem, 1961).

Kloft, Jost, *Inventar des Urkundenarchivs der Fürsten von Hatzfeld-Wildenburg zu Schönstein/Sieg*, Veröffentlichungen der Landesarchivverwaltung Rheinland-Pfalz, 22, 31, 34, 37, 47, 62, 6 vols (Koblenz: Selbstverlag der Landesarchivverwaltung Rheinland-Pfalz, 1975–1993).

Kluppel, Konrad, *Konrad Kluppels Chronik und Briefbuch*, in *Waldecker Chroniken*, ed. by Paul Jürges and others, Veröffentlichungen der historischen Kommission für Hessen und Waldeck, VII,2 (Marburg: Elwert, 1914), pp. I–XXXVII, 1–179.

Knipping, Richard, *Die Kölner Stadtrechnungen des Mittelalters, mit einer Darstellung der Finanzverwaltung*, PGRG, 15, 2 vols (Bonn: Behrendt, 1897–1898).

Koelhoffsche Chronik: see *Cronica van der hilliger stat van Coellen*.

Köln als Kommunikationszentrum. Studien zur frühneuzeitlichen Stadtgeschichte, ed. by Georg Mölich and Gerd Schwerhoff, Der Riss im Himmel, 4 (Cologne: DuMont, 1999).

Kooiman, P. 'The Letters of Rodolphus Agricola to Jacobus Barbirianus', in *Rodolphus Agricola Phrisius 1444–1485. Proceedings of the International Conference at the University of Groningen 28–30 October 1985*, ed. by Fokke Akkerman and Arie Johan Vanderjagt (Leiden: Brill, 1988), pp. 136–46.

Krafft, Carl, 'Mittheilungen aus der Matrikel der alten Cölner Universität zur Zeit des Humanismus', *Zeitschrift für preußische Geschichte und Landeskunde*, 5 (1868), 467–503. Also as *Aufzeichnungen des schweizerischen Reformers Heinrich Bullinger über sein Studium zu Emmerich und Köln (1516–1522) und dessen Briefwechsel mit Freunden in Köln, Erzbischof Hermann von Wied, etc. Ein Beitrag zur niederrheinisch-westfälischen Kirchen-, Schul- und Gelehrtengeschichte* (Elberfeld: Lucas, 1870).

——, 'Mittheilungen aus der niederrheinischen Reformationsgeschichte', *Zeitschrift des Bergischen Geschichtsvereins*, 6 (1869), 193–340.

——, and Wilhelm Krafft, 'Über Petrus Mosellanus' Studium in Köln 1512–1514', in Carl Krafft and Wilhelm Krafft, *Briefe und Dokumente aus der Zeit der Reformation nebst Mittheilungen über Kölnische Gelehrte und Studien im 13. und 16. Jahrhundert* (Elberfeld: Lucas, 1875), pp. 118–201.

Kremer, U.M., 'Mosellanus, Humanist zwischen Kirche und Reformation', *ARG*, 73 (1982), 20–34.

Kristeller, Paul Oskar, 'The Contribution of Religious Orders to Renaissance Thought and Learning', *American Benedictine Review*, 21 (1970), 1–55; repr. in Kristeller, P.O. *Medieval Aspects of Renaissance Learning*, ed. and trans. by Edward P. Mahoney, Duke Monographs in Medieval and Renaissance Studies, 1 (Durham, NC: Duke University Press, 1974), pp. 95–158.

Kuckhoff, Joseph, *Der Sieg des Humanismus in den katholischen Gelehrtenschulen des Niederrheins 1525–1557*, Katholisches Leben und Kämpfen im Zeitalter der Glaubensspaltung, 3 (Münster: Aschendorff, 1929).

——, *Die Geschichte des Gymnasium Tricoronatum*, Veröffentlichungen des Rheinischen Museums in Köln, 1 (Cologne: Bachem, 1931).

Kulturströmungen und Kulturprovinzen in den Rheinlanden: Geschichte – Sprache – Volkskunde, ed. by Hermann Aubin, Theodor Frings, and Josef Müller (Bonn: Röhrscheid, 1926; repr. Darmstadt: Wissenschaftliche Buchgesellschaft, 1966).

Kuphal, Erich, 'Das Urkundenarchiv der Stadt Köln seit dem Jahre 1397'. VIII. '1506–1540', in MStAK, 40 (Cologne: Neubner, 1929), pp. 5–161.

——, 'Die Archive der Universität Köln', in *Festschr. Köln*, pp. 548–637.

Kurkölnische Begräbnisordnung, 1688: printed broadsheet version of the *Erneuerte Funeral oder Begräbnüß Ordnung*, 1688. No title. Begins: 'Maximilianus Henricus Dei gratia Archiepiscopus Coloniensis, [...]'. Ends: 'Datum [...] Bonnae 28. Februarii 1688.'

Langen, Rudolf von, *Rhodolphi Langii Canonici Monasteriensis Carmina* (Münster: J. Limburgus, 1486); *Des münsterschen Kanonikus Rudolph von Langen Gedichte*, facs. repr. with transl. by Hermann Hugenroth (Münster: Regensberg, 1991).

——, *Rosarium [...] beatissimae virginis [...] Marie [...] Ad egregium virum utriusque iuris professione praeclarum Magistrum Petrum Rinck civem urbis sanctae felicisque Coloniae* (Münster: n.pr., [1493]).

——, *Horae de sancta cruce pindaricis versibus ac elegia de eadem* ([Cologne]: [Quentel], [1496]).

Lassotta, Friedrich-Arnold, *Formen der Armut im späten Mittelalter und zu Beginn der Neuzeit. Untersuchungen vornehmlich an Kölner Quellen des 14. bis 17. Jahrhunderts*, 2 vols (Cologne: Hundt, 1993).

Lea, Henry Charles, *A History of Auricular Confession and Indulgences in the Latin Church*, 3 vols (Philadelphia: Lea Brothers, 1896).

Das Leben in der Stadt des Spätmittelalters. Internationaler Kongreß Krems an der Donau 20. bis 23. September 1976, Österreichische Akademie der Wissenschaften, Philosophisch-historische Klasse, Sitzungsberichte, 325; also Veröffentlichungen des Instituts für mittelalterliche Realienkunde Österreichs, 2 (Vienna: Österreichische Akademie der Wissenschaften, 1977).

Leedham-Green, Elisabeth S., *Books in Cambridge Inventories. Book-lists from the Vice-Chancellor's Court Probate Inventories in the Tudor and Stuart Periods*, 2 vols (Cambridge: Cambridge University Press, 1986).

Liessem, H. J., *Hermann van dem Busche. Sein Leben und seine Schriften. Nebst einer Beilage: 'Die quodlibetischen Disputationen an der Universität Köln'* (Cologne: Kaiser-Wilhelm-Gymnasium, 1886).

Lodge, Gonzalez, *Lexicon Plautinum*, 2 vols (Leipzig: Teubner, 1924–1933; repr. Hildesheim: Olms, 1962).

Löfstedt, Bengt, 'Zur Lexikographie des deutschen Neulateins', *Latomus*, 60 (2001), 456–59.

——, 'Zum deutschen Neulatein', *Latomus*, 63 (2004), 725–29, 963–67.

Loesch, Heinrich von, *Die Kölner Zunfturkunden nebst anderen Kölner Gewerbeurkunden bis zum Jahre 1500*, 2 vols, PGRG, 22 (Bonn: Hanstein, 1907).

Lohr, Charles H., 'Renaissance Latin Aristotle Commentaries', *RQ*, 33 (1980), 623–734.

Looz-Corswaren, Clemens von, 'Die Kölner Artikelserie von 1525', in *Kirche und gesellschaftlicher Wandel in deutschen und niederländischen Städten der werdenden Neuzeit*, Städteforschung, A 10 (Cologne–Vienna: Böhlau, 1980), pp. 65–153.

Lurz, W., 'Heiliges Jahr', *LThK²*, V, cols 125–26.

Macardle, P.G., 'Our Reading of an Early "Documentary Drama": Schottennius's *Ludus Martius* (1526)', *Daphnis*, 18 (1989), 391–420.

———, 'Cologne Life and Cologne University Humanism. The *Confabulationes tyronum literariorum* (1525) and their Author Hermannus Schottennius Hessus', *HL*, 42 (1993), 126–59.

———, 'Matthias Wagener and Traces of Antonite Humanism in Cologne', *JWCI*, 57 (1994), 254–63.

———, *The Allegory of Acolastus. Biblical Allegoresis and its Literary Reflex in Gnapheus's Acolastus* (1529) (Durham: Centre for Medieval and Renaissance Studies, 2007).

Manitius, Max, *Analekten zur Geschichte des Horaz im Mittelalter* (Göttingen: Dieterich, 1893).

Manuale scholarium qui studentium vniversitates aggredi ac postea proficere in eis intendunt ([Cologne]: [H. Quentel], after 6 April 1490]).

Manuale scholarium, ed. by Friedrich Zarncke, in *Die deutschen Universitäten im Mittelalter: Beiträge zur Geschichte und Charakteristik derselben*, Erster Beitrag (Leipzig: Weigel, 1857), pp. 1–48, 221–32.

The Manuale Scholarium: An Original Account of Life in the Mediaeval University, trans. by Robert Francis Seybolt (Cambridge: Harvard University Press, 1921).

Massebieau, Louis, *Les colloques scolaires du seizième siècle et leurs auteurs (1480–1570)* (Paris: Bonhoure, 1878; repr. Geneva: Slatkine, 1968).

Die Matrikel der Universität Leipzig, ed. by Georg Erler, 3 vols (Leipzig: Giesecke & Devrient, 1895–1909; repr. Nendeln: Kraus, 1976).

Medieval Latin, ed. by K.P. Harrington (Chicago: University of Chicago Press, 1997).

Medieval Latin. An Introduction and Bibliographical Guide, ed. by F.A.C. Mantello and A.G. Rigg (Washington, D.C.: The Catholic University of America Press, 1996).

Mehl, James V., 'Hermann von dem Busche's *Vallum humanitatis* (1518): A German Defense of the Renaissance *Studia Humanitatis*', *RQ*, 42 (1989), 480–506.

———, 'Humanism in the Home Town of the "Obscure Men"', in *Humanismus in Köln / Humanism in Cologne*, ed. by James V. Mehl, pp. 1–38.

Meisen, Karl, *Nikolauskult und Nikolausbrauch im Abendlande. Eine kultgeographisch-volkskündliche Untersuchung*, Forschungen zur Volkskunde, 9–12 (Düsseldorf: Schwann, 1931).

Mering, Friedrich Everhart Freiherr von, and Ludwig Reischert, *Die Bischöfe und Erzbischöfe von Köln nach ihrer Reihenfolge, nebst Geschichte des Ursprunges, des Fortganges und des Verfalles der Kirchen und Klöster der Stadt Köln, mit besonderer Bezugnahme auf die Kirchen und Klöster der Erzdiözese* (Cologne: Lengfeld, 1844).

Meuthen, Erich, 'Die Artesfakultät der alten Kölner Universität', Gesellschaft für Rheinische Geschichtskunde, Vorträge, 25 (Düsseldorf: Droste, 1989), 367–93.

Mezger, Werner, 'Rückwärts in die Zukunft. Metamorphosen der schwäbisch-allemannischen Fastnacht', in *Fastnacht/ Karneval in europäischen Vergleich*, ed. by Michael Matheus, Mainzer Vorträge, 3 (Stuttgart: Steiner, 1999), pp. 121–73.

Middendorpius, Jacobus, *De celebrioribus universi terrarum orbis Academiis libri duo* (Cologne: P. Horst, 1567). *VD 16*, M 5184.

——, *Academiarum orbis Christiani libri duo [...]* (Cologne: M. Cholinus, 1572). *VD 16*, M 5180, M 5181.

Militzer, Klaus, *Die vermögenden Kölner 1417–1418. Namenslisten einer Kopfsteuer von 1417 und einer städtischen Kreditaufnahme von 1418*, MStAK, 69 (Cologne–Vienna: Böhlau, 1981).

——, 'Collen eyn kroyn boven allen steden schoyn. Zum Selbstverständnis einer Stadt', *Colonia Romanica (Jahrbuch des Fördervereins Romanische Kirchen Köln, e.V.)*, 1 (1986), 15–32.

——, *Kölner Geistliche im Mittelalter*, 2 vols. I. *Männer*, MStAK, 91 (Cologne: Historisches Archiv der Stadt Köln, 2003); II. *Frauen*, MStAK, 96 (Cologne: Historisches Archiv der Stadt Köln, 2004).

Die Mirakelbücher des Klosters Eberhardsklausen, ed. by Paul Hoffmann and Peter Dohms, PGRG, 64 (Düsseldorf: Droste, 1988).

Mischlewski, Adalbert, 'Der Antoniterorden in Deutschland', *AMKG*, 10 (1958), 39–66.

——, 'Die Antoniter und ihr Haus in Köln', in *600 Jahre Antoniterkirche in Köln*, ed. by Evangelische Gemeinde Köln (Cologne: Evangelische Gemeinde Köln, 1984), pp. 17–32.

——, 'Das Antoniusfeuer in Mittelalter und früher Neuzeit in Westeuropa', in *Maladies et société (XIIe–XVIIIe siècles). Actes du colloque de Bielefeld novembre 1986*, ed. by Neidhart Bulst and Robert Delort (Paris: CNRS, 1989), pp. 249–68.

——, 'Beobachtungen zur Erwerbspolitik und Wirtschaftsweise des Memminger Antoniterhauses', in *Erwerbspolitik und Wirtschaftsweise mittelalterlicher Orden und Klöster*, ed. by Kaspar Elm, Berliner Historische Studien, 17; Ordensstudien, 7 (Berlin: Duncker & Humblot, 1992), pp. 175–96.

——, *Grundzüge der Geschichte des Antoniterordens bis zum Ausgang des 15. Jahrhunderts*, Bonner Beiträge zur Kirchengeschichte, 8 (Cologne–Vienna: Böhlau, 1976).

——, 'Soziale Aspekte der spätmittelalterlichen Antoniusverehrung', in *Laienfrömmigkeit im späten Mittelalter. Formen, Funktionen, politisch-soziale Zusammenhänge*, ed. by Klaus Schreiner and Elisabeth Müller-Luckner, Schriften des Historischen Kollegs, Kolloquien, 20 (Munich: Oldenbourg, 1992), pp. 137–56.

——, 'Expansion et structures de l'ordre hospitalier de Saint-Antoine-en-Viennois', in *Naissance et fonctionnement des réseaux monastiques et canoniaux. Actes du premier colloque international de C.E.R.C.O.M., St-Etienne, 16–18 septembre 1985*, Travaux et recherches du Centre européen de recherches sur les congrégations et ordres religieux, 1 (St-Etienne, Université Jean Monnet, 1991), pp. 195–209.

——, 'Antoniter', in *Handbuch der Mainzer Kirchengeschichte*, ed. by Friedhelm Jürgensmeier, 3 vols in 5 (Würzburg: Echter, 1997–2002), I/2, pp. 830–40.

Mosellanus, Petrus (= Schade, Peter), *Paedologia Petri Mosellani Protegensis in puerorum usum conscripta & aucta. Dialogi XXXVII. Dialogi pueriles Christophori Hegendorphini XII. lepidi æque, ac docti* (Strasbourg: J. Knobloch, 21 June 1523).

——, *Paedologia*, ed. by Hermann Michel, Lateinische Litteraturdenkmäler des XV. und XVI. Jahrhunderts, 18 (Berlin: Weidmann, 1906).

Moser, Dietz-Rüdiger, 'Fastnacht und Fronleichnam als Gegenfeste: Festgestaltung und Festbrauch im liturgischen Kontext', in *Feste und Feiern im Mittelalter. Paderborner Symposion des Mediävistenverbandes*, ed. by Detlef Altenburg, Jörg Jarnut, and Hans-Hugo Steinhoff (Sigmaringen: Thorbecke, 1991), pp. 359–76.

Müller, Johann, *Vor- und frühreformatorische Schulordnungen und Schulverträge in deutscher und niederländischer Sprache* (Zschoppau: Raske, 1885–1886; repr. Leipzig: Zentralantiquariat der DDR, 1973).

Murmellius, Johannes, *Ioannis Murmelij Ruremundensis. cui titulus Pappa. in quo hec insunt. Variarum rerum dictiones latine cum germanica interpretatione Oratiuncule varie puerorum vsui exposite Precepta moralia [...]* (Cologne: P. Quentel, 1513). *VD 16*, M 6952. Twenty later editions (1513–1550) listed in *VD 16*, M 6953–70, 6972–73.

——, *Opuscula duo [...] ad tyrunculorum usum diligenter recognita. Vnum de uerborum compositis. Alterum de uerbis communibus, ac deponentibus* (Cologne: E. Cervicornus, 1519) *VD 16*, M 6944.

Nauert, Charles G., Jr, 'Humanists, Scholastics and the Struggle to Reform the University of Cologne, 1523–1525', in *Humanism in Cologne*, ed. by Mehl, pp. 39–76.

Neuenahr, Hermann von, *De nouo hactenusque Germaniae inaudito morbo [...] quem uulgo sudorem Britannicum uocant* (Cologne: J. Soter, 1529).

Niavis, Paulus, *Latinum ydeoma pro novellis studentibus* (Leipzig: K. Kachelofen, [ca 1488]).

Noreña, Carlos G., *Juan Luis Vives* (The Hague: Nijhoff, 1970).

Oediger, Friedrich Wilhelm, 'Die niederrheinischen Schulen vor dem Aufkommen der Gymnasien', in Friedrich Wilhelm Oediger, *Vom Leben am Niederrhein. Aufsätze aus dem Bereich des alten Erzbistums Köln* (Düsseldorf: Schwann, 1973), pp. 351–408.

Ong, Walter, *Ramus and Talon Inventory* (Cambridge, Mass.: Harvard University Press, 1958).

Orme, Nicholas, *Medieval Children* (New Haven–London: Yale University Press, 2001).
Paas, Theodor, *Das Alexianerkloster in Köln-Lindenthal in seiner geschichtlichen Entwicklung*, ed. by Bernhard Giergen (Köln-Lindenthal: Kloster der Alexianerbrüder, 1934).
Persius Flaccus, Aulus, *Satiren*, ed. and trans. by Walter Kißel (Heidelberg: Winter, 1990).
——, *A. Persi Flacci et D. Juni Juvenalis Saturae*, ed. by Wendell Vernon Clausen (Oxford: Clarendon Press, 1959; rev. edn 1992).
——, *The Satires of Persius. The Latin Text with a Verse Translation* by Guy Lee (Liverpool: Cairns, 1987).
Quarg, Gunter, *'Ganz Köln steckt voller Bücherschätze'. Von der Ratsbibliothek zur Universitäts- und Stadtbibliothek 1602–2002* (Cologne: Universitäts- und Stadtbibliothek Köln, 2002).
Ranke, Ermentrude von, 'Die wirtschaftlichen Beziehungen Kölns zu Frankfurt am Main, Süddeutschland und Italien im 16. und 17. Jahrhundert', *Vierteljahrsschrift für Sozial- und Wirtschaftsgeschichte*, 17 (1923), 54–94.
Reinsberg-Düringsfeld, Otto von, *Das festliche Jahr in Sitten, Gebräuchen und Festen der germanischen Völker*, 2nd edn (Leipzig: Barsdorf, 1898).
Rheinisches Wörterbuch, ed. by Josef Müller and others, 9 vols (Bonn: Bouvier, 1928–71).
Riecke, Jörg, 'Sebald Heydens "Formulae puerilium colloquiorum". Zur Geschichte eines lateinisch-deutschen Gesprächsbüchleins aus dem 16. Jahrhundert', *ZdPh*, 114 (1995), 99–109.
Röhrig, Hans-Hermann, 'Reste alter Bibliotheken in der theologischen Abteilung der Kölner Gymnasialbibliothek' (unpubl. dissertation, Bibliothekar-Lehrinstitut des Landes Nordrhein-Westfalen, Cologne, 1957).
Schaefer, Heinrich, 'Inventare und Regesten aus den Kölner Pfarrarchiven', I. *AHVN*, 71 (1901), 1–215; II. ibid., 76 (1903), 1–263; III. ibid., 83 (1907), 1–219.
——, 'Ein Verzeichniss von Kölner Prälaten- und Stiftsherrenbildern aus dem Jahre 1635', *AHVN*, 75 (1903), 94–105.

Schmid, Wolfgang, *Kölner Renaissancekultur im Spiegel der Aufzeichnungen des Hermann Weinsberg (1518–1597)*, Veröffentlichungen des Kölnischen Stadtmuseums, 8 (Cologne: Kölnisches Stadtmuseum, 1991).

———, *Stifter und Auftraggeber in spätmittelalterlichen Köln*, Veröffentlichungen des Kölnischen Stadtmuseums, 11 (Cologne: Kölnisches Stadtmuseum, 1994).

Schmidt, Oswald Gottlob, *Petrus Mosellanus. Ein Beitrag zur Geschichte des Humanismus in Sachsen* (Leipzig: Fleischer, 1867).

Schoeck, R.J., M. Rütt and H.-W. Bartz, 'A Step towards a Neo-Latin Lexicon: A First Word-List Drawn from *Humanistica Lovaniensia*', *HL*, 39 (1990), 340–65; 40 (1991), 423–45.

Schwerhoff, Gerd, 'Ein Blick vom Turm. Kölner Quellen zur historischen Kriminalitätsforschung', *GiK*, 27 (1990), 43–67.

———, *Köln im Kreuzverhör. Kriminalität, Herrschaft und Gesellschaft in einer frühneuzeitlichen Stadt* (Bonn–Berlin: Bouvier, 1991).

———, 'Das rituelle Leben der mittelalterlichen Stadt. Richard C. Trexlers Florenzstudien als Herausforderung für die deutsche Geschichtsschreibung', *GiK*, 35 (1994), 33–60.

———, 'Köln rüstet sich zur Gottestracht: Eine Morgensprache vom 23. März 1478', *QGSK*, II, pp. 129–35.

———, 'Insel des Friedens oder Brennpunkt der Gewalt? Die Reichsstadt Köln ca. 1470–1620', in *Unsichere Großstädte? Vom Mittelalter bis zur Postmoderne*, ed. by Martin Dinges and Fritz Sack, Konflikte und Kultur. Historische Perspektiven, 3 (Konstanz: Universitätsverlag Konstanz, 2000), pp. 139–56.

———, 'Vereinswesen und Religiosität in der spätmittelalterlichen Stadt. Eine neue Quellenedition zur Geschichte der Kölner Laienbruderschaften', *GiK*, 45 (1999), 107–21.

Schwinges, Rainer Christoph, 'Studentische Kleingruppen im späten Mittelalter', in *Politik, Gesellschaft, Geschichtsschreibung. Gießener Festgabe für František Graus zum 60. Geburtstag*, ed. by Herbert Ludat and Rainer Christoph Schwinges, *Archiv für Kulturgeschichte*, Beiheft, 18 (Cologne–Vienna: Böhlau, 1982), pp. 319–61.

——, 'Sozialgeschichtliche Aspekte spätmittelalterlicher Studentenbursen in Deutschland', in *Schulen und Studium im sozialen Wandel des hohen und späten Mittelalters*, ed. by Johannes Fried, Vorträge und Forschungen, herausgegeben vom Konstanzer Arbeitskreis für mittelalterliche Geschichte, 30 (Sigmaringen: Thorbecke, 1986), pp. 527–64.

——, *Deutsche Universitätsbesucher im 14. und 15. Jahrhundert. Studien zur Sozialgeschichte des Alten Reiches*, Veröffentlichungen des Instituts für Europäische Geschichte Mainz: Beiträge zur Sozial- und Verfassungsgeschichte des Alten Reiches, 6 (Stuttgart: Steiner, 1986).

Sheerin, Daniel, 'Christian and Biblical Latin', in *Medieval Latin*, ed. by Mantello and Rigg, pp. 137–56.

Siuts, Hinrich, *Die Ansingelieder zu den Kalenderfesten. Ein Beitrag zur Geschichte, Biologie und Funktion des Volksliedes* (Göttingen: Schwartz, 1968).

Smet, Gilbert A.R. de, 'Schöffer und die Nomenclatura von S. Heyden. Die Mainzer Bearbeitung von 1534', in *In diutscher diute. Festschrift A. van der Lee, Amsterdamer Beiträge zur älteren Germanistik*, 20 (1983), 141–54.

——, 'S. Heydens Nomenclatura rerum domesticarum in Köln', in *Verborum amor. Studien zur Geschichte und Kunst der deutschen Sprache. Festschrift für Stefan Sonderegger*, ed. by Harald Burger (Berlin–New York: de Gruyter, 1992), pp. 412–29.

——, 'Zur Geschichte der Pappa Puerorum in Köln', in *Vielfalt des Deutschen. Festschrift für Werner Besch*, ed. by Klaus J. Mattheier (Frankfurt am Main: Lang, 1993), pp. 193–208.

Sottili, Agostino, 'Codici del Petrarca nella Germania occidentale', *Italia medioevale e umanistica*, 11 (1968), 409–10.

Statuta seu decreta provincialium et dioecesanarum synodorum sanctae ecclesiae Coloniensis: ex pervetusto & authentico codice, qui in archivo archiepiscopali asservatur, aliisque vetustis exemplaribus restituta et emaculata [...] (Cologne: Heirs of J. Quentel, 1554). *VD 16*, K 1725.

Stohlmann, J., 'Zum Lobe Kölns. Die Stadtansicht von 1531 und die "Flora" des Hermann von dem Busche', *JKGV*, 51 (1980), 1–56.

Studien zum städtischen Bildungswesen des späten Mittelalters und der frühen Neuzeit. Bericht über Kolloquien der Kommission zur Erforschung der Kultur des Spätmittelalters 1978 bis 1981, ed. by Bernd Moeller, Hans Patze, and Karl Stackmann, Abhandlungen der Akademie der Wissenschaften in Göttingen, philologisch-historische Klasse, 3. Folge, 137 (Göttingen: Vandenhoeck & Ruprecht, 1983).

Streckenbach, Gerhard, 'Paulus Niavis, "Latinum ydeoma pro novellis studentibus" – Ein Gesprächsbüchlein aus dem letzten Viertel des 15. Jahrhunderts', *Mittellateinisches Jahrbuch*, 6 (1970), 152–91; 7 (1972), 187–251.

——, 'Das "Manuale scolarium" und das "Latinum ydeoma pro novellis studentibus" von Paul Niavis. Zur Interpretation mittelalterlicher Prosa', *Mittellateinisches Jahrbuch*, 10 (1975), 232–69.

Tentler, Thomas N., *Sin and Confession on the Eve of the Reformation* (Princeton: Princeton University Press, 1977).

Tewes, Götz-Rüdiger, 'Die Studentenburse des Magisters Nikolaus Mommer von Raemsdonck: Ein Konflikt zwischen Rat und Universität im spätmittelalterlichen Köln', *GiK*, 20 (1986), 31–66.

——, 'Deutsche Universitätsbesucher im Mittelalter. Die Kölner Universität im Vergleich', *GiK*, 23 (1988), 91–102.

——, *Die Bursen der Kölner Artisten-Fakultät bis zur Mitte des 16. Jahrhunderts*, Studien zur Geschichte der Universität zu Köln, 13 (Cologne–Vienna: Böhlau, 1993).

——, 'Die Universität Köln im Umbruch: Aus Protokollen des Dekans der Artisten-Fakultät, 1522–1526', in *QGSK*, II, pp. 161–67.

Thomson, D.F.S., 'The Latinity of Erasmus', in *Erasmus*, ed. by T.A. Dorey (London: Routledge and Kegan Paul, 1970), pp. 115–37.

Thorbecke, August, *Geschichte der Universität Heidelberg. I. Die älteste Zeit. 1386–1449* (Heidelberg: Koester, 1886). No further parts appeared.

Tondini, H., 'De Ciceronianae imitationis ortu et progressione', *Latinitas*, 7 (1959), 166–81.

Tournoy, Gilbert, and Terence Tunberg, 'On the Margins of Latinity? Neo-Latin and the Vernacular Languages', *HL*, 45 (1996), 134–75.

Tunberg, Terence O., 'The Latinity of Lorenzo Valla's *Gesta Fernandi Regis Aragonum*', *HL*, 37 (1988), 30–78.

——, 'Further Remarks on the Language of Lorenzo Valla's *Gesta Fernandi* and on *De reciprocatione "sui" et "suus"*', *HL*, 39 (1990), 48–53.

——, 'De locutionibus nonnullis humanisticis quae pro vestigiis linguarum nationalium habentur', *Vox latina*, 26:101 (1990), 415–30; 27:103 (1991), VIII (appendix).

——, 'The Latinity of Lorenzo Valla's Letters', *Mittellateinisches Jahrbuch*, 26 (1991), 150–85.

——, 'Ciceronian Latin: Longolius and Others', *HL*, 46 (1997), 13–61.

——, 'Quae Latinitas sit moderna?', *Retiarius* (January 1998), online at <http://www.uky.edu/AS/Classics/retiarius/ian 98-latin.html>.

——, The Latinity of Erasmus and Medieval Latin: Continuities and Discontinuities', *Journal of Medieval Latin*, 14 (2004), 147–70.

——, 'De Erasmi declamationibus deque declamatiuncula, quae *Oratio Episcopi* inscribitur', *HL*, 55 (2006), 9–24.

Vives, Johannes Ludovicus, *Exercitatio Linguae Latinae* (Antwerp: C. Plantijn, 1538), cited from Vives, *Colloquia sive Exercitatio Latinae linguae [...] notis illustrata* (Gouda: F. Hoola, 1662).

Vollmer, Thomas, *Agenda Coloniensis. Geschichte und sakramentliche Feiern der gedruckten Kölner Ritualien*, Studien zur Pastoraltheologie, 10 (Regensburg: Pustet, 1994).

Weingärtner, Joseph, *Das Kind und seine Poesie in plattdeutscher Mundart* (Münster: Aschendorff, 1880).

Werhahn, Heinz Martin, 'Die Bücher des Dr. Peter Rinck', in *Kölner Schule. Festgabe zum 60. Geburtstag von Rudolf Juchoff*, ed. by Hermann Corsten, Arbeiten aus dem Bibliothekar-Lehrinstitut des Landes Nordrhein-Westfalen, 7 (Cologne: Greven, 1955), pp. 179–88.

Wesseling, Ari, 'Dutch Proverbs and Ancient Sources in Erasmus' *Praise of Folly*', *RQ*, 47 (1994), 351–78.

——, 'Dutch Proverbs and Expressions in Erasmus' Adages, Colloquies, and Letters', *RQ*, 55 (2002), 81–147.

Winheim, Erhardus, *Sacrarium Agrippinae: hoc est designatio ecclesiarum Coloniensium praecipuarum reliquiarum [...] &c. [...]* (Cologne: B. Gualtherus, 1607), cited from the edition of Cologne: J. Steinhauss, 1736.

Wolff, E., 'Mots rares et mots nouveaux dans les *Colloques* d'Erasme', *Revue des études latines*, 69 (1991), 166–86.

Wrede, Adam, *Altkölnischer Sprachschatz. Auf Grund archivalischer Quellenstoffe der Reichsstadt Köln vom 12. Jahrhundert bis 1815 als Wörterbuch bearbeitet [...], Lieferung 1. a–amandel* (Bonn: Klopp, 1928). No further fascicles appeared.

——, *Neuer Kölnischer Sprachschatz*, 3 vols (Cologne: Greven, 1956–1958).

——, *Rheinischer Volksbrauch im Kreislauf des Jahres*, Rheinisches Volkstum, 4 (Düsseldorf: Schwann, [1935]).

Zender, Matthias, 'Eigenart und Entwicklung des Festtagsbrauchtums im Raum Euskirchen', in *640 Jahre Euskirchen 1302–1952*, ed. by Josef Franke, 2 vols (Euskirchen: Volksblatt, 1952–1955), II, pp. 279–98, quoted from repr. in Matthias Zender, *Gestalt und Wandel*, pp. 132–53.

——, 'Das Kölnische "Niederland" in Gestalt und Sonderart seines Volkslebens', *RVB*, 36 (1972), 249–80; repr in Matthias Zender, *Gestalt und Wandel*, pp. 94–122.

——, *Gestalt und Wandel. Aufsätze zur rheinisch-westfälischen Volkskunde und Kulturauffassung*, ed. by H.L. Cox and Günter Wiegelmann, Veröffentlichungen des Instituts für geschichtliche Landeskunde der Rheinlande an der Universität Bonn (Bonn: Röhrscheid, 1977).

Zimmern, Froben Christoph von, *Die Chronik der Grafen von Zimmern. Handschriften 580 und 581 der Fürstlich Fürstenbergischen Hofbibliothek Donaueschingen*, ed. by Hansmartin Decker-Hauff, 3 vols (Darmstadt: Wissenschaftliche Buchgesellschaft, 1964–1972).

EU authorised representative for GPSR:
Easy Access System Europe, Mustamäe tee 50,
10621 Tallinn, Estonia
gpsr.requests@easproject.com

www.ingramcontent.com/pod-product-compliance
Ingram Content Group UK Ltd.
Pitfield, Milton Keynes, MK11 3LW, UK
UKHW021942200326
4879IPUK00004B/53